Preface

This book is a companion to *Bob Dylan: What the Songs Mean*, published in November 2019, hence the intended similarity in cover design. That book put forward an interpretation of the human condition based on an analysis of Bob Dylan's lyrics. But other artists share that interpretation. What's more, their experience and its artistic expression widen the perspective, offering different insights. Playwright Harold Pinter, for instance, might be less comprehensive an artist than Bob Dylan, less all-encompassing, but he's more forensic in exploring the early stages of the artist's interior journey. This provided the initial impetus for *Artists*, which offers a detailed analysis of Pinter's great early plays, from *The Birthday Party* to *Betrayal*.

Subsequently, Bob Dylan, as he approached his 80th birthday, brought out a new album, *Rough and Rowdy Ways,* in which he set out to bring his vocation as a songwriter full-circle, using a lifetime's experience to go back to the beginning and discover its meaning for the first time. This summation needed, at the very least, to be explored as a kind of appendix to the earlier analysis of his lyrics. It also happens to be the case that Ian Curtis, singer and lyricist of 1970s rock band Joy Division, and singer-songwriter David Gray, of *White Ladder* fame, cover the same ground as Bob Dylan. An analysis of their lyrics, therefore, however brief, enables us to arrive at a more complete understanding of the human condition from the artist's point of view.

Finally, as a handy aide memoire, *Artists* concludes with a short summary of the life and work of Scottish painter James Cowie, who graphically illustrates that view in a handful of striking oil paintings.

Michael Karwowski

A Necessary Introduction

B iographers have a lot to answer for. This is particularly true of biographers of artists. Life isn't always about the personal. Sometimes it's about the philosophical. In fact, where the greatest artists are concerned, it's mostly about the philosophical. Of course, sex sells better than the soul. And, certainly, the artists whose work is analysed in this book all had personal histories. In some cases, this featured rather prominently in their life. Bob Dylan's affair with Joan Baez at the start of his career has absorbed many biographers, not to speak of readers, while Joy Division singer-lyricist Ian Curtis's marital situation was a focus of his best-known song, "Love Will Tear Us Apart" and of the 2007 biographical film drama *Control*. Sex also featured prominently in the life of playwright Harold Pinter, who divorced his first wife, actress Vivien Merchant, to marry historian Lady Antonia Fraser, and who acknowledged that he used details from a seven-year extra-marital affair with BBC TV presenter Joan Bakewell in his play *Betrayal*.

So, yes, of course, the personal is relevant to biography, even to critical biography. But it's not always primarily so. Often, it qualifies merely as background, dealing as it does with the existence of an artist rather than with their life. It involves their daily physical and emotional needs, the fleeting, but not their concern with the human condition, the abiding. And it's this that makes them an artist. In this respect, while the personal might provide material for an artist's work, the "details" in Pinter's word, it's not the meat, not what it's "about", any more than a scientist's daily life contributes significantly to their discoveries.

This applies equally to an artist's attitudes and opinions, insofar as they express any. T. S. Eliot is reported to have said that the person who writes a poem and the one who publishes it are not the same person. What this amounts to is that a person's soul, their philosophical side, so to speak, and their self, or personality, are two completely different and separate parts of that person, with minimal connection between them. This means that an artist's views, as well as their private life, bear no essential relationship to their work, if, that is, and it's a big if, they *are* a true artist. The veracity of that work, in other words, isn't affected by how they live their life. Biographers who spend their time trying to make connections between the two are missing the point. Artists aren't like other people.

This may appear rather contentious, indeed, downright false, but the purpose of this book is to set down some parameters for a reality where it makes perfect sense. It begins by defining the nature of an artist before illustrating that new reality in terms of five very different but nevertheless similar artists, similar because all true artists are essentially dealing with the same thing, i.e. the human condition. And, in doing so, this book attempts to shift the biographical balance away from sex and scandal towards the soul, at least where artists are concerned. At the same time, it tries to prove that philosophy can be as sexy as sex and scandal, although admittedly in a more spiritual way. Many mystics throughout history have seen their relationship with the divine as a love story and the artists in this book all have the same attitude towards truth. As for excitement, the French philosopher Simone Weil, who was very much an artist, is said to have assured a young boy pining for a life of adventure out in the world that he'd find infinitely more excitement, as well as joy, in the interior life. True philosophy can be every bit as passionate as a physical affair, with the added advantage that it lasts.

But what is true philosophy? Well, it's not the dry and dusty discipline taught in most educational establishments, that's for sure. While Kant and Confucius can leave the poor student confused and exhausted, true philosophy is all about waking up to the world, about feeling more alive, not less.

But can anyone practise such philosophy or is it only for a select few? The answer is that, yes, anyone can be a philosopher, although perhaps not everyone can be an artist such as those featured in this book since all five are exceptionally talented. But anyone can be a philosopher and express the fruits of philosophy in some way, perhaps not as well as Bob Dylan or Harold Pinter, but, who knows, perhaps better. So, if it's for everyone, how do we go about practising it? Surprisingly, perhaps, this is a lot easier than it seems. For a start, it needn't involve reading philosophical texts or considering so-called philosophical questions such as whether God exists. Paradoxically, it doesn't even begin with the philosophical but with the personal. It begins, in fact, with the simple question *why*. Why am I alive? What is the meaning or purpose of my life? Is there a meaning or purpose to my life? And, if so, is it possible for me to know what it is?

In turn, answering the question *why* involves understanding the nature of the human condition. This is to say the nature of reality with regard to human life. To know *why* we exist, we first need to know *what* kind of world we live in and, thus, perhaps, *who* we are. In contrast to the question *why*, which is personal, these are philosophical questions, underlining the fact that all humanity is in the same boat. Insofar as one of us can shed light on the nature of the human condition, that light is shared by all.

Acting philosophically, then, involves asking questions about the nature of human reality, about the world we live in, in an attempt to answer the question *why*. And if we ask these questions sincerely, honestly, with an open mind, with the sole intention of finding answers, whatever the consequences, then we inevitably find inspiration from the spirit of truth, which is the only way we can perceive reality.

The spirit of truth is an outside force that acts on any mind that seeks to understand the nature of human life by enabling it to see the reality of whatever aspect it might consider. That mind then confirms the perception through personal experience, which transforms the perception into knowledge. This knowledge or understanding then prompts another question, when the process is repeated.

The process of truth, then, is a circular process: question and answer, experience and understanding, question and answer, experience and understanding, and so on. Anyone involved will probably become aware, at least on a subliminal level, of this circular process. But that doesn't necessarily mean they'll be aware that it's the spirit of truth that's responsible. Neither is it necessary for them to know. Where the artists featured in this book are concerned, for instance, songwriters Bob Dylan and David Gray were each manifestly aware of the spirit of truth from very early in their career, Ian Curtis became aware of it during his short time as a lyricist, playwright Harold Pinter appears to have been familiar with it, while painter James Cowie was certainly aware of the circular process of truth, but, as to the spirit, there's no evidence.

In the case of Dylan and Gray, they signal their awareness by employing the image of a "wind" in their songs to symbolise the spirit. Bob Dylan's first major lyric, in fact, "Blowin' in the Wind", states categorically that the only way to answer all questions about the human condition is through the blowing wind of truth.

This image of a "wind" to express the spirit of truth, or the Holy Ghost, as it's also known, comes from *The New Testament*, specifically *The Gospel According to St. John* and *The Acts of the Apostles*. In the former, the spirit of truth is described in terms of a wind at the very outset by Jesus, also suggesting where Bob Dylan got the idea for "Blowin' in the Wind":

> "The wind bloweth where it listeth, and thou hearest the sound thereof, but canst not tell whence it cometh, and whither it goeth: so is everyone that is born of the Spirit," *John* (3:8).

In *Acts of the Apostles*, meanwhile, the "mighty wind" of the spirit of truth is depicted as a muse:

> "And suddenly there came a sound from heaven as of a rushing mighty wind, and it filled all the house where they were sitting…And they were all filled with the Holy Ghost, and began to speak with other tongues, as the Spirit gave them utterance," *Acts* (2:2-4).

The "wind" metaphor for truth was subsequently adopted by a number of artists including poets William Blake, Dylan Thomas and Edward Thomas, whose poem "Wind and Mist" is very specifically about the wind of truth:

"You would not understand about the wind.

It is my subject…

There were whole days and nights when the wind and I

Between us shared the world, and the wind ruled

And I obeyed it …"

The spirit of truth, then, is the incipient philosopher's muse in their questioning of the human condition. And what they sooner or later discover as the overriding fact of that condition is that there's a second force operating in the world, one which rules all human behaviour that isn't ruled by the spirit of truth. This force is that of the desire for power, which Jesus calls "the prince of this world" *John* (12:31). The fact that it has an overwhelming control over us is explained by our assertive pride in ourselves. Confirmation of this fact can be found by noting how often we refer to pride with approval. This pride has also been called "honour", largely in the past, and, in the present, "dignity". Honour and dignity, however, are merely synonyms for pride.

But it's not the fact that we're proud that's important to understanding the human condition; it's that this pride is assertive. This means that we're not satisfied with merely feeling proud of ourselves or trumpeting our dignity; we actively seek justification for that pride; we look for reasons to feel proud. And it's this assertive pride that finds an active response from the force of the desire for power, which presents itself to us as the way to justify our sense of pride, just as our need to know *why* finds a response from the spirit of truth.

As humans, then, we're all subject to two forces capable of acting on our mind. But, whereas the spirit of truth only becomes active if we effectively call upon it by questioning the human condition, the desire for power is relentless. It seems that human life and assertive pride are inextricably linked, a "long-time curse" as Bob Dylan calls it in his song "Just Like a Woman", and, as a result, the desire for power holds sway in the world, as Jesus observed. Much of what we think of as thought, in fact, is merely the operation of the desire for power on the human mind.

The existence of the two forces, however, does mean that we have a choice at any time to act in one of two different ways. This freedom to choose between desire and truth is the meaning of the term "free will". In answer to our assertive pride, we can respond to the desire for power. Responding in this way means that our mind is active as a "self" or "ego", so that we're acting as an egoist. On the other hand, in answer to the need to know *why*, we can respond to the spirit of truth. This is the meaning of the word "soul", and when our mind is directed thus we're a truth seeker, or, if we express the resulting knowledge creatively, an artist. In a nutshell, then, the human mind face to the desire for power is the self, face to the spirit of truth, the soul, and our ability to choose between them, free will.

Since an assertive pride appears to be our natural state and the force of desire constant in its pressure as a result, it is, of course, normal for this choice to prevail with most of us, the overwhelming majority, in fact. This pushes the truth seeker or artist to the margins of society, aliens few people can understand because their terms of reference are utterly foreign, especially as the desire for power's demands are so addictive. In the circumstances, any alternative, spiritual life is bound to appear nonsensical or eccentric at best.

We all know desire's demands because their satisfaction is what we mean by the term "happiness". We don't see happiness in this way, though, because the desire for power appears to each of us in terms of desires particular to ourselves. Happiness is not the same for everyone. The nature of the desires that each of us adopts to express the desire for power depends on our influences, especially in childhood. This is because it's in childhood that we're most susceptible to influence. As children, with no experience of the world, we're bound to believe that those on whom we depend know better than we do. Of course, as we grow older and more experienced, we might come to doubt this. But the damage has already been done: we've already accepted desire's terms of reference as the only ones that matter, even if the nature of our desires might change over time.

Another reason that we're ignorant of our attachment to the desire for power is that the satisfaction of the particular desires in which we see desire requires the realisation of certain conditions. The reality of the world, in other words, needs to be arranged in a certain way for our happiness to be fulfilled. What's more, we usually transform these conditions into handy aims, goals or ambitions, whose nature, like the particular desires in which we see the desire for power, depends on our influences, particularly in childhood. Interestingly, in contrast to the circular nature of the process of truth, the process of desire is linear, a straight line leading to happiness somewhere up in the distance, with the achievement of our aims stages along the way.

In turn, when setting out to achieve those aims, we're bound to subscribe to certain values, ideas which act as signposts or directions for their achievement, a blueprint for fulfilment. These values act as our moral compass in differentiating between actions we consider right, because they lead towards the achievement of our goals, and those we consider wrong, because they don't. This is the meaning of morality, which amounts to a table of do's and don'ts towards the achievement of the conditions for our happiness. Again, the values we espouse depend on our influences, particularly in childhood.

These, then, are some of the elements that make up the scaffolding, as it were, for building our happiness, elements that define our relationship to the world in which we see ourselves as living. But there's another essential element to add to our idea of happiness and how to achieve it. This is belief, because the conditions for the achievement of happiness can only be realised if the reality of the world is conditional, i.e. if it's a plastic medium that can be moulded into a particular shape in order to facilitate happiness.

Each of us, therefore, is bound to believe, firstly, that the reality of the world is conditional in principle, i.e. that the conditions for happiness are realisable in the first place, and, secondly, that the particular conditions for our own idea of happiness are realisable in practice. This is what we mean by having a belief system, whose nature, as with everything else, depends on our influences, particularly in childhood. Each of us, that is, believes that the reality of the world is such that the achievement of happiness is possible in general and that our own idea of happiness is achievable in particular.

But, and this is a central fact of the world view of the artists in this book, as well as many others, notably William Shakespeare, the reality of the world must, by its very nature, be unconditional. It must be absolute. It's what is. It's either this or it's that. Any conception of a conditional reality of the world, then, is an illusion. This isn't to say that the world that most of us live in all the time and artists and truth seekers most or at least some of the time doesn't exist. It's to say that it's not what we think it is. It's not built on solid philosophical foundations but on sand. The reality of the world isn't a plastic medium that can be moulded to deliver happiness on tap. It's not plastic but fixed, governed by absolute, immutable laws that make no concession to human pride or the desire for power.

Once we see happiness for what it is, sooner or later, through the inspiration of the spirit of truth, all this becomes apparent. The fundamental fact of life is change: we change, relationships change, we become ill, we lose our job, people die, accidents happen, disasters occur, etc. etc., and happiness depends on fixity, on everything being perfect forever, on living happily ever after, or at least until we die, which is why so many people choose to believe in an idea of heaven in which we achieve happiness after death. The reality is that the only way we could ever be lastingly happy is if we were God, or at least as that deity is imagined in many religions: a being in total control of everything, so that we could have everything exactly as we want it forever. But we can't.

What this means is that our beliefs, whatever they might be, whether religious, humanistic, success-related or whatever, are merely wishful-thinking. They amount to imagining a "reality" of the world that may be a perfect fit for the satisfaction of our desires but bears absolutely no relation to the reality that actually exists. What's more, if our beliefs are illusionary, it follows that whatever the nature of our conditions for the arrangement of this "reality", or the aims, goals and ambitions in terms of which we see those conditions, they're merely particular illusions arising out of the general illusion of our belief.

One way of expressing this is to say that any belief in a conditional reality of the world is tantamount to sleep, while our aims are dreams arising from this sleep. Again, as with pride, honour, or dignity, it's noticeable how often we speak of our dreams with approval, and, if we achieve one of our aims, how it's a "dream come true". But dreams don't come true, dreams only occur when we're asleep, and eventually we wake up and they dissipate, although we might remember them fondly as a time when we once felt happy. The proof is in the fact that no matter how many aims or ambitions we might fulfil, we're never satisfied; we never feel that we've achieved lasting happiness, only a temporary illusion of happiness.

This metaphor of sleep and dreams for our beliefs and aims is used by many artists, notably Bob Dylan, who also uses an alternative metaphor, which is a favourite of Shakespeare's. This is that, in acting as a self or ego, we're not real people but actors, relating as we do to the "stage" of an imagined world, rather than to the real world. And, like all actors, we act a number of parts, in our case, roles that correspond to the different desires that make up our desire for power. As Shakespeare has it in *As You Like It*: "All the world's a stage, And all the men and women merely players...And one man in his time plays many parts," (Act II, Sc. vii).

The French symbolist poet Arthur Rimbaud, on the other hand, in a letter written when he was just 16, dismissed the self or ego as "I is someone else", which relates to Eliot's comment that the poet and the person, soul and self, are not the same, that the self is essentially different from the soul. In this respect, it's interesting how often we use the word "soul" to express what we consider to be our true or inner self.

The human condition, then, is one of illusion. We have beliefs and aims that are all illusions and, as such, blind us, like the "mist" in Edward Thomas's poem "Wind and Mist", to the reality of the world, so that the meaning or purpose of human life is concealed from us, remains a mystery. And, as we've seen, these illusions arise from our pursuit of happiness, from the satisfaction of our desires, whose source is the force of the desire for power. It's these desires that attach us to the illusionary world in which we live. One image used by artists to express this is that the force of desire is a spider with our particular desires the attachments that make up the spider's web in whose coils we're enmeshed like flies. Thus, famously, Shakespeare, in *King Lear*, has: "As flies to wanton boys are we to the gods. They kill us for their sport." Similarly, Bob Dylan called his stream of consciousness prose poem *Tarantula* to express the same thing, while Harold Pinter's confined protagonist in *The Birthday Party* is surnamed "Webber". We all, however, also have a deep-seated need to know *why*, which explains the profound attraction to us of the word "soul". *And* we have the free will to set out to answer this need through the existence of the spirit of truth.

It's first necessary, however, that we detach ourselves from desire, at least sufficiently to be inspired by the spirit of truth. This is what Bob Dylan means in his song "Mr. Tambourine Man", which is about the nature of our relationship to the spirit of truth, when he writes: "with one hand waving free". We can't be attached to desire and committed to truth *at the same time* since desire and truth lead in opposite directions, the one towards illusion, the other towards reality. And as our attachment to desire arises from our assertive pride, so must any commitment to answering the need to know *why* involve an antidote to that pride, which is humility. By adopting a humble or childlike passivity, we open up a distance from desire, however temporary, that allows us to access truth. This explains Christ's insistence on humility as a prerequisite for the attainment of ultimate reality. Thus, we have: "And Jesus called a little child unto him, and set him in the midst of them, And said, Verily I say unto you, Except ye be converted, and become as little children, ye shall not enter into the kingdom of heaven," *Matthew* (18:2-4). Again: "Take my yoke upon you, and learn of me; for I am meek and lowly in heart, and ye shall find rest unto your souls," *Matthew* (11:29). All this is simply another way of saying that we need, as any scientist knows, to have an open mind in questioning the nature of reality, to want to know the answer whatever the consequences. And, if we do, we set in motion the circular process of truth and a growing understanding of the human condition. What's more, the proof is in the doing. As science fiction writer Frank Herbert wrote in his 1965 novel *Dune*: "The mystery of life isn't a problem to solve, but a reality to experience."

Our attachment to desire, however, is deep and wide, so it's essential that we maintain any commitment to truth because, the moment we let up on it, we inevitably slip back into our old habits in the pursuit of happiness. Bob Dylan was referring to this when, in an interview with *Playboy* magazine in 1966, he said: "Out of all the people who just lay around and ask *why*, how many do you figure really want to know?"

If we do maintain our commitment, though, it's inevitable that we'll arrive at the first great turning point in our journey along what Bob Dylan calls the "road" of truth. This is the perception that the world we've lived in all our life, the world we've always believed to be real, is, in fact, an illusion. We've been living a lie. To say that this experience is disquieting would be an understatement. It's shattering, like something out of a Hollywood horror movie, as we're suddenly plunged into darkness, the false lights of illusion that have illuminated our life up to that point having all been extinguished in one puff of the wind of truth. We have, in 16th century Spanish poet and mystic John of the Cross's famous phrase, entered "the dark night", popularly known as "the dark night of the soul".

This "dark night" has more than one meaning. It's dark because, having perceived our beliefs to be false, mere wishful-thinking, we can no longer rely on them to light our way in life, and, as a result, we have to seek the reality of the world without them; "we must seek the light in darkness", as John expressed it. But it's also dark because our darkness means that we're obliged unconditionally to trust the spirit of truth to lead us out of that darkness towards the light of reality. This is the meaning of faith, faith as trust, not as belief. John of the Cross expresses this in his poem "The Dark Night": "On a night of darkness…My only light and guide/The one that in my heart was burning." By "heart" here he means his commitment to truth, his soul, and by "light" he means that spirit of truth.

Recalling the beginning of this introduction about the personal and the philosophical, it's interesting to study this disturbing period in any artist's life, prompting, as it does, frenzy from biographers seeking to discover what personal trauma could possibly have produced such an extreme reaction in their subject, most famously, perhaps, with Shakespeare, whose *Hamlet* is probably the best description of the experience ever written. Ironically, however, it might be said that the biographers do have a point, even if it's not the one they're looking for. This *is* a time when philosophy gets really personal, because it's only then that we realise exactly how the human condition applies to each one of us and how we can't escape its consequences.

As we come to terms with the experience and proceed along the road of truth, we also realise the *degree* to which philosophy is a personal matter. This is because, since it's our illusions that blind us to the reality of the world, so does true philosophy amount to a process of disillusionment. This *is* deeply personal. We need, that is, to use the wind of truth to blow away the illusions of our own personal ideas of happiness as it's these that separate each of us from reality. Thus, the quote earlier from Edward Thomas's

"Wind and Mist" concludes: "…the wind ruled/And I obeyed it *and forgot the mist.*" Similarly, this is what William Blake means in "The Marriage of Heaven and Hell" when he writes: "If the doors of perception were cleansed, everything would appear to man as it is, infinite." The "doors of perception" here are the eyes of the soul and infinity a synonym for reality.

What this means in practice is that we need to question the nature of our personal beliefs and conditions for happiness in order that the spirit of truth reveal their illusory nature, perceptions that we can then transform into knowledge through our experience of them. It involves, that is, travelling deep into the "dark night" of our illusions in order to dispel them, which, in turn, will reveal the reality they conceal. This is another meaning of John of the Cross's "we must seek the light in darkness".

And since the roots of our illusions lie in our childhood influences, so must we use the spirit of truth to counter those influences in order to uproot them. This is precisely what Marcel Proust's great 20th century novel *À la recherche du temps perdu* (In Search of Lost Time) is about, the last of its seven volumes being *Le temps retrouvé* (Time Regained or Redeemed). Bob Dylan refers to this in his last album, 2020's *Rough and Rowdy Ways*, when he seeks in "Crossing the Rubicon" to "redeem the time" in the "dark days" of a "world so badly bent". Again, in "I Contain Multitudes", he writes: "I go right where all things lost – are made good again." And as, through the circular process of truth, we dispel the illusions, so do we free ourselves from our desires as we come to fully understand how they separate us from reality. Jesus Christ expressed this in the *St John Gospel*: "And ye shall know the truth, and the truth shall make you free," (8:32), "…now shall the prince of this world be cast out," (12:31).

All this seems simple and straightforward, a walk in the park with its fresh air and open skies in place of the close confinement of our dark dungeon of attachment to the desire for power. It's a fact, though, that a great many artists give up their commitment to answering the question *why*, some surrendering to addictions, such as alcoholism, for instance, others returning to their pre-truth life in the pursuit of happiness. And there's a very good reason for this. This is that the nature of our desires depends on influence, particularly in childhood, and our susceptibility to influence at such an early age transforms this influence into conditioning or "brain washing". In turn, this conditioning leads us to love our desires as a guarantee of happiness, investing them with comforting warmth, as warm as the deepest sleep and sweetest dreams of the beliefs and aims they instigate. As a result, disillusionment is bound to appear as a move towards something alien and cold, prompting a profound reluctance to proceed further along the road of truth. As we'll see, the artists in this book make much of this contrast between the welcome warmth of illusion and the harsh cold of reality.

The strength of our reluctance to persevere with truth as a result of our conditioning is best appreciated if we relate it to the instinct for self-preservation, since disillusionment amounts to deconstructing the self or ego: our attachment to the desire for power, since it's this that's the source of our imprisonment in illusion. We must, that is, extinguish or "kill" the self: *disillusionment means self-extinction*. One of the most pressing impressions of the sudden arrival of the "dark night", in fact, is an overwhelming sense of the proximity of death. Naturally, we associate this sense with that of our physical death since, at this stage, we still identify with the self rather than with the soul. But, as we've seen, the self is not who we are in reality: "I is someone else," as Rimbaud expressed it. Rather, the self is our proudly assertive identification with the desire for power. Many people are prepared to die physically in order to preserve this, suicides or war heroes, for instance, hence the phrase "I'd rather die than…," suggesting that the instinct for self-preservation is stronger than the animal fear of death.

The upshot of the appearance of this impediment in our interior journey is that we're suddenly brought up short. Just as we're quickly disabused of any misapprehension that philosophy is a purely cerebral matter when we first set out to answer the question *why*, so, now, we discover that there's no question of our idea of self remaining untouched by the process of truth; far from it. The process involves total transformation, the death of the self, and few of us there are who are prepared for such a metamorphosis, as Franz Kafka's short story calls it, hence our hesitation. But then the pressing need to answer the question *why* re-establishes itself. Now, we see a deeper meaning to Bob Dylan's rhetorical question: "Out of all the people who just lay around and ask *why*, how many do you figure really want to know?"

At this stage of their interior journey, the artist is, according to Dylan Thomas in his poem sequence "Altarwise by Owl-light", in a "half-way house", or as Harold Pinter expresses the same thing in the title of his play, in a "no man's land" between self and soul, caught between two worlds, one of seductive illusion, familiar and warm, and one of uncompromising reality, alien and cold. Put simply, faced with the need to answer the question *why* and the opposing instinct for self-preservation, the artist inevitably feels that they're facing a life or death decision, one between worldly life and spiritual life, one, moreover, in which the pressing nature of the contending parties is such that they veer from one side to the other, from expressions of despair at the prospect of self-extinction one moment, to the production of inspired creations the next as they make the case for the primacy of the soul.

There's absolutely no doubt that this is the most pressing philosophical question that we can face in life, a drama so gripping that it explains many of the greatest works of art ever created, not least Shakespeare's *Hamlet*: the quintessential expression of existential indecision between self and soul; also the late chamber works of both Beethoven and Schubert, considered by many to be high points in the history of classical music; also many of the iconic works of modern art, Edvard Munch's painting, *The Scream*, for instance, as well as much of the work analysed in this book, particularly that of Harold Pinter, where the philosophical dilemma facing the artist or truth seeker is analysed in depth over six great plays; not that it's not the elephant in the room in the work of Bob Dylan, Ian Curtis, David Gray and James Cowie.

While popular creative works such as Hollywood movies or blockbuster novels generally deal with the so-called triumph of the human spirit, which is to say the removal of obstacles to the self's acquisition of power, to happiness, this conflict between the force of desire and the spirit of truth, expressed in the personal space of our mind, is the true subject of art and, thus, the preoccupation of all true artists, the ones in this book being no exception. Initially, the conflict is defined in terms of whether we want to answer the question *why* at all, considering what it means for the self, as a matter of principle, that is. How much does true philosophy matter to us, in short, which is what Bob Dylan meant when he made his comment in his 1966 interview. But, if our answer is that it matters more to us than anything else in life, i.e. more than the pursuit of happiness, that's not the end of the matter, far from it, because throughout the entire process of truth, our commitment to truth will constantly be questioned anew as we seek freedom from each one of the desires that make up our perception of desire itself until we're free of them all.

Perhaps no one has better explained this than that master of the soul's journey towards freedom from the tyranny of desire than John of the Cross, who actually appears to have found that freedom, and who saw the struggle in terms of a bird tethered to the earth, which is to say to the illusionary world of desire, by manifold strings, all of which need to be cut before we're free to fly. Ultimately, it makes no difference whether we're attached to many or merely to one since our confinement remains the same. John, who was a mystic, saw the freedom of the soul to fly not in terms of arriving at ultimate reality or answering the question *why* but of "divine union", which he considered to be the meaning or purpose of human life. The terms used, however, make no difference to what's at stake:

> "The soul that is attached to anything, however much good there may be in it, will not arrive at liberty of divine union. For whether it be a strong wire rope or a slender and delicate thread that holds the bird, it matters not, if it really holds fast; for, until the cord be broken, the bird cannot fly. So the soul, held by the bonds of human affections, however slight they may be, cannot, while they last, make its way to God."

This idea has been taken up by a number of artists, Bob Dylan and David Gray, for instance, as we'll see, but also by songwriters such as Gavin Sutherland with "Sailing", made famous by Rod Stewart, and Townes van Zandt with "To Live is to Fly". The former song recreates the wonderful sense of a growing freedom for the soul through the dying of the self in its soaring music and lyrics: "flying like a bird...to be free...through the dark night...dying, forever crying, to be with you..." The ambiguous "forever crying" beautifully captures the eternal need to answer the question *why* along with the painful price for its fulfilment, a price van Zandt insists is worth paying as he counsels that "it don't pay to think too much on things you leave behind".

Ultimately, it's this that defines the greatness of an artist, or, indeed, a truth seeker: the degree to which they're willing to identify with the soul rather than with the self. Disillusionment, and its ultimate destination: self-extinction, may be difficult and painful at times, but it's essential to keep in mind that the pain is merely the birth pangs of the soul. Mothers throughout history have considered these a small price to pay for new life. Similarly, the artist must be a mother to the soul.

Harold Pinter

Illustratio interruptus

Playwright Harold Pinter is unquestionably a giant of world literature. His career spanned the whole of the second half of the 20th century, leading to a Nobel Prize in 2005. Probably few would disagree, however, that it's on a handful of plays that his reputation rests, from *The Birthday Party, The Caretaker,* and *The Homecoming* in the late 1950s and early '60s, to *Old Times, No Man's Land,* and *Betrayal* in the '70s. The phrase most often associated with his plays is "comedy of menace", with the pause often as powerful as action or dialogue.

In his later years – he died on Christmas Eve 2008, aged 78 – his celebrity depended more on his politics than on his plays. The master of the dramatic pause became a rebel without a pause, taking every opportunity to make pronouncements on current affairs.

This new role as moral chorus in the wings of the political stage coincided with something of a drought in his playwriting. Not only did his plays become few and far between, they were also invariably short and politically-inspired, agitation rather than art. Pinter was also prepared to re-interpret his greatest stage plays in political terms, as an incipient expression of his condemnation of injustice. This new interpretation of his *oeuvre* as essentially political, at least in spirit if not always in practice, was enthusiastically taken up by many critics and academics. The evidence of the time, however, contradicts this view. In an interview published in 1961 as *Writing for Myself*, for instance, Pinter could hardly have been clearer: "No, I'm not committed as a writer, in the usual sense of the term, either religiously or politically. And I'm not conscious of any social function. I don't see any placards on myself, and I don't carry any banners. Ultimately, I distrust definitive labels."

Just in case anyone failed to appreciate this apolitical point of view, Pinter clarified it even further the following year in a speech published as *Writing for the Theatre*, summing up the "warnings, sermons, admonitions, ideological exhortations, moral judgements" indulged in by playwrights, in and out of their plays, in one phrase: "*I'm* telling *you!*"

His stated attitude to this response was: "Beware of the writer who puts forward his concern for you to embrace, who leaves you in no doubt of his worthiness, his usefulness, his altruism, who declares that his heart is in the right place, and ensures that it can be seen in full view, a pulsating mass where his characters ought to be. What is presented, so much of the time, as a body of active and positive thought is in fact a body lost in a prison of empty definition and cliché…Ideas endlessly repeated and permutated become platitudinous, trite, meaningless."

Again, in an interview in 1969, he said: "I'm not interested in ideology. You can't expect this to be in any way a just world. I have no expectation of the world getting better in any way."

The most compelling evidence of the apolitical nature of Harold Pinter's great stage plays, however, is in the plays themselves. "Never trust the artist. Trust the tale," as D.H. Lawrence advised. "The proper function of the critic is to save the tale from the artist who created it." There can hardly be a better way to protect Pinter's great plays from any misinterpretation than by setting out to explain what Pinter clearly intended them to mean when he wrote them. To quote Pinter himself on the subject: "I think I can say I pay meticulous attention to the shape of things, from the shape of a sentence to the overall structure of the play. This shaping, to put it mildly, is of the first importance." As we'll see, he wasn't kidding. And to understand what Pinter meant provides definitive proof that his celebrated early plays are the works of a true artist, just as his later works, and his belated re-interpretation of his early plays, are products of his self, rather than of his soul.

What's remarkable about Harold Pinter's literary career, in fact, is that they reveal what might be termed a cancelled artist, i.e. an artist who simply abandoned his journey along the road of truth. In this respect, his first three great plays tell us about that journey up to and including its cessation, while his next three, correctly nominated "memory plays", have him remembering aspects of his early artistic life in order to produce new plays. In this respect, Harold Pinter and Samuel Beckett are brother-artists, Pinter recognising the Irish playwright and novelist as his precursor and identifying with him as a result. Indeed, Pinter and Beckett apparently even sent each other drafts of their work-in-progress for comment.

The Birthday Party

One proof that Harold Pinter has attained the status of a literary "great" is the fact that the first appearance of his work on a national stage, *The Birthday Party,* has become legendary. This legend is that of the misunderstood work of genius.

Written in 1957 when Pinter, as an actor, was on a British tour of a comedy play, *The Birthday Party* was presented at the Lyric Hammersmith in London in May 1958 only to be taken off after a few nights as a commercial and critical flop. Its demise was followed soon after by a glowing review in *The Sunday Times* whose drama critic, Harold Hobson, wrote in what was effectively a eulogy: "I am willing to risk whatever reputation I have as a judge of plays by saying…that Mr Pinter, on the evidence of this work, possesses the most original, disturbing and arresting talent in theatrical London. Mr Pinter and *The Birthday Party*, despite their experiences last week, will be heard of again."

He was right. Like Samuel Beckett's *Waiting for Godot*, which similarly elicited no little degree of incomprehension on its first appearance, *The Birthday Party* rose from the dead and is now widely considered a modern classic.

So what's it about? Again, returning to the literary legend theme, most people with any interest in drama know the basic plot. An erstwhile piano player in his late 30s, Stanley Webber, is living in a seaside boarding house run by Meg, a woman in her 60s, who is married to Petey, a deckchair attendant. Two sinister strangers, Goldberg and McCann, arrive unexpectedly. They interrogate and terrorise an increasingly erratic Stanley before staging a birthday party for him in which he snaps and tries to strangle Meg during a power-cut. The next morning, they take Stanley, reduced to an automaton, away for treatment after Petey tries, and fails, to stop them.

According to theatre critic Michael Billington, who wrote Harold Pinter's authorised biography, the play deals with a hero who is forced to conform to conventional society. Not so, said Pinter, who is quoted from a 1960 interview as saying that many people have adopted this interpretation but that wasn't his intention at all. There was no question of hero and villain.

i

Stanley

So, once again, what's the play actually about? In fact, *The Birthday Party* depicts how fear of the death of the self, the instinct for self-preservation, can persuade a human mind to abandon an incipient commitment to truth, whatever their idea of truth may be: whether an outside spirit as described in the *New Testament,* or merely a magical or mysterious form of inspiration; but, however conceived, always a means to enable the perception of reality. One indication that Harold Pinter's status as an artist is limited to his early plays is that they're often centred on an insecure or lapsed artist or truth seeker. In the case of *The Birthday* Party, we actually have two such individuals, suggesting that this was Pinter's focus when he wrote the play. The first of these is Stanley.

That Stanley is a man who is caught in a tug of war between a commitment to truth and the attachment to desire is expressed in his name. "Stanley" is an allusion to the famous 19th century explorer who discovered the "lost" missionary David Livingstone in the African jungle; and a commitment to truth involves an exploratory journey into the dark jungle of illusion, which, in turn, is symbolised by Stanley's surname, "Webber", since, as we saw in the Introduction, attachment to desire involves entrapment in a web of illusion from which the commitment to truth promises freedom.

Pinter demonstrates that Stanley is in a halfway house between reality and illusion – at once committed to truth and yet still caught in the web of illusion – in the fact that, on his first appearance, he's in a pyjama jacket and wears glasses. The pyjama jacket is a clear allusion to sleep and hence illusion, while Stanley's glasses are shown throughout the play as representing his commitment to truth, to seeing clearly the reality of the world.

The most precise statement of this dichotomy facing Stanley is made in the scene in Act 1 in which he asks the play's object of desire, Lulu, whose name suggests the femme fatale of Alban Berg's opera, to go away with him. When she asks where, he replies: "Nowhere," because, he says, there's nowhere to go, to which she answers by asking him if he's obliged to wear his glasses and he replies: "Yes." What this means is that at this point in the play Stanley is unwilling to give up his commitment to truth and, as a result, is unable to really believe in any illusionary world promising happiness.

Compare this to Stanley's reply later in the play when Goldberg asks him what he can see without his glasses: "Anything," he says. Without his commitment to truth, symbolised by his glasses, in other words, Stanley could, like anyone uncommitted to truth, be influenced to believe in any conditional reality.

Perception, however, is not knowledge, and only knowledge brings disillusionment. This is Stanley's predicament: perception without knowledge. He is, in other words, in that early stage of the artist or truth seeker's journey in which he's seen that the reality of the world is absolute and, hence, that any conditional reality must be false. It follows that happiness is an illusion. Yet he's lived his whole life up to that point believing in happiness: an absurd situation.

Not surprisingly, this explains the so-called "Theatre of the Absurd", of which Beckett and Pinter are prime exponents. Thus, in his initial dialogue with McCann, Stanley describes the boarding house in which he's living as "ridiculous", "ridiculous" being a synonym for "absurd". The question McCann asks in reply: "Why?" underlines the fact that it's because he first set out to answer the question *why* that Stanley is aware of the absurdity of a world based on the fulfilment of happiness. This idea of the absurdity of Stanley's position is echoed at the end of the play when Petey's proposal that he remain in the house to recover from his breakdown is dismissed by Goldberg as "silly", another synonym for "absurd".

Stanley shows his own understanding of the implications of his intermediate situation when he tells McCann that he's changed but that he's still the same man that he always was, i.e. he hasn't changed irrevocably through experience, only tentatively through perception. Stanley's repetition of "I mean" and "really" draws attention to the fact that he's talking about meaning and reality.

The idea of a man changed in principle, through perception – Stanley also repeats: "to look at me" – but not in practice, through experience, is also suggested in his initial dialogue with Meg, in which he says that he didn't sleep at all and then that he's been dreaming all night long. When Meg points out the contradiction, he tells her that he's been day-dreaming all night. This supposed paradox only makes sense as a spiritual metaphor: the light of truth has been cast on his world yet Stanley is still in the grip of the night of illusion and, hence, dreaming.

Stanley's predicament, then, is clearly expressed in the play in several ways. We know his state of mind. What's more, Pinter also makes clear how Stanley arrived where he is through a number of comments he makes to Meg early in the play and later to McCann and Goldberg. That his comments are made in a confused manner is typical of a mind that has suddenly become aware of the absurdity of a life lived in relation to an illusionary world. As we saw in the Introduction, the perception involved is so revolutionary that it's bound to leave the mind in a state of shock. At the same time, the mind is also aware that an urgent life and death decision is called for, which, allied to the confusion, explains Stanley's erratic behaviour throughout the play.

Nevertheless, it's possible to piece together the sequence of events in Stanley's life preceding his first appearance in *The Birthday Party*, although it's necessary to separate what actually happened from what Stanley wants to believe happened or wants others to believe happened: we're all prey to wishful thinking.

The crucial passage dealing with Stanley's early life comes in the dialogue with McCann in Act II, whose greatest revelation is in the trite phrase: "No place like home", which, significantly, Stanley follows with a laugh. It's significant because it shows that Stanley has seen the illusory nature of the world of his childhood conditioning. The phrase, in other words, means that, as far as Stanley's concerned, in reality there's no such place as "home", rather than the accepted meaning of there being no *better* place than home, although, faced with the menacing McCann, there's no doubt that's what Stanley wants him to think he means. It's just that he can't help laughing when he says it because of his awareness of the literal truth of the phrase.

We know that Stanley feels threatened by McCann because the rest of his statement is an attempt to persuade the persuader that he intends to return home quietly and stay there this time. In the process, however, he reveals two things. The first is that he'd once believed completely in the world of his early conditioning, "played records, that's about all", as he says, i.e. suggesting a passive acceptance of what his mind had recorded. This is followed by: "Everything delivered to the door", which suggests that Stanley never ventured outside his conditioned world.

However, Stanley then admits to McCann that he would never have left his home except that "business calls", specifying, moreover, that his business was "private", suggesting that it related to the soul rather than to a self created by outside influences. This equates to Bob Dylan's "something calls for you" in the song "It's All Over Now, Baby Blue" on 1965's *Bringing It All Back Home* album, this "something" being the need to answer the question *why*, which, because it's a perennial question facing mankind, is phrased by both Pinter and Dylan in the present tense. Stanley follows this with a similar statement in the past tense to convince McCann that answering the question *why* is now in the past as far as he's concerned.

This "private business", as in "that's my business" as opposed to a business completely owned by one person, involved playing the piano to express the reality of the world that Stanley perceived through the inspiration of truth. We know this because he tells Meg that he had a unique touch in his playing, "absolutely unique", just as the real world is unique, absolutely unique; it's the way things are, as opposed to any self's conditional reality of the world, which, as we've seen, can be anything, depending on the nature of that self's desires (as, for instance, in song titles such as "A World of Our Own" or "Welcome to My World").

As for Stanley's playing being inspired by truth, Stanley tells us as much during his interrogation when Goldberg asks him his trade and he answers that he plays the piano. Goldberg then asks Stanley how many fingers he uses, to which Stanley replies: "No hands!" This expresses Stanley's experience that his playing doesn't come from himself but from truth. Thus, when Goldberg then asks Stanley what he uses for pyjamas, he replies "Nothing", because pyjamas are associated with sleep and, hence, illusion, in contrast to the reality he perceives through truth.

But, as was suggested in the Introduction, the road of truth is a long and difficult road and the temptations of desire unrelenting. As a result, the artist or truth seeker's self often hopes for some proof as to the viability of their commitment to truth, i.e. that it will actually lead to their answering the question *why*, what might be termed the "doubting Thomas syndrome". In effect, this means that they seek some acknowledgement or appreciation from their fellow-men and also sometimes, perhaps often, from God, or however they might conceive the source of the spirit of truth. As we'll see, this was a major factor in Bob Dylan's career. In this respect, Stanley is no exception.

This explains Stanley's "absolutely unique touch" comment to Meg being followed by his remembering or, perhaps more likely, imagining, the distinguished audience at what appears to have been his only concert, at Lower Edmonton in north London, coming "up" to him to say that they were "grateful", before toasting him with champagne. Stanley also remembers that his "father" nearly came "down" to hear him, but didn't.

The "up" and "down" here suggests that Stanley's concert performance rather went to his head so that he imagined his audience celebrating him for his inspired playing, with perhaps also the "Our Father" of God almost coming down from his elevated position to hear it. The "father" in question, of course, could also be his biological father, to whom Stanley first says that he "dropped him a card", before definitively correcting himself that he didn't contact him at all: "No, I – I lost the address, that was it." This suggests that, in line with his conflicted nature between desire and truth, self and soul, which accounts for the "I – I", as "Webber", he wanted his father's approval but, as the artist

"Stanley", had to admit that he'd "lost the address" because, as he later tells McCann, there's "No place like home".

Stanley's repetition of the fact that the concert was at *Lower Edmonton* immediately after the "lost the address" comment appears to be significant here because it underlines the fact that he's at an early stage of the road of truth and pretty naïve as a result and hence particularly vulnerable to the force of the desire for power. As the English poet Alexander Pope wrote in *An Essay on Criticism*: "A little learning is a dangerous thing...shallow draughts intoxicate the brain...," which explains the proverb: "A little knowledge is a dangerous thing."

This is a vital point in the play, perhaps *the* vital point of *The Birthday Party*, as we'll see later, because Pinter clearly sees the soul's inspiration as an overwhelming temptation to the self to take advantage of the unique perceptions the mind receives for its own power-related ends. This may well be true. Any truth seeker knows how persistent the force of desire is in not giving up its control on a human mind. But it's also very much a perception of which Pinter the artist seems to be acutely aware. It doesn't seem to be typical of many other artists.

What's certain is that Stanley, whatever his creative talents, set out on the road of truth and had some kind of success as a pianist, enough to impress Meg anyway. The success went to his head, leading him to "sell out", in common parlance, to the desire for power, specifically power over people's minds. Now committed only to pursuing the adulation of an audience – the perennial theme of many performers as the perfect power fix – he found, like many before him, that success is not a given and life can be a bitch. The upshot was that he succumbed to the conspiracy theory of history. This arises when someone sets out to acquire power over people's minds, fails to acquire that power, and believes, in consequence, that others have the power and are conspiring against them to ensure that they don't acquire it.

In Stanley's case, he believes further that those others are out to humiliate him for his presumption in trying to take their perceived power away. As he tells Meg, they want him to "crawl". This underlines the fact that Stanley understands that the desire for power arises from the self's assertive pride.

Stanley's perception that the powers that be are out to get him is crucial to understanding *The Birthday Party*. It explains his dialogue with Meg in which he tells her that "they", who are "looking for someone", are "coming today". Soon after this, Goldberg and McCann arrive, looking for Stanley, and one of the first things Goldberg says is: "Take my tip", recalling Stanley's "I can take a tip" in his conspiracy speech.

Returning to the events in Stanley's life that preceded *The Birthday Party*, it's clear that he worked for a time as a pianist in a show on the pier of the seaside town in which he's now living. This job came to an end and he's now been staying in Meg's boarding house for a year, as she tells Goldberg, and living off "a small private income", as he tells McCann.

Yet he still dreams of a resumption of his artistic career, fantasising to Meg of having been offered a job, "a good one, too" – a phrase that re-occurs almost immediately with his account of the Lower Edmonton concert, introducing morality and, hence, desire and illusion to the equation – playing the piano in a Berlin nightclub on a "fabulous" salary, "fabulous" signifying the fantasy. Warming to his flight of fancy, he imagines his German gig as part of a round-the-world-tour.

Just as the crucial phrase with regard to his London concert involves his "absolutely unique touch", so, now, the crucial phrase describing his Berlin residency is: "And all found". This is highly ambiguous and it's in that ambiguity that its significance lies, indicating Stanley's conflicted nature; because the word "found", as the contrary to "lost", can just as easily relate to reality as it does to happiness, where it means with board and lodging provided free.

Of course, the fact that it occurs in a deluded rant anchors it firmly in the illusionary world of happiness. But the connection to his concert, where Stanley believes his playing was an expression of truth, suggests that *he* relates it to reality, as, indeed, does the suggestion of the circular nature of truth in the perceived tour being "round the world". Stanley believes, in other words, that his playing is the fulfilment of his vocation as an artist.

Although both the concert at Lower Edmonton, if it ever took place, or, more pertinently, if it was as successful as Stanley imagines, and the Berlin residency and subsequent world tour are full of patent absurdities, Stanley's perception of himself as an artist is nevertheless as crucial to the meaning of *The Birthday Party* as his belief that the powers that be are out to get him.

For, as we shall see, the play is very much concerned with the earthly battle between the desire for power and the spirit of truth, illusion versus reality, and Stanley does represent the latter as best as he's able in his conflicted state. And that best is not inconsiderable. But, remembering Harold Pinter's comments about the meaning of the play, that doesn't make him a hero. A hero belongs firmly to the world of pride and power, and artists and truth seekers are humble servants of the spirit of truth, whose purpose is to free them from that world.

The fact is that Stanley is most definitely a truth seeker and possibly an artist, too; we don't have any real evidence about his talent as a pianist, inspired or not. But that's not essential to the meaning of the play. Indeed, Stanley's unspecific relationship to truth makes him more relevant to all of us, talented or otherwise, which may well have been Pinter's intention.

What's certain is that, when we first meet him, Stanley is mired in a state of chronic indecision similar to that of Shakespeare's Hamlet, one that prevents him from actually doing anything. This indecision arises from his being trapped in a vice between the equal forces of truth and desire and his manifest unwillingness to resolve his dilemma by choosing the one or the other irrevocably because he wants both.

In short, he's lost, hence the wishful thinking of: "And all found". The physical expression of his state is in the fact that he's dirty and unshaven, spends hours in bed or sitting around Meg's boarding house, as we see and learn from various characters. As an alternative to doing nothing, he spends his time drinking, as he admits to McCann, no doubt in an attempt to forget his predicament.

It's this desperate rudderless state that has led him to accept a role defined for him by Meg. Unable to decide what to do, he does what Meg wants him to do in fulfilment of her desire for happiness.

ii
Meg

Harold Pinter tells us enough about Meg for us to know that her conditions for happiness arise from her childhood conditioning. It's her relationship with her father, in fact, that underlies her idea of happiness. The crucial details are expressed when Meg describes to McCann during Stanley's birthday party how her father cared for her as a little girl. This involves a favourite Pinter image, that of a closed room where everything's rosy – she even had a pink carpet and curtains in her little bedroom – where happiness reigns and nothing threatening is allowed to enter. She also tells McCann that her father once gave her a stool, a symbol of inferiority and dependence, thus conveying the idea that he, "a very big doctor", as she describes him, treated her as a precious possession, which clearly led her to worship him as a superior being.

However, Meg tells McCann that her father once went away without her, which obviously affected her, but her protected childhood nevertheless left its mark, conferring the illusion that she once was happy. As an adult, she wants to recreate this world, but now with *her* providing the shelter for a child of her own, who, because this is a mirror-image of her childhood, has to be male, like her father. For Meg dreams of having a child, as we see in the opening dialogue of the play between her and Petey, even though she's in her 60s, and, as she says, she'd much rather have a little boy.

This relationship is crucial to the meaning of the play because it's Meg who declares that it's Stanley's birthday, in spite of the fact that he states categorically that it's not. Meg, however, wants it to be his birthday because she wants him to be born again as the epicentre of *their* new world together in *her* house, a world, moreover, that won't involve a leaving as it did with her father: her happiness, as she states in her birthday speech, is based not only on Stanley being "my Stanley now" but also on him "not gone away". Happiness has to be permanent, "happily ever after", to be happiness.

Goldberg, too, underlines the fact that Meg's relationship with Stanley is based on desire and, hence, on the fulfilment of her need to justify an assertive pride, when he sums up her birthday speech in terms of devotion based on pride. Goldberg's take-over of the occasion by calling for a party to celebrate Stanley's birthday, moreover, signals his intention to ensure that Stanley's rebirth will be on his terms rather than Meg's.

The connection between Meg's childhood conditioning and the resulting memory of happiness and her current illusion of happiness is also made through the relation between two images: Meg's evening dress at the party, which her father gave her, as she tells Goldberg when she agrees with him that it's "wonderful" and "out of this world", and the boy's drum she gives Stanley as his present at the birthday party. Meg's entrance at that party, moreover, occurs in a manner resonant of pomp and circumstance, a loud drumbeat off-stage preceding her appearance holding sticks and drum, which, she states, makes a beautiful noise.

"To beat one's drum" is a phrase meaning to express the self or ego; and Meg clearly connects the idea of her own grand entrance in the evening dress her father gave her with the memory of herself as his precious possession and with her own possession of Stanley, for whom she bought the boy's drum. The fact that Meg thinks that the "noise" made by the drum is "beautiful" signifies her belief that the fulfilment of her happiness is good, a value judgement connected to her calling Stanley "a good boy", although "sometimes...bad" when he doesn't agree with her that she knows him "better than all the world". The contrast with Stanley's remembrance of his piano concert performance as "absolutely unique" could hardly be more obscene.

The boy's drum Meg gives Stanley as a birthday present, in fact, is essential to understanding why Stanley fits the bill as the answer to all the dreams of her childhood conditioning; for he appears to Meg as a musician; no, more than a musician, as a celebrity musician. As she tells Petey in their opening dialogue, she liked *watching* Stanley play the piano. In other words, it's not the music that matters, his "unique touch", but him playing. The crucial relationship with her childhood is that, as she tells McCann, she had musical boxes all over her bedroom that played her to sleep. This relationship between music and illusion, moreover, she associates with her glamorous father, whom she mentions immediately after.

The connection between her father and Stanley is reinforced by Meg's comment to Petey that Stanley, "of course", didn't sing. This is because, as Meg tells McCann, her nanny, a domestic servant, sang songs to her, while her father, the nanny's employer, supplied her with music.

It's clear that Stanley is well aware of the power that Meg's idea of his celebrity status gives him over her. When he feels that his shelter in her house is threatened, he responds by emphasising the distance in status between them by calling her "Mrs Boles", instead of the more egalitarian "Meg", when asking her if she realises who she's talking to when she addresses him. Meg, in turn, acknowledges the unspoken assumption of his superiority by asking when he'll play the piano again. Stanley responds with the brainstorm about his world tour.

He also exploits Meg's fear of losing him with his suggestion that "they", who are "looking for someone", are "coming today." This fear of Meg's, as we've seen, is based on the fact that she was clearly affected by her father's once going away without her, but also on the fact that Stanley, the progenitor of her happiness, once left her, too, as she says just before his terrorising of her: "Don't you go away *again*, Stan."

Meg's belief that she's found happiness with Stanley, however, is clearly not reciprocated. Lost, Stanley found a refuge with Meg. Like Meg, with her childhood rosy room that stored happiness, Stanley may for a time have believed that he'd created a room of his own with Meg. When we first meet him in *The Birthday Party*, however, there's little doubt that his credulity at the permanence of his refuge is strained to the utmost. This provides no little comedy at the outset of the play, accounting for some of the first part of that "comedy of menace" tag.

Before we even meet him, however, we're given strong indications about the nature of Meg's relationship with Stanley in her opening dialogue with Petey. Meg's calling him "that boy", a bizarre epithet considering that Stanley is in his late 30s, and a manifestly regular occurrence of bringing him a cup of tea in bed, suggests a theme of mother and surrogate son.

When he does arrive on stage, Stanley's dissatisfaction with Meg's provision of an at-least bearable refuge is first intimated by his distaste with the breakfast she offers him. His cornflakes are "horrible" because "the milk's off", and, when Meg, stung into action, gives him fried bread, he's disgusted.

There are intimations of sexuality between the two centred on Stanley's use of the word "succulent" and her sensually stroking his arm and reminding him of the "lovely afternoons" they've spent in his room, which leads him to recoil from her hand in disgust.

It's clear that, although Stanley still needs Meg, he's reaching the end of his tether with his role in *her* world. Pinter makes this clear by means of an amusing riff based on the English expression "not my cup of tea", which means something that doesn't suit.

Thus, Stanley begins by saying that he doesn't know what he'd do without Meg when she brings the teapot in, Pinter's stage direction: "(absently)" underlining the metaphorical nature of the statement. But he ends by expressing how tired he is as he, again metaphorically, puts his head in his hands. That Pinter means us to see the interplay over the tea as a metaphor is made even plainer in Act II when Stanley tells Goldberg that "this house isn't your cup of tea".

What's more, the interplay with Meg over the tea also includes Stanley's rejection of Meg's coming "into a man's bedroom", i.e. not the bedroom of "that boy" as she calls him to Petey, and waking him up with a morning cuppa. The deeper significance of this is that, rather than waking up from his sleep of illusion to see the light of truth, Stanley perennially wakes up only to dependency in Meg's illusionary world. Pinter suggests this through Stanley wiping his eyes under his glasses immediately before this interchange with Meg, as if wiping the sleep of illusion from his eyes and also through Meg calling him "Stanny" immediately after the above exchange, since his connection to truth, as we've already suggested, is symbolised by Stanley's first name. Indeed, she calls him "Stan" and "Stanny" when she first shouts upstairs for him to come down, rather than "Stanley".

Stanley's dependency is also manifested in Meg's demands that he say "please" and "sorry" in their interplay preceding the introduction of the teapot, a superficially amusing dialogue that ends, less superficially and less amusingly, in her observation that he deserves "the strap".

Finally, all the intimations that Stanley is nearing the end of his tether with Meg are brought to a climax. This follows his explicit demand for "a new room". He stands and exits quickly by the door leading to the hall, the street door slams...and Stanley returns!

Meg's asking him whether the sun is shining is Pinter's ironic comment on the significance of this return. Almost immediately, Meg mentions that two gentlemen are coming to stay. Stanley is first afraid that his refuge is under imminent threat and then takes refuge in self-delusion. However, faced with the prospect of being forced to leave Meg's, he suddenly finds that it is his cup of tea after all: cue an amusing interplay about his right to his cuppa. This is then followed by Stanley asserting the authority of his celebrity status over Meg to ensure that she continues to provide him with a refuge.

Just prior to the arrival of Goldberg and McCann, we have the dialogue between Stanley and Lulu in which he asks her to go away with him because "It's no good here", but that there's nowhere else to go, showing his complete understanding of the fact that all attempts at happiness are futile, an understanding underlined by his affirmation that his glasses, his connection with truth, are essential to him.

If Stanley refuses to give up his tentative commitment to truth, however, he's not prepared to commit himself irrevocably because he wants the prospect of happiness, too. Clearly, then, he's in a chronic state of indecision that creates tension both for himself and for the audience. It's this tension that's first heightened by the appearance of Goldberg and McCann and then broken as Stanley is broken.

iii
Goldberg

Although *The Birthday Party* may be said, with good reason, to be "about" Stanley, Goldberg is undoubtedly the principal character through whom Harold Pinter expresses much of the play's meaning. It's no coincidence that Pinter played Goldberg in a TV adaptation.

From the action of the play, it's clear that Goldberg and McCann represent the powers that be or Establishment and, as such, are puppets of the force of the desire for power, "the prince of this world". They're antagonistic to Stanley because the Establishment sees him as a threat, essentially from his soul's incipient commitment to truth, but, practically, from the danger that he could influence others in this respect.

Stanley threatens the Establishment through his perception of illusion, which rubbishes any idea of position in the world, something for which McCann vaults Goldberg on their first entrance. Their assignment, therefore, is to persuade Stanley to abandon his insight and return to their "reality" in which the fulfilment of the desire for power, or happiness, is not an illusion.

The fact that Stanley could actively use his insight, moreover, against the Establishment by obtaining power over people's minds means that they must snuff out this potential threat by breaking the assertive pride that would underlie any such desire, something of which Stanley is acutely aware even before they arrive.

This two-pronged attack to ensure Stanley's mental and physical obedience – his independence extinguished and his pride broken – is precisely what happens in *The Birthday Party*.

However, if the play was only about a battle for power it wouldn't rank as the major work of art it undoubtedly is. What lifts it to the level of art is the fact that Pinter reveals how Western Civilization, indeed, any civilization, although he's concerned with the one he knows best, is based on illusion through its attachment to the force of desire and how this affects its members. He does this by making Goldberg and McCann operate on two levels. On the one hand, they're symbols; on the other, characters in their own right.

As with Stanley, their symbolic nature is suggested in their names. Goldberg is a Jewish name and, as such, he may be said to represent the Old Testament tradition in Western Civilization, just as McCann is Irish and a Catholic, representing, therefore, the New Testament tradition. Just to make it clear, they represent how religion is an essential part of civilization, the part that replaces the purpose or meaning provided by the spirit of truth.

The names also have a further symbolic role to play, however. For a "berg" is a hill or mountain. This might refer to Mount Sinai, where according to the Old Testament, Moses received the Ten Commandments, and it could, as a result, be seen as referring to Western Civilization's system of values. But it's far more potent as an image representing aspiration or ambition, "getting to the top". This interpretation is supported by the fact that the "berg" in question is "gold", which is associated in the West with wealth and power.

Moreover, Pinter's use of this "mountain" image occurs in three other instances in the play, demonstrating how precise and thorough his construction of the play is. The first is the venue for Stanley's concert, which could have proved to be the first step on his rise to fortune and fame. The venue is Lower Edmonton and "mont" is French for mountain. The "Lower", in this respect, passes comment on the lowly level of human influence Stanley enjoys in contrast to Goldberg's.

The second time is when Goldberg and McCann take the broken Stanley away to "Monty", whom Goldberg describes as the best person for "special treatment" or "brain-washing".

Finally, the third time is when McCann, on his first meeting with Stanley, reminds him of his childhood aspirations by whistling "The Mountains of Morne".

McCann's name, too, is manifestly symbolic. The significance is in the first three letters: M.C.C., which stand for Marylebone Cricket Club. Pinter makes this clear by having Goldberg refer to the M.C.C. shortly after his entry. Goldberg also uses cricketing metaphors throughout the play. But it's in his explanation to McCann of how he reached his position that Goldberg conjures up the most telling cricketing metaphors by relating them to values, quoting from Sir Henry Newbolt's poem, "Vitaï Lampada", in which a future soldier learns commitment to duty in cricket matches, "Play up, play up, and play the game", and from American sportswriter Ford Frick's "Keep your eye on the ball", here related to cricket, both of which Goldberg connects to one of the Ten Commandments and to following "the line" so that "you can't go wrong".

As we saw in the Introduction, values are the criteria which act as the signposts delineating the straight road or "line" the egoist believes they must follow in order to realise the conditions for the fulfilment of happiness, and it's clear that Goldberg is using images associated with cricket as metaphors for values espoused by Western Civilization.

Similarly, Meg's surnames is Boles, which may be taken as another cricketing metaphor relating to values as she claims to be a moral person and an excellent wife.

As Goldberg's name expresses the idea of ambition, then, so does McCann's conjure up the idea of values and, therefore, morality. Where Catholicism is concerned, throughout history this has always meant loyalty to the Church, or orthodoxy, representing right, and disloyalty, or heresy, representing wrong. However, Pinter doesn't get too hung up about the precise meaning of the two names, rather, they're meant to be taken loosely to suggest all that's involved in the desire for power in the context of Western Civilization, which is what Goldberg and McCann represent on a symbolic level. Thus, McCann compliments Goldberg shortly after their first appearance on being "a true Christian", with Goldberg replying "in a way", although he's manifestly Jewish.

This isn't to say that Goldberg and McCann don't represent very different strands within the Establishment of Western Civilization. The distinction is made in a sharp exchange between them at the beginning of Act II, when McCann's tearing a sheet of newspaper into strips is dismissed by Goldberg as childish and pointless. McCann's paper-tearing is clearly meant as a metaphor for censorship, a forcible control by the Establishment of what's permitted. A similar situation occurs with McCann's breaking of Stanley's glasses, which he does without Goldberg's knowledge or, presumably, approval.

This idea of censorship is very much in McCann's character, which is that of a loutish bully boy. His idea of control is manifestly a combination of the Spanish Inquisition and the IRA, as are his values. The images he uses are all connected with violent retribution towards anyone who steps out of line. Similarly, he expresses the self-righteous brutality of the bigot towards Lulu.

Goldberg, in contrast, regards censorship as childish and pointless because he believes in the power of persuasion. Since he specifies that he chose McCann to help him bring Stanley back into line, Goldberg clearly thinks that censorship, whether of word or action, might have a part to play. But censorship only controls the actions of a rebel, not their thoughts, which is what concerns Goldberg throughout the play. He wants to persuade Stanley that he's wrong and they're right because of their greater understanding of reality and, hence, of the purpose of life. His attitude, in other words, is psychological rather than physical.

This brings us to Goldberg's character. Paradoxically, the essential factor in this character is his fundamental connection to Stanley. The two, in other words, have a lot in common. Thus, he tells McCann on their first entrance that when the Stanley job came up, he was "naturally" approached to take care of it.

As we'll see, it's natural for him to be the one to bring Stanley back into line because he himself was once out of line just as Stanley is now out of line. He is, in other words, naturally qualified to understand Stanley's position and, hence, how to undermine it.

If there are definite similarities between them, however, there are also differences. Pinter makes this point of similarity and dissimilarity in Act III when Goldberg enters following a dialogue between Meg and Petey. Meg tells Goldberg that she thought it was Stanley entering and he asks her if she finds a resemblance between them. When she says that they look quite different, he agrees that their "build" is different. Goldberg's reply suggests that he doesn't deny that there's a resemblance between himself and Stanley, only that they have a "different build", by which Pinter seems to mean that they have a different history.

The same point is made in Act I when McCann asks Goldberg whether the job they are on will be like anything they've done before and Goldberg answers that it'll be different but that certain elements will have similarities.

The point Pinter is making here is essential to understanding *The Birthday Party*. It's that the need to justify an assertive pride and the need to know *why* are fundamental to the human condition. They apply to everyone. This accounts for the similarities. However, there are differences between one individual and another which depend on the particular nature of each individual's history. These differences may be summed up as the choices we make at any time between our attachment to desire and any commitment to truth. Knowing the process from personal experience and, hence, Stanley's state of mind, Goldberg tells McCann following their exchange described in the previous paragraph that everything depends on the attitude of their subject, i.e. which choice Stanley makes when they confront him. Incidentally, this also explains why Goldberg needs McCann's strong-arm support: as insurance that, whatever choice Stanley makes, their mission will be accomplished without too much trouble if his own persuasive tactics prove insufficient.

Returning to the similarity between Goldberg and Stanley, what evidence does Pinter provide? Well, just as it's possible to piece together Stanley's past from the information he supplies, so, too, is it possible to work out Goldberg's history or the "build" that made him who he is. Stanley's history might be said to consist of two distinct phases: his upbringing and his reaction to that upbringing. Goldberg's, on the other hand, consists of three separate phases. Pinter makes this point very strongly in the play by having Goldberg refer to himself at different times by three different names: Nat, Simey, and Benny.

The name Benny is probably meant to provide a connection between Goldberg and his Uncle Barney, about whom he offers an affectionate monologue on his first appearance on stage. This monologue provides a number of hints that the uncle filled young Goldberg's head with ideas that ultimately led him to question the meaning of his conditioned upbringing. Perhaps the clearest is the fact that he recalls his uncle regularly taking him to the seaside. This remembrance clashes with Goldberg's speech to McCann about values in Act III, where he cautions against going too near the water.

In turn, it recalls his attempt, moments before, to get Petey out of the way by trying to persuade him to go to the beach to prepare his deck chairs, asserting that the seaside crowds will be "lying on their backs, swimming out to sea". This smacks not only of absurdity, the perception of which is a by-product of a connection to truth, but also of being lost or going nowhere, a state with which Goldberg seems familiar as he follows it with the exclamation: "My life...," just as his lesson to avoid going too near the water suggests a lesson learned from painful experience. The overall impression is that Uncle Barney's influence led Goldberg to abandon the dry land or firm ground of his childhood values.

Again, his uncle is said to be both cultured and cosmopolitan, suggesting an understanding not bound by the narrow confines of his upbringing, and also, more pertinently, "an all-round man", which clashes with Goldberg's advice to "follow the line". This is important because it contrasts the linear process of fulfilling happiness and the circular process of fulfilling the need to know *why*, a suggestion almost certainly confirmed by the hint of truth and meaning in the rhetorical question "what do you mean?" that Goldberg adds to "all-round man".

The connection to truth is suggested in other ways such as Goldberg's description of himself as an apprentice, which follows "take a chance, let yourself go, what can you lose." A more obvious hint, however, comes with a reference to the fact that Barney had a house just outside Basingstoke, as this chimes with Stanley, who later tells McCann that he had lived for many years in just that town.

Another connection Pinter clearly means us to make is with Stanley and Goldberg's singular public performance. Any reaction against conditioning is defined by that conditioning because you remain under its influence until you're completely disillusioned, which takes time. The nature of any such reaction, therefore, is defined by what you're reacting against. With Stanley, Pinter expresses his conditioning in terms of "played records", so that his reaction, playing the piano at his concert in Lower Edmonton, is compatible.

This relationship between conditioning and reaction applies equally to Goldberg, who expresses his conditioning in terms of a philosophy or ethics based on the *Bible*. His reaction is also philosophical or ethical because it's to speak at the Ethical Hall, Bayswater, on the Necessary and the Possible. Goldberg also tells us what his talk was about by conveniently using its central premise in the interrogation of Stanley, which can hardly be a coincidence: "We admit possibility only after we grant necessity. It is possible because necessary but by no means necessary through possibility."

This relates to the fact that we're bound to believe that it's possible for the necessary conditions for the fulfilment of our happiness to be realised. In short, the necessity produces the possibility or it's possible because necessary. The second part, that it's not necessary through possibility means that, even if happiness were possible, it wouldn't be necessary for us to choose happiness because we have an alternative, which is to set out to answer the question *why*, and we might choose this rather than happiness.

If it isn't clear enough, it should now be obvious that Goldberg, like Stanley, was once committed to answering the question *why* because he couldn't have lectured on the subject he did at the Ethical Hall without having once been inspired by the spirit of truth!

What's more, this final proof also provides a link with Goldberg's Uncle Barney, the suggested progenitor of that commitment. The connection is made in two ways, firstly the fact that Goldberg gives his talk in Bayswater, which calls to mind his trips to the seaside with Barney. In the second instance, the only other time Goldberg mentions Barney is when he recalls his father's death, which is also the one time he refers to himself as Benny.

In the speech, his dying father appeals to him to return to his wife and to do his duty and, should he ever be in any difficulties, to rely on his Uncle Barney. It's clear from this that Goldberg rejected his conditioned world or "home" and that the uncle knows something about it but ultimately sides with the world Goldberg has abandoned; for if Uncle Barney set young Goldberg on the road to a commitment to truth that led him to perceive the absurdity of his conditioned reality, that clearly wasn't his intention. Uncle Barney may have been an "all-round-man", but he was also "respected by the whole community". Pinter suggests that Barney's questioning of accepted values was at best blinkered – the deck chairs he and young Goldberg sat in on their seaside jaunts had "canopies" – so that rather than going all out to see the nature of reality, he merely dipped his toes in the water: "we'd have a little paddle", as Goldberg remembers it.

Goldberg, on the other hand, went much further, leading to his rejection of his conditioned world, hence his lecture at the Ethical Hall, which, as we've seen, chimes with Stanley's concert in Lower Edmonton. Thus, just as Stanley has two distinct phases in his life, so Goldberg has the same two phases. What's more, like Stanley, who sees his piano playing as having an "absolutely unique touch" but with "no hands", so did Goldberg believe that in rejecting his conditioned world he'd committed himself to truth, which is shown by the subject he chose for his lecture. And, again, he was right, but only for a time. Because, like Stanley, the reaction he received from his audience, or believed he'd received, went to his head, tempted him, and he fell.

What Goldberg believed was a commitment to truth henceforth became the expression of his attachment to a desire for power over people's minds. Pinter makes the point that

Stanley and Goldberg's situations were precisely the same in this respect by having each remember their big night with the same expression: "They were all there that night."

This, then, is the "resemblance" between them. But Pinter also emphasises their "different build". For, whereas the play shows us Stanley's forcible return from the second phase of his life to the first, it's also clear that Goldberg is in a third phase that's different from the two phases he shares with Stanley. This point is made through the fact that his first name at the time *The Birthday Party* takes place is Nat, while Pinter makes clear that the name associated with Goldberg's conditioned existence is Simey.

This first phase of Goldberg's life is associated with the two women in his life, his mother and his wife, one being merely an extension of the other, as Pinter tells us by having Goldberg tell Petey that they were "the same" and "identical" and by him recalling his relationship with each in identical terms: "Simey! My old mum (or "my wife") used to shout, 'quick before it gets cold'." On both occasions, the same observation is made, firstly by McCann, then by Lulu: "I thought your name was Nat," and Goldberg replies: "She called me Simey."

Goldberg allows us a number of glimpses into the world he lived in as Simey. He tells Meg that he used to be in the business of dressmaking, a typically Jewish occupation, and by using Jewish expressions and referring to Jewish delicacies served up by his mother and wife implies that he lived a conventionally Jewish life. Perhaps the essential phrase he uses to describe this life is "Not size but quality", while a strong connection is established with Stanley's early life in that both mention "Fullers" teashop and "Boots Library", suggesting a similar background.

However, Goldberg's references to his life as Simey certainly no longer apply to his life as Nat. The "little Austin" he tells us "satisfied" him earlier provides a glaring contrast to the big car he has now and which he boasts about in the play. This provides the clue to the difference between Goldberg's old life as Simey and his current life as Nat. For, while the references to the former are all intended to convey an impression of respect for the influences of his conditioned environment and knowing his place, of a life lived in his "bungalow with the flat roof", his current life as Nat is clearly based on overweening power and pride. It follows that Goldberg's references to his earlier life are clearly hypocritical, his cynical seduction of Lulu, for instance, being in stark contrast to his reminiscences of himself as a youngster who never took liberties with women.

Goldberg's manifest contempt for the life of his conditioned childhood environment is expressed most forcefully through his extraordinary outburst in Act III when McCann calls him Simey following his admission of fatigue. Goldberg grabs McCann by the throat and murderously screams at him never to call him by a name that he clearly equates with subservience, which is why he hates to be reminded of it. Clearly, his abandonment of his earlier life for his current role as a "persuader" under the name Nat was a reaction against that subservience by choosing perceived strength and power. Indeed, there's even a suggestion that he murdered his wife in order to remove an impediment to his climbing the greasy pole of the Establishment, Lulu's questions about his role as a husband eliciting his reply that he gave her a good funeral. His only recollection of his wife in the play, in fact, is either as a provider of food on a plate, implying his dependence as an acquiescent husband, or of burying her. Goldberg also makes much of Stanley having murdered his wife, even though Stanley denies ever having had a wife.

The name "Nat" testifies to his new role, conjuring as it does the word "gnat", in his case of the blood-sucking variety, a derivation which is supported by his reference to his teeth, which he equates with his lofty position in the exchange with McCann following his outburst. In turn, this suggests the idea of a bloodthirsty animal, which is supported by his sinister correction of McCann when the two are seducing Stanley with dreams of power at the end of the play and his mention of "animals" is repeated by his subordinate to his annoyance.

Pinter also provides evidence as to what prompted Goldberg to adopt his role as Nat, with the seed of his third coming, as it were, being planted during his talk at the Ethical Hall. As we've seen, this was the product of a commitment to truth, but led him to acquire a taste for the acquisition of power; and he tells us that this came about through his discovery of a talent for speaking, a gift of the gab. We see this in the play when Lulu compliments him on being a marvellous speaker and, Goldberg, clearly flattered, remembers the "wonderful opportunity" of his lecture, which, he says, he'll never forget. And on this occasion, at least, he means what he says.

Thus, while Goldberg's lecture on the Necessary and the Possible was, initially at least, the expression of a truth seeker against the established state of affairs, directed towards divorcing people from their illusions – Goldberg tells Lulu that "It went like a bomb," suggesting the seditious anti-Establishment attitude of the anarchist – yet it was followed by its exact opposite: "Since then I always speak at weddings," which suggests cementing people to their dreams of happiness.

Yet if this was all there is to *The Birthday Party*, it would be a pretty depressing play. Fortunately, it isn't. For if Goldberg has largely replaced truth with power, something which also has an appeal for Stanley, yet he can't get over his past love of truth and what it taught him about the world. We see this again and again. With Goldberg, it's a pretty distant prospect; his lecture, as he tells Lulu, was "a good while ago". Stanley, on the other hand, still has a pretty close relationship with truth, in spite of the temptations of power. Whereas Meg's questions about the weather to Petey, for instance, are all phrased to receive the answer she wants to hear, Stanley's are more scientific. And, as we've seen, even when desperate, he still can't kid himself that there's anywhere to go with Lulu to escape his predicament.

Goldberg, too, can be pretty scientific, but his relationship to truth is stained by his longstanding loyalty to a lust for power. Thus, when Lulu complains about his cynical seduction of her, his replies put her right where the facts are concerned, but the honesty he reveals is brutal. The point is made with devastating truth when Lulu asks him why he took such liberties with her and he replies that he did it because she wanted him to. In short, she got what she deserved: "That's fair enough," as McCann comments.

Their dialogue in Act III is clearly intended by Pinter to provide a contrast with Lulu's dialogue with Stanley in Act I. Nat seduces Lulu, Stanley doesn't. This illustrates the difference between them. Goldberg is irredeemably committed to his lust for power, Stanley isn't, at least not initially.

However, if Goldberg consciously rejected truth, the dilemma he faced when he moved away from his conditioned environment and set out to express what truth had taught him about the nature of reality is patently still unresolved. This is the essential truth about Goldberg. The differences between himself and Stanley are secondary when compared to this similarity.

Pinter expresses this similarity between their states of mind through a telling detail. This occurs at a point in Act III following a dialogue between Goldberg and Petey when Pinter tells us through a stage direction that Goldberg is "uneasy", indeed, he's probably at his most uneasy throughout the entire play. It's then that he smokes his one and only cigarette in our experience of him.

Stanley smokes two cigarettes in *The Birthday Party*, both at moments of intense emotion connected to the conflicted state that's threatening to tear him apart and leads to a nervous breakdown at the end of Act II. This conflicted state, as we've seen, arises from his questioning the idea of a conditional reality of the world. The fact that the Jewish Goldberg is still, for all his perceived self-confidence, in the same conflicted state is expressed in the play by the Egyptian – i.e. what might be perceived on historical grounds as "anti-Semitic" – brand of cigarettes he smokes: Abdullahs.

The connection between Stanley's cigarette smoking and Goldberg's, therefore, draws attention to the particular significance of what Goldberg is saying at the time that he feels obliged to smoke.

This is his explanation to Petey of what happened to Stanley at the end of the birthday party. It was, he says, purely and simply, a nervous breakdown. Petey asks what brought it on so suddenly and Goldberg's reply reveals the essential factor about himself. When speaking about something of extreme delicacy that involves us, we often pretend to be speaking about someone else, a fact with which audiences, in the theatre as in life, are generally familiar. This is what Goldberg does on this occasion. And what he says is that a friend of his was telling him, "only the other day", about a similar case, i.e. his own, not entirely similar, but quite alike.

This friend told him that such cases sometimes happen "gradual" and at other times all at once. The essential fact, however, is that "with certain people...it's a foregone conclusion." It's then that, "unsteadily", he takes out his cigarette case.

The "friend" to whom he's referring is probably Monty, to whom Goldberg and McCann take Stanley at the play's conclusion for what might be termed "mental reconditioning". This is suggested by the association of Goldberg's "nervous breakdown" speech with what he says immediately before. This is that he isn't really qualified to say whether Stanley is any better, which is the question Petey asks him, because he hasn't the requisite qualifications, the "letters after his name".

Pinter is suggesting, then, that Goldberg, "only the other day", found himself facing the same conflicted state between desire and truth as Stanley, that he was unable to resolve the dichotomy and was forced to consult a superior authority. This interpretation is underlined by Goldberg's lapse into ungrammatical English, with his "gradual", to suggest his ignorance and consequent need to place his trust in someone more lettered.

As we've seen, Goldberg believes himself to have given up any commitment to truth many years before, his lecture being "a good while ago". From the above, however, it's clear that truth continues to haunt him. Indeed, even though he might believe that his recent treatment by Monty or whoever has silenced truth's echo in his mind – or why would he think that he's the right man to bring Stanley back to the straight and narrow? – his belief is manifestly delusional.

Pinter establishes this in a number of ways. One is Goldberg's lapse into slang or ungrammatical English, in line with his "gradual" in the speech above. This is meant to provide a glaring contrast to his gift of the gab, which is now entirely in the service of the desire for power. It occurs in Act II when he lauds Meg for her birthday speech to Stanley by giving his hypocritical speech about quality rather than size, "a little Austin" and so on, which concludes with: "We all wander on our tod through this world. It's a lonely pillow to kip on."

Having committed himself to the Establishment in fulfilment of his overweening pride, Goldberg appears, on the surface at least, supremely confident that there's no other choice. This admission of lack of direction and alienation: "wander" and "tod", arising from a life lived in sleep or illusion: "a lonely pillow to kip on", suggests the opposite.

Again, Goldberg's confidence in the strength of his commitment to the desire for power accounts for his air of invincibility, allowing him to assure McCann when he's "all over the place" that bringing Stanley to heel will be a stroll in the park. Yet the action of the play, involving the confrontation of power and truth, clearly shatters this confidence, leading Goldberg to admit, as he does to McCann, that he feels uncommonly "knocked out". It's only McCann's threatening his position by calling him Simey that brings him back to himself.

It's at this time that Goldberg reasserts his commitment to the values of his conditioned world: "Play up, play up, and play the game". This seminal speech includes: "Nothing's changed", which chimes with Stanley's "I suppose I have changed, but I'm still the same man..." Moreover, just as Stanley's assertion to McCann is insincere, so, too, is Goldberg's. For the latter's "Nothing's changed...All my life I've said the same...And don't go too near the water" clearly refers to his commitment to truth, which did change him and continues to haunt him by reminding him of the absurdity of his conditioned world. This prevents him from truly believing in any conditional reality, leaving him, like Stanley, in a no man's land between truth and desire.

Thus, Goldberg's passionate speech about the values that guarantee happiness ends with a pathetic attempt to re-establish his belief in a conditional reality of the world. Pinter makes the point with stage directions that descend to a climax: from "vacant" to "desperate" to a cacophonous "lost".

This failure leads him to recollect his promise to his dying father to reject his life as Benny, a life in which Goldberg had committed himself to truth. Again, he tries to justify the wisdom of that rejection, but fails completely because he can't forget his perception of the absurdity of his conditioned world that truth revealed to him.

Thus, he can't forget his father's death-bed confession: "I lost my life in the service of others", even as he pleaded for his son's unquestioning loyalty to family values. Then Goldberg's attempt to justify his belief in that world on the grounds of ancient tradition swiftly descends into farce as he locates the roots of that tradition in a "great-gran-granny". Pinter's stage direction here pointedly links Goldberg's "triumphant" expression with "vacant".

With this empty justification for his life, which is justification for a life wasted, "lost time", in Marcel Proust's novel sequence *In Search of Lost Time*, Goldberg rises from his recumbent position of exaggerated respect to pronounce that it explains why he's reached his position of power, blind to the fact that all his so-called philosophical efforts to give his life meaning merely serve to prove how self-deceiving are all his boasts of strength and power.

Impelled by the strength of his creative inspiration, Harold Pinter couldn't help at this point to bring the whole absurd situation to active life on the stage by having Goldberg's empty boasts of power graphically illustrated by one of the most bizarre occurrences ever depicted on a theatre stage. This involves

Goldberg asking his subordinate, McCann, to blow into his mouth, which, he does, twice.

Thus, finally, Goldberg is reduced to bolstering his faltering ego by feeding on what he sees as the breath of McCann's life, which is an unswerving belief in the unquestionable Authority of the Establishment of which Goldberg is a leading member. Considering that Goldberg's whole position is based on a dogmatic certainty that his philosophical attitude represents the true attitude to life, to which everyone must defer once they're made aware of it, the only certainty we're left with is how absolutely illusory it is.

iv

McCann

McCann provides a contrast to Goldberg, not only symbolically in terms of coercion and persuasion, but also as a character. It's no coincidence that, during Stanley's birthday party, he and Meg are paired because, like Meg, McCann yearns for the environment of his childhood conditioning. Called upon to sing a song, he sings "Come Back Paddy Reilly to Ballyjamesduff" by James McEleney, a song about returning to one's early home, which is equated with the Garden of Eden.

This longing differentiates McCann from the mindless hit-man. When Goldberg absurdly and hypocritically recalls his own childhood environment, McCann responds sincerely with a recollection of his home in Ireland. Goldberg's dismissing the comparison merely provides an ironic comment on his own insincerity.

We know, then, that McCann is profoundly homesick through his consciousness that he's lost his "home". It's this sense of loss that accounts for his dissatisfaction throughout *The Birthday Party*. He agrees with Goldberg when he laments the loss of love and affection our mothers taught us in the nursery and, hilariously, answers "Never" when Goldberg asks how often one meets someone it's a pleasure to meet. He also agrees with Goldberg's assertion that everywhere he goes is like a funeral.

His sense of the loss of a world in which he fundamentally believes also explains his uncertainty about the value of his current life. This, in turn, explains the nervous fear that underlies all his actions in the play, an anxiety apparent from his first entry on stage. He correctly explains his situation to Goldberg as only being "all right" once he knows what he's doing. The problem is that he has serious doubts about what he's doing.

The doubts resurface in Act III when they produce a manifest distrust of, and hostility towards, Goldberg, that lead to open warfare between the two as McCann can't wait to finish the job. It's then that he taunts Goldberg by reminding him of his humble beginnings as Simey and Goldberg responds by re-establishing his authority.

There's no question that Goldberg has the power over McCann; but Goldberg's a persuader; he doesn't believe in an authority based solely on force. So he sets out to persuade McCann to follow his orders. He does so through an appeal to McCann's attachment to the values of his childhood conditioning, calling him "Seamus" in the process. On the job, though, McCann's first name is "Dermot".

The two names, Seamus and Dermot, signify the two separate phases in McCann's life, his current one as a hit-man for the Establishment, under the name Dermot, and a previous one, that of his childhood conditioning, as Seamus. The name "Seamus" may even be meant to convey a connection with the name that distinguishes Goldberg's phase of attachment to his childhood conditioning: Simey.

The reason for McCann's move is that, like Goldberg, he's been seduced by the desire for power to the point where he now considers that his childhood home offers him too little scope for that desire: witness his admiration for Goldberg's "position" and his appreciation for what Goldberg has done for him. But it's obviously not enough to dispel his doubts. And it's these doubts that lead McCann to accuse Stanley of having betrayed Ireland, the IRA, and the Catholic Church, all elements of his early world with which McCann himself identifies. The accusations are given their force, that is, by the fact that they apply to himself, not to Stanley. He is, in short, deflecting his self-criticism onto another in order to make himself feel less burdened. In this respect, it's highly significant that his accusations against Stanley are followed by McCann's nostalgic reminiscences of his early life.

McCann, then, is tortured by the uncomfortable feeling that he has sold out and it's this sense of betrayal that also accounts for his violence. Feeling bad about himself, he takes it out on others, particularly Stanley, but also Goldberg. When Stanley tricks him, for instance, he responds with a hysterical violence that even takes in his boss.

However, the reverse of this violence is a reluctance to represent a cause towards which he has no fundamental commitment other than personal ambition. Even the cynicism acquired from his current environment cannot insulate him against the consciousness of that fact. This explains his contradictory attitude towards Goldberg, but also towards Stanley. McCann follows Goldberg in setting out to pacify him, but it's clear that he bears him no personal animosity, which explains his haste in wanting to get the job done and go.

If Stanley and Goldberg are both divided, then, McCann is equally divided. But whereas, with them, the division arises from their tentative commitment to truth, with McCann it comes from his indecision as to how best to achieve happiness: whether through a return to his roots or the continued enjoyment of his status as a hit-man for Goldberg's employers. McCann's divided nature serves to render ironic Goldberg's injunction for him to blow into his mouth. For it invests McCann with a single-minded loyalty to the Establishment and its values which he clearly doesn't feel at the same time as it underlines Goldberg's own divided mind.

Thus, if Goldberg and McCann symbolically represent the Authority and Establishment of Western Civilization, they're also as divided as the rebel they've come to return to that Civilization. The doubts of these Establishment stooges, however, are kept just sufficiently under control to justify Goldberg's assertion to McCann "that the assignment will be carried out and the mission accomplished"; not, however, "with no excessive aggravation" to them, as Goldberg hopes, or to Stanley, indeed, especially not to Stanley.

v

The Birthday Party

Goldberg and McCann's breaking of Stanley is based on the carrot and stick strategy of persuasion and coercion. As we saw in the Introduction, disillusionment often appears to the self as the abandonment of the idea of "home", of all the ideas we received from our childhood conditioning which are comfortingly familiar, warm as sleep, for a move towards what, in contrast, appears alien and cold. As such, it inspires reluctance in the conditioned mind. At its deepest level, this reluctance amounts to a fear of self-extinction that triggers the instinct for self-preservation.

Stanley being in precisely this situation of reluctance and fear enables the pair to tempt him to return "home" – that's the carrot – and terrorise him with the prospect of self-extinction – that's the stick.

Thus, on the first meeting between Goldberg and Stanley, the former speaks lyrically about childhood, which he pointedly associates with warmth in "hot water bottles", "hot milk" and "soap suds". Goldberg and McCann's subsequent interrogation of Stanley takes a brutally contrary direction. This starts by alluding to his hopeless drifting, which he can hardly deny, and concludes with questions about his identity that lead to concerted assertions that he's dead. Similarly, in Act III, before they take Stanley away, they tell him that he's "a dead duck" but that they can save him "from a worse fate", which is the death of his self.

The birthday party they throw for Stanley signifies a celebration of his rebirth, not the rebirth of his soul into reality, which he'd first set out to achieve on committing to truth, but the rebirth of his rejected self into his conditioned childhood environment, i.e. his return "home" after mental reconditioning to remove any traces of truth. Significantly, Goldberg lyricises the significance of a birthday in the only dialogue he and Stanley share in the play as escaping self-extinction – "what are you but a corpse waiting to be washed?" – by waking up in his own home in the morning.

Goldberg and McCann's strategy is so precisely calculated to work with Stanley because Goldberg, having been there himself, knows his man. Stanley, who is acutely aware of the dichotomy he finds himself facing, knows that sooner or later he must decide between self and soul, desire and truth. As a result, he only needs to hear Goldberg's name to know that the decision he's desperately been avoiding is now upon him. As Goldberg tells Meg, if they hadn't come today, they'd have come tomorrow. He's glad, though, that they came just in time for Stanley's birthday.

The pivot of *The Birthday Party*, then, is Stanley's decision between truth and desire. As Goldberg tells McCann, everything depends on their subject's attitude. And, from the outset, there's little doubt as to Stanley's decision. No sooner does Meg mention that two gentlemen are coming than he's taking refuge in illusion.

Ironically, it's Meg, who believes that she knows Stanley "better than all the world", knows him as the son she's always desired as a means of her own rebirth, who welcomes Goldberg and McCann into her home so that they can take him back to the home to which they know he belongs: "I know him!" as McCann tells Stanley. Thus, Meg's question to Stanley after remembering Goldberg's name: "Do you know them?" asks the fundamental question of the play. The fact that Stanley subserviently sits down immediately on learning Goldberg's name already suggests the answer. Shortly after, Meg introduces the theme of his erroneous birthday and gives him his present, a boy's drum, as a self-serving replacement for his piano.

Stanley's reaction provides the climax to Act I, which encapsulates his predicament. The absurd reminder of his piano-playing, which Stanley saw as the expression of his commitment to truth, reveals to him what he has become at Meg's: a caricature. This leads him to try and leave the cosy illusionary world she has created for him as he heads for the front door. But he can't leave unless he resolves his dichotomy, and as he won't, so he returns and asks her if he should hang the drum around his neck, an admission of his dependency. At first, he beats the drum regularly, an action play of the life she wants him to live with her. But the beat becomes erratic, savage and possessed. This expresses Stanley's de facto admission of the reality of his situation: the fact that his commitment to truth was scuppered by his continuing possession by the force of the desire for power. Unwilling to commit absolutely to truth through his fear of self-extinction, he is ripe for the breaking by Goldberg and McCann.

Act II begins with Stanley's meeting with McCann. The latter introduces the theme of the lyrically remembered aspirations of a conditioned childhood environment by whistling "The Mountains of Morne", with which Stanley joins in. Stanley tries to trick McCann by insisting that he can be trusted to return "home" without outside interference, but McCann makes it brutally clear that he cannot do so on his own terms. This introduces the carrot and stick theme of Stanley's seduction, which is then played out with the entrance of Goldberg, who, rather than McCann, will set the terms of Stanley's return. McCann is just there as the "muscle", the censor, symbolised by his torn newspapers.

During Stanley's interrogation, faced as he is with renouncing truth, so does Stanley re-discover his commitment, at least for a while. This is essential for Harold Pinter to demonstrate what such a commitment can reveal about the human condition, which, for him, was the whole point of *The Birthday Party*. We know this because that's what the play does and Pinter, as was quoted earlier, paid a meticulous attention to the shape of things, to put it mildly.

Thus, when Goldberg and McCann ask who Stanley thinks he is, he tells them that they're "on the wrong horse". This is because he sees his commitment to truth as leading him towards reality and away from illusion and, hence, towards who he really is rather than a person his conditioning leads him to think he is.

Stanley's reasserted commitment then leads him to give absurd answers to their next questions, testifying to his rejection of their world on the grounds of its absurdity. But his commitment to truth is so shaky that, almost immediately, he's struggling. However, he perseveres. This explains his rejection of McCann's assertion that he knows him and his telling Goldberg that he can see "Anything" without his glasses. His stumbling attempt to retrieve his glasses, when McCann snatches them, expresses how desperately he's trying to maintain his hold on truth, prompting Goldberg's assertion that he's a fake, i.e. his commitment to truth is merely a pose.

Again, Stanley rallies under the barrage of questions, telling Goldberg that he forgot his other name when asked why he changed it. This refers to the fact that Stanley identifies with this name, which signifies his truth-seeking, rather than with his "other" name, "Webber", which signifies his ensnarement in the web of desire and illusion. In this respect, it's significant that both Goldberg and McCann refer to Stanley as "Webber" until after their interrogation, by which time Stanley has lost his tenuous hold on truth so that their references to his first name in terms of "Stan" or "Stanny boy" amount to a mocking taunt. Similarly, McCann calls Stanley "sir" on their first meeting as an ironic comment on his reduced circumstances.

Goldberg then asks Stanley what his name is now and he replies "Joe Soap", which is rhyming slang for a stooge or a scapegoat, "Joe" being an ordinary person and "Soap" a rhyme for "dope". What Stanley means is that he might be "Joe Soap" in Goldberg's eyes but, really, he's Stanley, which signifies his commitment to truth, a name he won't use with Goldberg because *he* is a stranger to truth in his role as a persuader.

This stings Goldberg to unleash the gift of the gab he discovered at the Ethical Hall, Bayswater. He is, in other words, measuring up against Stanley in the philosophical stakes. And he does so by asking Stanley if he recognises an external force. Stanley, of course, does. He recognises two: the force of the desire for power and the spirit of truth, which is why he responds to Goldberg's question with one of his own: "What?" by which he means: "Which one?"

But that's not what Goldberg means. He's referring to the "God" of Western Civilization, served by the Establishment of Judaism and Christianity, which promises salvation from "sin" and entry to "heaven", which explains Goldberg's accusing Stanley of stinking of sin. This theology is related to happiness, as we see when Goldberg follows it with his philosophy of the necessary and the possible. Stanley's reply that it's late amounts to his saying that he's gone beyond all such religious nonsense. He has moved on to a direct relationship with the spirit of truth, however he envisages this, rather than trusting in an authoritarian intermediary.

However, this is almost Stanley's last attempt to reassert his tentative commitment to truth. His collapse is prepared by hints from Goldberg about the necessary and the possible, which suggests that a commitment to truth necessarily excludes an attachment to desire and, hence, the possibility of happiness. Stanley's insistence that he can have both is rejected by Goldberg, who is, of course, right, as he and McCann affirm to Stanley. This suggestive approach is calculated to have a maximum effect on Stanley by echoing the agonising conflict going on in his mind. For, at this early stage of his commitment to truth, Stanley is still confused about the implications.

Stanley does make one last effort to cling to truth with his assertion that he plays the piano with "no hands" and has no use for pyjamas, but his goose is cooked when Goldberg first plays on his ignorance with his questions about why the chicken crossed the road, "chicken" referring to Stanley's terror of self-extinction and "road" to the road of truth, and then when Goldberg and McCann drop their suggestive approach and home in directly on his terror.

This process effectively removes Stanley's option to commit irrevocably to truth, leaving only two options: a return "home" or a bid for power in revolt against the Establishment. The latter is the option initially chosen by Stanley. Thus, he kicks Goldberg in the stomach and takes on McCann. A loud drumbeat preceding Meg's entrance with the boy's drum testifies not only to the fact that Meg is expressing herself, but also that Stanley is now all self, his soul no longer active: as we've seen, "to beat one's drum" is an idiom for expressing the self.

The rest of the play deals with Goldberg and McCann's combination of coercion and blandishments aimed at convincing Stanley that he can't hope to win by taking on the Establishment and should just give in to them. Throughout this time, Stanley never speaks coherently on stage again, testifying to the fact that what made him "Stanley" is no longer capable of expression.

The birthday party itself provides Pinter with an opportunity to show how each of the characters, with the exception of Petey, who leaves before the party begins, lives in their own illusionary world. The party ends when they play blind man's buff. Lulu explains the game in terms of becoming blind if one is touched, "touched" referring to the attachment to desire and "blind" to ignorance of reality, which handily describes what happens to Stanley in the final confrontation with Goldberg and McCann.

The latter wants to play hide and seek, which is how, unaware as he is of truth, he sees the game being played with Stanley. Goldberg, however, who has a deeper understanding of what's going on, approves Lulu and Meg's enthusiasm for blind man's buff. Blindfolded, McCann touches Stanley's glasses, offering a symbolic representation of the action of the play, i.e. Stanley's incipient commitment to truth is the central driver of the plot. McCann then breaks the glasses and places the boy's drum, symbolising Stanley's refuge at Meg's, in his path. Stanley walks into the drum and falls over with his foot caught in it. His refuge is lost. His reaction is to turn on Meg, whom he feels has betrayed him by letting Goldberg and McCann into the house. He tries to strangle her.

Throughout the party, the light outside the window has been fading, symbolising the slow strangulation of Stanley's soul, i.e. his commitment to truth, as he comes to terms with the denouement of his interrogation by Goldberg and McCann. Suddenly, the lights go out in the room, which coincides with the fading of light outside. The stage is in total darkness: truth has left the building. It's at this point that Stanley takes control. Freed from the indecision that has paralysed him for so long, he's now single-mindedly dedicated to achieving power. Unlike his piano playing, however, he no longer labours under the illusion that this is the expression of a commitment to truth. The motivation is now laid bare for what it is. This is expressed through his sharp and sustained hammering on the side of the drum, while Goldberg and McCann are on their knees looking for the torch which someone, probably Stanley, has knocked from McCann's hand.

For a moment, Stanley achieves power in the darkness of illusion and sets out to take his reward by attempting to rape Lulu, adding further fuel to Pinter's refutation of the theory that the play provides an instance of a villain society and hero individual. The attempted rape underlines the change that has occurred in Stanley since Act I, when he propositioned Lulu, only to see the futility of going away with her. Now, without his glasses, his desire for sexual power over her is uncomplicated by his tentative commitment to truth. When McCann's torch captures him in its beam, he giggles. Seeing himself cornered, his need to know *why* frustrated, his desire for power frustrated, he reaches the end of his tether and breaks down.

Act III begins with Goldberg and McCann to all appearances in total control. Meg has nothing for Petey or Stanley's breakfast, the two Establishment figures having eaten it all. The change in Stanley's status is also clearly implied: McCann prevents Meg from giving him his early morning cup of tea. She overhears him talking to McCann in his room. This suggests that he's in his power. Pinter underlines the change even further with Goldberg's entrance, when, at the same point in Act I, it was Stanley who made his entrance.

Goldberg easily handles Meg's anxious questions about Stanley as a result of her misguided faith in him. But when she goes out to do her shopping, Goldberg finds himself facing Petey.

vi
Petey

Petey is the only character in *The Birthday Party* who's not actually present at the party itself. Indeed, it's he who, arriving late, finds all the other characters in darkness. He puts a shilling in the electricity meter, the lights come on, and he finds the party over. This is crucial to an understanding of his role in the play, for it shows him as someone who sheds light on darkness. Petey, in short, is uncomplicatedly committed to truth. As such, he acts as a criterion by which the delusions of the others may be seen in their proper light. Nowhere is this more telling than in the scene involving him with Goldberg in Act III when with one word he demolishes Goldberg's credibility.

The dialogue follows Goldberg's contention that a commitment to truth must inevitably lead to a nervous breakdown, the result of the unbearable tension between the opposing forces of truth and desire. Petey's one-word interrogative: "Really?" not only questions the truth of Goldberg's contention, it also points out its fallacy and the direction in which the answer may be found, i.e. towards reality and away from illusion. Petey, that is, unlike Goldberg and Stanley, is uncompromising in adopting the view of the soul. He doesn't see disillusionment coloured by the instinct for self-preservation but as the prerequisite for the fulfilment of the mind's need to know *why* through the discovery of the reality of the world.

As was shown in the Introduction, the commitment to truth must involve a concurrent detachment from desire, which amounts to the adoption of a humble passivity that quietens or stills the assertive pride of the self, the motive behind the mind's attachment to desire. This humble passivity is Petey's customary state of mind throughout *The Birthday Party*. It may easily be mistaken for inertia and, hence, weakness, but when compared to the attitudes of all the other characters, shows them up for what they are, which is deluded.

Petey's attitude of detachment is symbolised by his occupation, deck-chair attendant, which, for him, amounts to a vocation, as we see when Meg tells Goldberg that "he's out in all weathers" and he replies: "Of course."

The absurdity of this dialogue: one expects a deck-chair attendant to work exclusively in fine weather, hardly "in all weathers", points up the fact that Petey's occupation says more about his philosophy than it does about his job. This is confirmed by what happens in Act III when Petey feels Stanley's need for help and refuses to be put off by Goldberg, who tries to get rid of him by referring to the warm weather and the need for deck-chairs on a crowded beach. When Petey tells him that he put them all out and Goldberg asks him who is to take the tickets, Petey nonchalantly dismisses his concern.

It's plain that Petey has little concern for the financial implications of his job. What Pinter is telling us through Petey's occupation is that his commitment to truth is expressed through a call to detached contemplation symbolised by a deck-chair. This, in turn, provides a connection with Goldberg, the roots of whose own early commitment to truth were bound up with the contemplation implied in a deck-chair: "Breathe in, breathe out…let yourself go" he says in reminiscing about his trips to the seaside with his Uncle Barney.

Petey's spiritual bent is also expressed in his fondness for gardening, which brings to mind's Voltaire's prescription for achieving philosophical detachment: "Cultivate your garden."

Petey, then, acts as a detached observer of the delusions of the other characters in the play, much as Shakespeare's clown does in *King Lear*. Far from being critical, he sees their actions as merely the inevitable consequence of their attachment to desire and, hence, understands their predicament, suggesting how we, the audience, would see the actions of others if we had his detachment. This explains Petey's calm tolerance of Meg's manifest delusions, which constitutes the final scene of *The Birthday Party*, and his sympathetic attitude to Stanley's agonised indecision.

Similarly, with Goldberg, Petey reacts to his using childhood conditioning to try to seduce Stanley by hinting instead that a little detachment would be more in order. He does this by rising from the table and leaving, in contrast to Goldberg's reminiscences of sitting at the table to eat his mother and his wife's delicacies in the years of *his* response to his childhood conditioning.

But it's in the scene with Goldberg in Act III that Petey makes his most telling comment on delusion, for, while Goldberg appears to be in total control, a sophisticated puppet master, Petey reveals that he was the only one who knew how to shed light during the blackout at the party. Petey's "shilling in the slot", moreover, is contrasted with Goldberg's deluded "I could have sworn it was a fuse." "Blowing a fuse" calls to mind Goldberg's previous speech about the inevitability of the nervous breakdown, while Petey's light of truth is contrasted with Goldberg's darkness of power.

This dialogue between Goldberg and Petey sets a completely different slant on what appears to be the Establishment's triumph at the conclusion of the play. In the first instance, it's Petey's contribution that first reveals the sham of Goldberg's certainty and strength, a façade that begins to slip immediately after their talk: he's irritable with McCann, rejects his questions, and then admits to feeling "knocked out".

This, in turn, underlines the absolute absurdity both of Goldberg and McCann's attempts to bolster their convictions and of their ultimate wooing of Stanley.

Finally, Petey's confrontation with Goldberg and McCann as they take Stanley away for treatment is not the defeat for truth that it appears to be. Pinter's stage direction for Petey: "broken", as he appeals to Stanley to not let them tell him what to do might suggest so. But Goldberg and McCann don't drag Stanley away. They persuade him. In the end, he goes with them willingly. And that's the point. Stanley, like Goldberg before him, freely chooses to renounce his commitment to truth. It's just that Petey momentarily forgets Stanley's free will and tries to act for him through his own love of truth, which equates with Christ's tears at the prospect of Jerusalem's future destruction or his anger over the moneychangers in the temple.

Petey's grasp of reality, however, quickly reasserts itself during the final dialogue with Meg, when he tells her that Stanley is "still asleep", testifying to his acceptance of the other's decision to choose illusion. His earlier lapse was merely a dramatic necessity, allowing Pinter to provide a climax to the play whilst opening up the debate between truth and power in the minds of the audience.

The Caretaker

If an analysis of Harold Pinter's first great play, *The Birthday Party*, provides a rejoinder against any belated political afterthoughts on what might be termed his classical works, then an understanding of the second, *The Caretaker*, categorically demolishes any moral interpretation of his art.

The playwright's most universally performed work and the one generally considered as quintessential Pinter, *The Caretaker* was the play that made its author famous.

Premiering at the Arts Theatre Club in London's Soho in April 1960, almost two years to the day after the premiere of its predecessor, it soon transferred to the Duchess Theatre in Covent Garden where it ran for 444 performances. A move to New York followed in 1961 and a film version based on a screenplay by Pinter two years later.

That *The Caretaker* has proved such an abiding classic is apt. For Pinter's central theme in the play is one which is so common that it characterises practically every religious and non-religious creed of recent centuries, one which most people seem to accept as essential to the meaning of life. Yet it's a theme that has rarely, if ever, received serious treatment in the theatre. This makes the play unique.

What, then, is Pinter writing about in *The Caretaker*? As with *The Birthday Party*, the meaning can be found in the play's title. For while, on one level, the caretaker referred to in the title is in the dictionary sense of someone who takes care of a property, on a more significant level the word refers to one who takes care of another human being, one who is "caring", i.e. one who acts in the interest of others.

In *The Caretaker*, then, Harold Pinter presents us with a dramatic exploration of altruism. This theme, moreover, is worked out in different ways according to the play's three characters: Aston, Davies, and Mick.

The plot of *The Caretaker* could not, on the surface, be simpler, or, indeed, more familiar. Aston, a mentally-fragile recluse living in a junk-filled attic, brings home Davies, an exploitative old tramp, and invites him to stay. The house is owned by Aston's younger brother, Mick, a builder, who, in an echo of Aston's philanthropy towards the down-and-out, lets his sibling stay there.

Mick's is the most obvious type of altruism dealt with in the play, that of family responsibility. "If you got an older brother, you want to push him on, you want to see him make his way," as he tells Davies. It's this possessive attitude towards his brother that leads Mick to resent Aston's relationship with Davies and to work to sever it by winning the tramp over to his side through pretended altruism and turning him against Aston in the process. This opens Aston's eyes to the fact that he's been acting under an illusion in his own charitable concerns. At this point, Davies tries desperately to save the situation by adopting an altruistic mantle himself. "You been a good friend to me," he tells Aston. "You took me in...you give me a bed...But listen. I'm with you..."

This is the second expression of altruism dealt with in *The Caretaker*, the pretence of caring about another's self-interest in order to disarm them and gain an advantage. And, again, just as Aston's altruism towards Davies is echoed by Mick's towards Aston, so is Davies's pretended care for Aston an echo of Mick's previously pretended care for Davies. But it's too late. Aston has seen the light. Davies's plea falls on deaf ears, underlining the significance of Mick's last word to his brother as he leaves the house: "Look..."

So what does Aston see? What does he see that leads him to turn his back on his former protégé and look instead out of the window, a favourite Pinter image for the apprehension of reality, of the way things are as opposed to the way we would like them to be?

Just as *The Birthday Party* is concerned with insecure or lapsed truth seekers, from Stanley to Goldberg, with even Petey periodically vulnerable to desire and illusion, so, in *The Caretaker*, we have a lapsed truth seeker in the shape of Aston. Aston's allegiance to truth is expressed most manifestly in a lengthy monologue that concludes Act II: "I used to get the feeling I could see things...very clearly... everything used to get very quiet... all this...quiet...and...this clear sight...it was...but maybe I was wrong."

When we first meet him in the play, however, Aston has already abandoned his tentative commitment to truth and is searching for a substitute to fill the resulting void. This substitute is altruism. That this is an attempted replacement for his former allegiance is demonstrated through Pinter's use of imagery in the play, particularly of the Buddhist and Christian variety.

Throughout history, there have always been two contrary elements in the major religions of the world. One is based on duality, on the perception of an inevitable separation between man and God or, not to be too theological, between man and ultimate reality. This duality underlies established religion. The other is based on the possibility of a direct approach to God or ultimate reality through the inspiration of the spirit of truth and is usually called "mysticism". In established religion, the dynamic of a movement towards God or some ultimate reality is replaced by an approach to it by being moral or "good", i.e. by being caring or charitable towards others.

The point that Aston is moving away from truth and towards altruism is made through the image of the Buddha he keeps in his room and the Oriental screen with which he intends to break up a room in the house into two parts, creating a separation or duality in the process. For if, in the mystical tradition, Buddhism relates to the contemplation of truth through a retreat from the loud diversions of worldly illusions, bringing "quiet...and clear sight", in the established religion it relates to duality and its concern with altruism.

This is even more obvious through the Christian imagery used in the play, as when Davies says to Aston at the climactic confrontation between the two: "Christ, you say that to me!" – "that", in this instance, referring to a distinctly uncharitable remark and "Christ" to Aston in his charitable role, hence the exclamation mark intended to underline the contradiction.

The point that the mystical tradition is essentially different from a concern with altruism, however, is best exemplified in the play by the tramp's hilarious story to Aston about his visit to a monastery in search of a pair of free shoes. For mysticism is most often associated in both East and West with monasteries.

The upshot of the story is that the monks first tell him to "Piss off" and then dismiss him like "a dog".

It's important to realise, however, that Pinter isn't dealing with altruism purely in a religious sense in *The Caretaker*. Aston, for instance, shows no interest in conventional religion in the play. The point is not to associate altruism with religion or otherwise but to relate it to reality and thereby dispel the illusion that it's somehow "metaphysical" or superior to "mere" self-interest.

In the first instance, Pinter does this through couching Aston's charitable invitation to Davies to stay in the room in terms of: "Would you like to sleep here?" According to Pinter's image system, where dreams are synonymous with sleep, this amounts to an invitation to Davies to share his dreams or illusions. Thus, when Davies is found out and pretends to adopt Aston's altruism, he says: "Christ, we'll change beds!"

The Caretaker, however, is a play and not a philosophical dissertation. As such, Pinter is at pains to demonstrate, rather than suggest, that altruism is not a different kind of activity to self-interest, but simply a different expression of the same thing. He reveals the motives of his characters through their actions. Where Aston is concerned, Pinter shows that his altruism arises from a desire to fulfil his vision of himself as a carpenter, which was Christ's worldly occupation, and one which Aston believes will give him a physical purpose in life, "Working with...good wood", as he puts it, as the flip side to his so-called metaphysical purpose in life.

This vision is centred on his building a shed in the badly overgrown back garden, the image of an abandoned Garden of Eden, as a first step to "doing up the upper part of the house" for Mick. Anyone who has seen the play, however, will know that Aston is obviously living under an illusion with regard to his talents as a handyman. Much of the humour of the play is based on his incompetence in this respect. Lacking confidence in his vision, then, he "charitably" invites Davies, who is even more lost than he is himself, to be his caretaker, i.e. superficially to look after the house, but, figuratively, to bolster or "care for" his perception of himself as a carpenter; in short, to share his illusion in order to make it "real". This is echoed by Mick's cynical offer to Davies to be *his* caretaker. That Davies knows on some subliminal level what Aston's offer really amounts to is revealed when he faces expulsion from the room and tells him: "I'll give you a hand to put up your shed…I'm with you…We'll do it together!"

Similarly, Mick's supposed care for Aston is revealed as being fundamentally self-interested. For this, too, is about Mick's need to bolster his vision of himself as a man of means: "I'm a tradesman," as he tells Davies. "I've got my own van." As such, he can afford to be charitable towards Aston, who, in return, supports Mick's view of himself: "He's got his own van," as he tells Davies. This dynamic between the two brothers is expressed in the battle between them over the bag of clothes Aston offers Davies and which Mick grabs. A tug of war develops as first Mick and then Aston and then Davies each claims the bag. It's only when Aston gives the bag to Mick that Davies receives it. This establishes Mick's position of power, not only over Davies, but also over Aston. This is underlined by Pinter's stage direction: "Mick looks at Aston."

All the expressions of altruism in the play, then, whether as family responsibility, as adopted philosophy or theology, or as political tactic are shown as amounting to nothing more than self-interest. In a word, all are false. In the event, Aston accepts that his attempt to substitute altruism for truth has failed when he expels Davies after the tramp transfers his allegiance to Mick.

Similarly, Mick, too, accepts that his "care" for his brother has failed. Symbolically smashing the Buddha in his frustration, he tells Davies about his brother: "I thought I was doing him a favour, letting him live here. He's got his own ideas. Let him have them. I'm going to chuck it in."

But if Aston and Mick both have their altruistic illusions shattered, it's truth that's ultimately the winner, the truth that altruism and self-interest amount to the same thing when they're seen for what they are. Moreover, we know what Aston has seen when Mick says to him: "Look…", not just by his banishing Davies, but also by his last words in the play, given in final explanation of that banishment: "You make too much noise." This recalls the "quiet and clear sight" Aston has now recovered, at least to the extent of freeing himself from the illusion of altruism as a substitute for truth.

Significantly, Pinter suggests that this liberty is precisely what Aston needs to enable him to find creative fulfilment, as his gradual disillusionment from his charitable concerns is shown to coincide with a new-found determination to get his shed up. Similarly, Mick's disillusionment with his supposed altruism towards Aston frees him from his own possessiveness towards him, allowing Aston to have "his own ideas". Even Davies might have learned something through the process of disillusionment as the last lines of the play show that he might, just might, be willing to abandon the false identity he tells us he has assumed and reclaim "papers" in Sidcup that prove his real identity.

The one mystery in the play is the "faint smile" that Mick and Aston exchange after Mick's machinations over Davies have reached their goal. Does this tell us that blood is thicker than water or are they now brothers in truth? In the context of the play, it seems clear that it's the latter. The only genuine altruism,

Pinter is suggesting, is in the sharing of the truth that leads to reality. The only charity is art.

The Homecoming

By the time Harold Pinter's third great stage play, *The Homecoming*, opened in London in 1965 he was a celebrated playwright. *The Birthday Party* had been watched by 11 million viewers on TV in 1960 and *The Caretaker* produced all over the world. Pinter had also moved into films with an award-winning screenplay for *The Servant* (1963). His new play's treatment of family values, moreover, couldn't help but add to his celebrity, or notoriety, as it turned out.

Yet again, as with his earlier classics, the plot of *The Homecoming* is as familiar to theatregoers as the plot of many Shakespeare plays. Teddy, a philosophy professor at an American university, visits his childhood home in north London with his wife, Ruth, a local girl and mother to their three children. The large house is home to his father, Max, a retired butcher and widower, his Uncle Sam, a chauffeur, and two younger brothers, Lenny, a pimp, and Joey, an apprentice boxer and demolition worker. The visit ends abruptly when Ruth accepts Max and Lenny's proposal that she remain with them and fund her upkeep as a sex worker. The homecoming turns out to be Ruth's rather than Teddy's.

This final plot twist is what audiences almost certainly remember best about the play and on what critics have largely focused. But, as we've already seen with his first two masterpieces, Harold Pinter was an artist and nothing is as it seems.

For a start, *The Homecoming* is entirely consistent with its predecessors, containing essential elements of both. Lenny's monologue to Ruth in Act I, for instance, about the difficulty of helping an old lady move her iron mangle, returns us to the theme of altruism. It ends with Lenny proposing that the lady stuff the mangle up her arse and replace it with a modern spin drier. This echoes Aston's misguided altruism towards Davies in *The Caretaker*, which prevents a more natural outcome to his creative endeavours.

Similarly, the significance of a return to their childhood home that affects several characters in *The Birthday Party* is also clearly at play here with both Teddy and Ruth. Again, Stanley's telling Meg that he didn't sleep and has been day-dreaming all night long is echoed by Lenny, who says he can't sleep and keeps waking up, either that or he's sleepwalking.

In short, *The Homecoming* is packed with metaphors which suggest, like its predecessors, that its concern is with working out philosophical conundrums within a search for meaning. And, as the play's time-and-place is the human condition, so must that concern involve the essential facts of that condition, which are the desire for power and the need to answer the question *why*.

The long opening scene of Act I – the play is in two acts and, as with all Pinter's classical plays, is beautifully constructed – reveals a battle between an ageing Max and a Lenny poised to take over as head of the family, a kind of working class *King Lear* of alpha males. Yet the absence of Max's dead wife, Jessie, hangs heavy over the heartless house: "Go and find yourself a mother" Max tells the others, this in spite of intimations of Jessie's adultery with his best friend, Mac, and of doubts over his sons' legitimacy.

The relatively leisurely introduction is followed by two rapid scenes, a monumental set-piece, and a brief final confrontation, a sequence repeated in Act II. We have Teddy and Ruth's arrival to a sleeping house, a "ships passing in the night" meeting between Teddy and Lenny, a battle for supremacy between Lenny and

Ruth that rises to an unforgettable climax and coda, before Ruth's introduction to the rest of the family and yet another confrontation, this time between Teddy and Max.

Each scene propels the plot and meaning of the play forward with the sure hand of genius. Thus, Ruth's "I'm tired" on her arrival, along with signs of tension between the married couple, prepare us for what follows in Act II. There's then a suggestion that Teddy and Lenny, like Aston and Mick, are brothers in truth as well as siblings, with Teddy detached and Lenny half-awake to the ticking clock of existence.

The centrepiece of Act I, however, is unquestionably the confrontation between Lenny and Ruth, whose opening exchange: "Good evening." – "Morning, I think," lights the match to the fire fight that follows while suggesting a metaphor for its outcome. The conflagration involves all-out attacks on Ruth's sang-froid by Lenny, countered by her imperturbable defence, and ends with Ruth's total victory as she quenches her thirst with the glass of water he offers her as a potential weapon in his onslaught.

Teddy's plan to surprise Max, who was ignorant of his eldest son's marriage, follows a similarly unexpected course in the morning. Max first angrily accuses him of bringing "a pox-ridden slut" into his house, echoing Lenny's story to Ruth earlier about rejecting advances from one of his sex workers after deciding she was "falling apart with the pox". He then violently, but shakily, attempts to assert his faltering authority over his family before inviting Teddy to a "cuddle and kiss". Teddy, at first angrily defensive of his maligned wife, reasserts his own authority by facing up to Max – "Come on, then" – who responds by chuckling and gurgling that Teddy still loves his father.

Pinter's themes here of male chauvinism and the absurdity of "happy families" are developed to hilarious effect in the first scene of Act II. This opens with the men standing around like millionaires lighting post-prandial cigars.

Coffee served by Ruth, Max waxes lyrical about his family, particularly his dead wife, Jessie, who, he says, taught his sons every bit "of the moral code they live by". Considering that Lenny revealed himself to be a vicious pimp with a penchant for mind games in the previous act and Joey is a brute, this appears to belong to the increasingly absurd family reminiscences that follow, reminiscences that veer wildly between saccharine sentimentality and savage censure. However, it has to be remembered that, where Pinter the artist is concerned, morality merely means values espoused as signposts to happiness. Morality is scaffolding for illusion, nothing more.

All this is necessary preparation for the demolishing of conventional family values and their replacement by something more brutal but realistic that follows.

Max goes on to admit that Jessie was "the backbone to this family", a woman "with a will of iron, a heart of gold and a mind". He emphasises the mind. This recalls Lenny's rhapsodising to Ruth earlier about Teddy, his "favourite brother", being a Doctor of Philosophy, "a very sensitive man", and having often wished he was as sensitive. "Have you?" Ruth asked pointedly and, when Lenny replied that he wished he could be more sensitive, she asked "Could you?"

Sensitivity to atmosphere, as Lenny describes it, to what's actually going on: awareness of reality, in short, whether in the realm of desire or of truth, is a fundamental theme of *The Homecoming*. This applies, initially at least, with particular reference to Ruth so that this whole opening scene of Act II can be seen as one long preamble to Ruth's reversal of the status quo in this London family, but also in her own family in America.

The overturning of conventional values continues with Max asking Sam: "Who did you kill?" when he insists that he fought in "the bloody war", revealing the reality of the battle for power everywhere, whether between nations or within families. Max then turns to marriage, specifically Teddy's to Ruth, and to wishing that his "two youngsters" could also get married because "it makes life worth living".

Ruth questions her fitness to be an ideal for other wives to follow. Max's reply that she's "a charming woman" echoes Sam's about Jessie in Act I. The family is about to discover that "charm" where women like Ruth and Jessie are concerned signals siren magnetism rather than compliant accessory.

Before we reach that conclusion, however, Pinter needs to provide the final building blocks to the validity of family values before tearing them down and rebuilding from the ground up. Thus, we have both Max and Teddy's ripostes to Ruth's claim that she was different when she met Teddy.

First, Max doesn't realise the shattering repercussions of what he's saying when he tells Ruth that no one can afford to live "in the past". This is followed by Teddy's claim that Ruth is a great help to him over in America, a wonderful wife and mother, and that they have everything they want in "a very stimulating environment". Teddy and Lenny's cigars subsequently go out, signalling the extinguishing of their pretensions to power and happiness. This reminds us that Max stubbed his cigar out earlier after admitting that his own pretensions to wealth and a wonderful family life were frustrated.

The scene is now set for a denouement. As *The Homecoming* is a work of art and, as such, concerned with philosophical realities rather than with a group of men and a woman in north London in the mid-1960s, Pinter now introduces the audience to some up-front philosophy for their consideration. In questioning Teddy about his philosophical teaching, Lenny suggests that Christianity contains a "certain logical incoherence" in that "the unknown", which is to say "God", can't merit reverence. You can't, that is, revere something of which you're ignorant.

In the context of *The Homecoming*, this means that the idea of the sacredness of marriage is nonsense. In other words, forget the "What God has joined together let no man put asunder" of the marriage ceremony. How can we know that "God" approves of marriage, that he gives it his blessing, if we don't know God? In this respect, all we have is belief, which only amounts to wishful thinking without knowledge. If we believe that marriage is sacred, it's because we want to believe it, not because it is.

We don't actually know whether Teddy and Ruth were married in a religious ceremony or in a purely civil ceremony, or, indeed, whether they were married at all. Teddy merely tells Max that their wedding took place the day before they left for America and that no one else was there. His angry insistence at the end of Act I, however, that Ruth is his wife and that they're married would suggest they are. Ultimately, it doesn't really matter, at least not for *The Homecoming*, which is concerned with marriage itself, rather than with Teddy and Ruth's marriage. If truth be told, Pinter is probably more concerned with making the point that Teddy's marriage to Ruth represents his attachment to desire, since marriage is unquestionably an attempt at achieving happiness.

In any case, Lenny's philosophical bombshell effectively removes the essential difference between religious law and secular law where marriage is concerned. Ruth may well be

Teddy's "lawful wife", as Sam claims later in the play, but this involved a decision she made "in the past". There's nothing to stop her changing her mind. And there's absolutely no doubt that she does because, as the men make fun of what passes for philosophy in academic circles, Ruth changes the subject as she begins to exert her erotic charms. This is followed immediately by her claim that she was born "quite near here".

Like McCann in *The Birthday Party*, who feels awkward and out of place in his new world and dreams of a return to his childhood "home" in the old, Ruth now reveals that she feels the same. Whereas McCann finds greater scope in his adopted world for the desire for power, however, Ruth feels the exact opposite. America, she says, is all "rock and sand" with "lots of insects".

This concludes the scene, which is followed by two short scenes that propel the plot forward at a rate of knots. The first, like its equivalent in Act I, involves Teddy and Ruth. Their earlier tension now takes a turn for the worse where Teddy's concerned as his suggestion to Ruth that they cut short their visit triggers a confrontation. This centres on Teddy's telling Ruth that "It's so clean" in America, which prompts Ruth to ask him if it's dirty "here" in London. At first, he denies this, saying only that it's cleaner there. But, later, pressed by Ruth, he compares the pool in America where their boys swim to the "swimming bath down the road", which, he says, is like "a filthy urinal". As for his plea that she rest, in response to the "I'm tired" of the equivalent scene in Act I, it falls on deaf ears. It's clear that rest is now the last thing she wants. Similarly, his promise that she can help him with his lectures on their return elicits no reply.

Where the second rapid scene in Act I involved Lenny and Teddy, the equivalent in Act II involves Lenny and Ruth. Teddy is now effectively out of the family equation, both in London, with

Lenny, and in America, with Ruth. In turn, Lenny and Ruth are now to form the kernel of a new family unit, which begins to take shape in this scene.

Ruth reveals that the life she lived before she met Teddy and was seduced into a new life with him, one she believed would offer greater scope for the desire for power, for happiness, involved her role as a porn or glamour model. What's more, she now clearly realises that she prefers this siren role to that of being a mother: paradoxically, the images she associates with her previous life all involve water, and so fertility, in contrast to the images of aridity she associates with America. This preferred siren role is now to be replicated in her homecoming but in a different way because, as Ruth tells Lenny, her previous role was before she had "all my children"; in short, her body has changed with childbearing, but not her mind.

The next scene, which begins with Teddy trying to prise her away and Ruth opting instead for an erotic dance with Lenny, corresponds to the mammoth scene in Act I between Lenny and Ruth, which is now revealed to have been the first stage of a courtship of sorts. We know this because Lenny's fantasising in that scene about visiting Venice as a participant in the last war's Italian campaign was echoed by Ruth at the conclusion of her scene with Teddy earlier. Ruth obviously prefers the macho environment in London to the "insects" in America.

Whereas Act I's centrepiece was concerned with Ruth's homecoming, however, ending with her quenching her thirst after the desert of "rock and sand" she found "over there", Act II's equivalent scene is concerned with working out the implications of the homecoming for Teddy. Indeed, just as Pinter prepares us for the scene in Act I by having Ruth sit down on her arrival in the house and Teddy ask her if she's tired, so does he have

Ruth ask Teddy in Act II, on his suggesting their early return to America, if he doesn't like his London family as much as he thought he did.

This Act II centrepiece is unlike its equivalent in Act I in that it has several phases. There's much coming and going of characters so that it appears to be several different scenes. But Teddy is on stage throughout. For him, it's one mammoth scene, beginning with his coming down the stairs with the suitcases for an early exit with his wife and ending when he leaves alone.

In between, we have Ruth's siren seduction of Lenny, followed by that of Joey, and the proposal that she remain, with different suggestions from the men about her new roles. Naturally, such goings-on can result in us seeing Teddy as something of a secondary figure, as merely Ruth's rejected husband. Teddy's role, however, is as crucial to the meaning of the play as Petey's is to that of *The Birthday Party*. Both might appear to be peripheral figures in the drama, but being on the periphery is essential to observing it objectively, and, indeed, both *are* on the outside looking in.

Teddy, then, is something of a Greek chorus to *The Homecoming*. But he's also a character in his own right, one who is profoundly affected by the actions of the play. And just as Ruth finds a new accommodation in her life, he does, too. The difference is that hers is with desire, his with truth.

The homecoming of the play's title may, ultimately, be Ruth's, but that wasn't Teddy's intention when they stopped off in London on their return to America from a week's holiday in Venice. Numerous references in the play, including the one above about not liking his family as much as he thought, testify to Teddy's homesickness for his early conditioning. Like Ruth, he wasn't as happy in America as he thought he would be. Indeed, on arrival, he's clearly suffering from what might be termed sentimental delusions about his London family. His characterisation of them to Ruth as "very warm people, really" could hardly be further from the experience of the audience. As if at a Christmas pantomime, their reaction to Teddy's: "They're not ogres" would most likely be: "They are!"

We also learn that Teddy had written to his father a few times from America and we know that he didn't tell him about his new family, which can only be because he still felt a part of the old and wanted his father to know that, and only that. He later also wrote to Sam, and it's his uncle who tells him that not only is he his favourite nephew but was also "the main object" of his mother's love. This places Teddy centre stage in his London family as Lenny and Max also clearly consider him special, witness their references to his "Doctor of Philosophy". It seems clear that Teddy's illusions about his family are rooted in his being rather spoilt in his early life. This has given him delusions of grandeur that colour his family impressions.

Where truth is concerned, then, he needs his eyes opened to this fact, a painful experience, but necessary on the road to reality. And, in this respect, he's fortunate, because what's most significant about his London family, which explains Ruth's feeling so much at home there, is the relative nakedness of the power struggle involved, which wasn't her experience in America. As Teddy tells Ruth, America is "behind the time here...It's so clean there," with "clean" meaning civilized, modern, progressive; "behind" meaning earlier in the day, morning relative to London's late afternoon, and, hence, with a brighter future: "Sun", as he says. But when "behind" and "clean" are connected in the light of truth, Pinter clearly means that, metaphorically, "clean" is "behind", or lower down the reality scale than "dirty", which is precisely how Ruth sees it, judging by her negative response, precisely the opposite reaction to the one Teddy intended.

The upshot of London's being less encumbered with reality-distracting civilization is that the moment Ruth turns on Teddy his family falls on him like a pack of wolves savaging their wounded leader. And, in doing so, they also reveal that his view of his family life with Ruth in America is just as deluded as his view of his family in London. "You've made a happy woman out of her…something to be proud of," Max tells him ironically, before Ruth, having established her dominance over Teddy's London family, something she clearly didn't have over his family in America, asks him: "Has your family read your critical works?" This is the equivalent of McCann questioning Goldberg when he finds life in his new world unbearable. In Ruth's case, she clearly felt excluded from her husband's inner life: witness Teddy's repeated assurances that she's a "great help" to him "over there" and that he'd be "so grateful" for her help with his lectures. This can only be because he's aware that Ruth doesn't agree that living with him and their children in America is "a very stimulating environment".

Now, just as McCann's turning on Goldberg wakes him up to the reality of his situation, so does Ruth's wake Teddy up. But whereas Goldberg's awakening is to the desire for power, Teddy's is to truth. This allows Pinter to state the case for true philosophy, in contrast to the academic variety rubbished earlier in the play when Lenny asked what a table is, philosophically speaking, and Teddy answered: "A table." Teddy explains that his "province" has "nothing to do with the question of intelligence", suggesting that academic philosophy is about being "clever" with ideas, but with a way of looking at the world, through detachment, that enables him "to *see!*"

This speech recalls Aston's in *The Caretaker* about *his* ability to "see things…very clearly", about his "clear sight", linking the two as similar artists or truth seekers at the centre of two very different plays, or not that different, since both deal with the apprehension of reality, as, indeed, do all Harold Pinter's great plays. The fact that Aston is a mentally fragile individual and Teddy a University professor differentiates them less than the fact that, as Teddy says, his philosophy, and, indeed, Aston's, has nothing to do with intelligence, merely involving detachment, which anyone is capable of, whatever their level of intelligence. It involves avoiding losing one's soul in the self's day-to-day existence, i.e. in the pursuit of happiness. Aston, being a simple soul, expresses this in terms of "quiet", Teddy, being an academic, in terms of maintaining "intellectual equilibrium". But the two things amount to the same thing, which is detachment.

We all, that is, have the free will to choose truth over desire and thereby to escape the resulting imprisonment in illusion by seeing it for what it is, even though we're still in it when we see it. Where Teddy's soul is concerned, this means that, while his self might still cling to the illusion of the "happy family" he thought he'd found in America or, indeed, to the happy memories of his early years in London, he "won't be lost in it". He always has a chance of freedom, or being found, which is the contrary of "lost", through truth. In short, while Ruth's homecoming is to the rediscovery of her self, Teddy's is with the rediscovery of his soul.

This leads him to tell his London family that they're "way behind", just as Ruth sees her "happy family" in America as "behind" that of a potential new family in Teddy's London home; and, of course, they're both right. If, for Ruth, however, the naked power relationship of her new family in London is superior to her "happy family" in America because nearer to the reality of power, Teddy's ability to see the reality of both families through detachment is infinitely superior to Ruth's perception because it exchanges the reality of power with the reality of truth, which offers the possibility of escaping the illusion that underlies all happy families, rather than of merely exchanging the power relationships of one with that of another, when both are illusions.

Teddy's own disillusionment from the idea of his "happy family" in America, however, unlike Ruth's, is not the subject of *The Homecoming*. If he continues to have the commitment to truth that resurfaced from the trauma of Ruth's rejection of that family then he could emerge from that illusion through experience. But the play is only concerned with Teddy and Ruth's London homecoming, not with Teddy's American homecoming on his return after the events of the play. That's another story, one we'll never know.

Pinter does suggest, however, that the naked power struggle Teddy finds on his return to London will do him the world of good in that respect. The clear implication is that our search for purpose is better served by facing up to the reality of the world than by setting out to make it a better place. Remember Harold Pinter's quote from that interview in 1969: "I'm not interested in ideology. You can't expect this to be in any way a just world. I have no expectation of the world getting better in any way." Finding a purpose to human life, in short, is about understanding, not about any ideology for promoting change for the "better", not about so-called progress.

This idea is absolutely crucial to the meaning of *The Homecoming*, indeed, is its essential focus, what it's "about", to which the theme of family values is secondary or constituent. Pinter makes this clear in an extended exchange between Teddy and Lenny that occurs soon after Teddy's "I won't be lost in it" speech. In between, there's a brief heart-to-heart between Teddy and Sam, who asks him if he remembers Mac and whether he took to him. Surprisingly, perhaps, Teddy replies in the affirmative, despite the fact that Sam had earlier described Mac as "a lousy stinking rotten loudmouth", which relates to the "dirty" of London in contrast to the "clean" of America in the Teddy-Ruth exchange, in which Teddy categorises the local swimming bath as "a filthy urinal". Now, however, after his awakening in the previous scene, Teddy is shown, at the very least, as having an awareness of an opposite viewpoint.

This contrast between "clean" and "dirty", a progressive New World, as in America, for instance, and an Old World of regressive values, such as in London, Europe, for instance, is now developed in the Teddy-Lenny dialogue. Pinter's choice of America in this respect is inspired because, while America has always represented a new world of opportunity for downtrodden Europeans, progress, in a word, it also includes the pursuit of happiness as one of the God-given rights in its Declaration of Independence, enshrining illusion and, hence, absurdity in its founding document.

Thus, Lenny begins, absurdly, with a jibe about Teddy's supposedly superior life in America: "Still here, Ted? You'll be late for your first seminar," "late", as in "way behind", being the operative word since Teddy trumpeted this earlier to affirm his superiority to his London family. This is clearly an attempt to stick a verbal knife into Teddy, whose pride Lenny believes has been wounded by Ruth's infidelity. Lenny then discovers that a cheese-roll he prepared for himself earlier has disappeared. Teddy tells him that he took it. Lenny makes much of the effort involved in preparing the roll in order to make the point that Teddy's taking it was theft and, hence, wrong. Teddy asks him what he's going to do about it. This prompts Lenny pompously to demand an apology, which amounts to his asking Teddy to abase himself before him for violating a morality based on altruism that we know Lenny doesn't believe in. His indignation, in other words, is pure hypocrisy. Here is the vicious pimp with a penchant for mind-games we encountered in Act I, who is now pathetically attempting to conceal his impotence when faced with a challenge to *his* wounded pride to which he has no defence.

Teddy's response, that he took the roll deliberately, twisting the knife into Lenny's wound by raising the stakes in what is now a face-off between the two, leads Lenny to accuse him of vindictiveness, when it's clearly Lenny himself who is feeling vindictive towards his brother, while also trying, and failing, to provoke such vindictiveness in Teddy by stealing his wife and taunting him about it. Pinter flags the hypocrisy by having Lenny add that he's "bowled over", a reference to the cricketing metaphor for values that played such a crucial role in *The Birthday Party*, a metaphor also used by Joey, "bowling down the road", in a later development with reference to his and Lenny's virtual rape of two women, revealing their true values.

The confrontation between Teddy and Lenny is an echo of that between Lenny and Ruth in Act I, which ended with Lenny's total defeat, as does this one. Lenny's mind games with Teddy, and with Ruth earlier, merely reveal his naivety, for all his pretensions to a Machiavellian sophistication. As we've seen, Ruth easily saw through this in Act I, as Teddy does now in Act II. The simple fact is that both Teddy and Ruth operate on a deeper level than Lenny, and what applies to Lenny applies equally to Max, Joey or Sam.

Lenny's self-righteousness over Teddy taking his cheese roll, however, is merely an immediate reaction, fluff floating on the superficial froth of pride and desire. It reveals his self, not his soul, and, whatever we might think of him, he does, as we all do, have a soul, or, at least, a soul-potential. And what's interesting about this scene is that Pinter reveals that Lenny, like the rest of us, can veer between self and soul.

Thus, in the midst of the above confrontation between the two, Teddy's admission that he'd seen his brother put the cheese roll into the sideboard, was hungry, so he ate it, also prompts Lenny to respond by calling this "barefaced audacity", adding that it was "something approaching the naked truth…in the land of no holds barred." This is an extremely apt description of the naked power struggle that the house of Teddy's homecoming represents in the play and reveals Lenny's own sensitivity to atmosphere, his openness to reality, for which he extols Teddy to Ruth in Act I while wishing that *he* could be more sensitive, which prompted Ruth to ask him whether he could be. And, sure enough, he now reveals that, yes, he can be. For, in the context of Teddy "thieving" his cheese roll, Lenny's comment amounts to his saying that the sensitive Teddy has rejected altruism, "barefaced audacity" relating to "naked truth", just as Lenny revealed that he, too, had rejected it, in his monologue to Ruth about moving the iron mangle.

On the profound level of the reality underlying worldly illusion, the scene confirms the suggestion in Act I that they are, like Aston and Mick in *The Caretaker*, brothers in truth. This explains Lenny's earlier admission to Teddy that "some kind of tick" keeps waking him up. He is, in other words, questioning the purpose of life in the ticking clock of existence. This was then developed by Lenny in a coda following the climax of his confrontation with Ruth, a coda full of the feelings of futility typical of a mid-life crisis – he talked of "people of my age" – in which he asks Max, in "a spirit of inquiry", about the circumstances surrounding his conception on the "night" he was made "in the image" of "two people *at it.*"

Lenny, in other words, has been bitterly asking himself why he was ever born, what's the point of living, when he manifestly hates his life, more than ever at that time, having just been humiliated by Ruth. Max's reply to Lenny that he'll drown in his own blood suggests the conditioning of children by their parents, "in the image" of their "own blood", in order that they espouse certain values, "the moral code" that Jessie taught the "boys", values that blind children to truth, leading to their drowning in illusion. And Jessie, as Max said earlier, not only had a will of iron and a mind, but also "a heart of gold", which implies altruism. Both Teddy and Lenny, however, have now clearly escaped this illusory trap, using their mind, their sensitivity to atmosphere, their openness to reality; in short: an attachment to the spirit of truth, whether they're actually aware of the existence of that spirit or not. And it's clear that, in this respect, Lenny was following in the footsteps of his elder brother, "old Ted", whose sensitivity he extolled to Ruth, "old", in this context, clearly meaning wiser, as in "older and wiser".

Lenny's considered soul-response to the revealing interchange with Teddy is then followed by two monologues in which he contrasts the so-called progressive attitudes of Teddy's New World in America to the so-called regressive attitudes in his London family's Old World.

The first monologue outlines Teddy's family life in the "clean" United States of America, which Teddy had earlier idealised to the family and to Ruth and which Lenny now absurdly extols to Teddy in similar terms of "sun" and "open spaces", "stimulation" and "all the intellectual life out there", which recalls Teddy's description of his philosophy of truth as nothing to do with intelligence. This point is made through Lenny's repeated use of the phrase "on the old campus", which, here, is clearly an ironic riposte to Teddy's jibe to the family that they are "way behind", Lenny openly questioning the idea of America being a more advanced society, where reality is concerned, particularly as one of three times he uses the phrase occurs in relation to "all the intellectual life out there". He also mentions "fun…down by the pool", which recalls Teddy's efforts to persuade Ruth to rush back to America with him.

Significantly, Lenny also mentions "tons of iced water", which recalls his offer to Ruth of ice cubes in terms of "On the rocks?" to accompany the whisky she'd earlier demanded as a tribute following her siren seduction of himself and Joey. "What do you know about rocks?" Ruth had asked him in reply, recalling her characterisation of America as "all rock".

Naturally, the monologue is heavily ironical, which is expressed through the multiple absurdities, such as "all the comfort of those Bermuda shorts", with Lenny adding "on the old campus". Lenny is clearly scorning Teddy's vaunting of a society which he, with his clear admiration of "something approaching the naked truth", considers inferior. But the monologue has a serious purpose, which is no less than to save his brother's soul. For, as Lenny now admits to Teddy, he looks up to him and does his best to follow the example he sets. This serious purpose is expressed in Lenny's clear sincerity in his surmise at the outset of the monologue that Teddy has grown "sulky" and "inner" and "less forthcoming", which, in terms of Lenny following his brother's example, amounts to his saying that Teddy has become less committed to truth in America.

Lenny, then, is disappointed with his "sensitive favourite brother" and it's this that accounts for the list of absurdities that follow, absurdities that Lenny acknowledges at the outset by pointing out that Teddy's sulkiness is "funny", a synonym for "strange", considering his six years in the United States of America, which, if it was truly superior, should have made him "more forthcoming, not less". This is then followed by a list of the supposed advantages of that nation which, on the surface, amount to the enthusiastic description of a convert to the American Dream, but, in reality, amount to grounds for disillusionment. Lenny, in other words, is saying that Teddy was seduced by this dream to the detriment of his relationship to reality. And, in this respect, what the monologue reveals is how well Lenny knows his brother because Teddy *is* clearly becoming disillusioned with America, or why would he be so initially enthusiastic about his homecoming to his birthplace? Yes, Lenny knows his man and desperately wants him to become again the person he once respected.

The monologue about Teddy's America is then followed by another, this time about his family home in London, "the land of no holds barred", which Lenny characterises as "a closer life", closer, that is, to reality, to "something approaching the naked truth". Lenny clearly intends this "closer" to provide a stark contrast to his characterisation in the previous monologue of Teddy's life in America as full of "open spaces", which, in this context, can be taken to mean emptiness, a void, or the desert of "rock and sand" described by Ruth, particularly as the "open spaces" phrase is followed, for the first time, by "on the old campus", which, as we've seen, Lenny uses to express the fact that America is "way behind", as Teddy disparaged his London family.

Like the American monologue, this monologue is also full of absurdities because Lenny is referring to the pursuit of happiness of Teddy's London family, just as he was earlier referring to the same pursuit of Teddy's American family. But, like that earlier monologue, this one also has the same serious purpose, which is to recall Teddy to who he really is, which is a philosopher of truth. Lenny makes this point by using Teddy's absence from London as a metaphor for his absence of soul, which he expresses in terms of "an empty chair", that, he says "is in fact yours". That "in fact" is highly significant in this respect because it means "in reality".

The point is given added resonance by having Teddy's empty chair standing "in the circle" of chairs occupied by the family members as they regularly sit "round" the backyard having a "quiet" look at the "night sky". From what we know of Teddy's London family, it seems highly improbable that Lenny is describing an actual series of events. What *is* highly likely, however, is that Lenny is recalling Teddy to Aston's "quiet" detachment and the circular process of truth in the "dark night". There may be an element here of Pinter speaking through Lenny to make his point, but it's not as if Lenny is speaking out of character, only that his choice of words can be interpreted on a deeper level.

That this is Pinter's purpose is clear. For Lenny specifies that his metaphor of the empty chair in the family circle is intended to illustrate that they are "a unit" of which Teddy is "an integral part", by which Lenny clearly means as its philosopher, its model or guide. Thus, he tells his brother, that when he at length returns, they expect some reassurance, whose nature he details in a series of expressions that amount to synonyms for "forthcoming", as in an example to follow, as in an artist pursuing his vocation from which others can learn. These expressions are "a bit of grace", "generosity of mind", "liberality of spirit" and, most pertinently, "je ne sais quoi", which literally means "I don't know what" and refers to Teddy's earlier defence of his philosophical vocation, which began: "You wouldn't understand my works." As for "grace", "mind" and "spirit", they clearly suggest that Lenny equates Teddy's description of his philosophical "province" or vocation as "a way of being able to look at the world" with some kind of spiritual inspiration. Lenny then asks Teddy whether that's what he's given them.

Teddy answers Lenny's question simply with "Yes" because his return *has* provided reassurance to his London family as the conflicts we observed at the outset of the play will melt away to be replaced by a new order, one "closer" to the reality of family life, of human relations.

Henceforth, following his affirmative, Teddy acts largely as a chorus to this process. As for himself, it's true that he continues throughout to cling to the hope that Ruth will return with him to America, to their "happy family", but in a noticeably more detached manner. The anxiety he revealed in Act I, for instance, chewing his knuckles after Ruth steps out for "some air" instead of going to bed with him, and his angry outburst over the "filthy urinal" in Act II have now been dissipated to some extent by the events of the play, including Ruth and Lenny's rejection of the American Dream and, especially, their brutal and ironic reminders, respectively, that he was in real danger of losing his soul-sensitivity, which have clearly provided him with something of a reality check.

But Teddy is not the only one to have benefited from events. Certainly, where Lenny's concerned, Teddy's return is shown to *have* provided the reassurance he was seeking, as the bitter, self-hating, despairing savage of Act I, sleepwalking in a haze of futility, is transformed by a clear sense of purpose, although in a more humble role to the one he may have envisaged as head of the family at the outset of the play. This new sense of purpose immediately begins to reveal itself on Joey's entrance following Teddy's "Yes."

We learn that Joey has been upstairs in bed with Ruth for two hours. Teddy, meanwhile, in his overcoat and with the suitcases beside him, has been waiting for her. Lenny now begins to question Joey about how he got on in the same scientific way that Stanley questioned Petey about the weather in *The Birthday Party*. Indeed, Lenny treats us to "What do you mean?" not once, but twice, an ongoing process of seeking the "closer" reality of the situation into which Joey and, later, Max also enter. In short, the family, with the exception of Sam and, of course, Teddy, come together in a collectively inquiring way to work out a new family order, one in which Lenny and Max, formerly bitter antagonists, co-operate creatively.

It transpires that Joey didn't get all the way, didn't, that is, manage to have sexual intercourse with Ruth, to which Lenny responds by questioning whether Ruth is "a tease". Teddy comments that perhaps Joey doesn't have "the right touch". As with the game of blind man's buff in *The Birthday Party*, which was also about being "touched", this amounts to saying that Joey doesn't know how to arouse Ruth's desire for power, for happiness, as Teddy did when he seduced her to America as his wife and subsequently to produce three children, to her abiding regret at what it did to the beauty of her body.

Lenny responds with his story about sex with the two girls in the rubble of a bomb site, a clear reference to the "old" world of Europe in which rape and destruction seem to go together. Lenny then asks Joey whether he can be satisfied "without going the whole hog". Joey replies that sometimes it's possible to be happy "without going any hog", i.e. without acting as an animal.

Lenny questions this by staring at Joey. The significance of this exchange is immediately brought home by the entry of Sam and Max, who asks whether "the whore" is still in bed, commenting that she'll make them all animals, which, as we've just seen, is clearly not the case. Indeed, as we're about to find out, Ruth will bring them closer as a family unit, of which *she*, rather than Teddy, will be the integral part, and, what's more, as a present, rather than absent, landlord.

The first step in this process occurs when Max suggests that it might be a good idea to have a woman in the house, that they keep Ruth. Teddy, supported by Sam, puts forward a counter-proposal that she return to America with him to their three children, to which Max responds by asking Teddy what he knows about what Ruth wants, which is clearly true. Max, in other words, is more in tune with the reality of the situation than Teddy, who continues to be blinded to a certain extent by his own desire for that "happy family" in America.

Max and Joey then discuss paying Ruth to stay with them and how much she would need. When Lenny asks where the money will come from, Max responds by telling him not to forget the "human considerations", which reveals that he's moved on from his "whore" and "animals" jibe towards the idea of a new family unit.

It's then, however, that Lenny, conscious of the reality underlying civilized behaviour and conscious of the need for domestic economy, proposes putting Ruth "on the game" as a sex worker in a flat in Soho, the centre of the sex industry in 1960s London: she'll earn her keep. The men discuss the commercial considerations. Max flags a possible fly in the ointment relating to her supposed "teasing", which could preclude her attracting fees from satisfied customers. Teddy, as the chorus to this flesh-trading, supposes that it was "just love play", which, as well as foreplay, could mean any number of things, its very ambiguity perfectly encapsulating Ruth's Machiavellian mastery, in contrast to Lenny's incompetence in that respect.

Teddy's comment, revealing that all their attempts to lord it over him in what they consider to be his downfall have fallen on stony ground, prompts Max, Lenny and Joey to taunt him about his wife's many business obligations in the sex trade. Teddy responds with a choral comment that Ruth would get old very quickly. As so often with Pinter, this is ambiguous. On the surface, of course, it means that she could be worn out if supplied with too many customers. On a deeper level, however, the "old" here recalls Lenny's "on the old campus" and means, therefore, "way behind", less in tune with reality, which, as this reality is that of the desire for power, means less in control of the family situation. Significantly, Max's riposte that Ruth will have "the time of her life" coincides with her entrance, dressed and smiling. This isn't a woman who intends to get old very quickly. No one, in fact, is more in tune with the reality of this family's situation than Ruth.

An exchange now takes place between Teddy and Ruth in what Pinter clearly intends as New World terms, as opposed to the Old World terms of "the land of no holds barred" that we have become accustomed to throughout the play. Thus, moments after hearing the men joke about working Ruth half to death "on her back" to maximise her earnings, Teddy puts this to Ruth in terms of "the family" inviting her to stay "for a little while longer…as a kind of guest", to which Ruth replies, in equally civilized terms, that she considers this "very nice of them", that laughably inappropriate "nice" being compounded moments later when she uses the word "sweet" to describe Max's "offer from our heart". Teddy's detachment is expressed in his saying that he doesn't mind, if she likes the idea. They can manage "very easily" in America until she returns.

This is followed by Max's connecting Ruth's stay to Jessie, recalling his "Go and find yourself a mother" in Act I, when he tells her that she's kith and kin, that she belongs with them, which is precisely what the play has revealed and why the homecoming is essentially Ruth's. Her reply, that she's "very touched", as in *The Birthday Party*'s game of blind man's buff, referring to the attachment to the desire for power, to her commitment to *this* idea of happiness, underlines the fit.

Continuing in his nicest New World terms, Teddy then introduces the theme of prostitution in terms of Ruth having to "pull your weight a little, if you stay". The monstrous Max, who moments earlier had been talking in international terms and a waiting list for Ruth's sexual services along with her "obligations this end as well", now echoes Teddy's "little" with his "a few pennies".

Teddy's repeating the alternative of her returning "home" with him introduces real competition for Ruth's services between himself and his family and leads, as a result, to Lenny's constantly increasing his offer to Ruth over the terms of her stay in London as she drives an increasingly hard bargain, pointing out that she would "need an awful lot" or wouldn't be "content". Lenny promises her "everything", which recalls Teddy's "we've got everything we want" earlier. Ruth muses that "it might prove a workable arrangement".

This prompts Max to mention Ruth's daytime domestic arrangements, which includes his suggestion that she could "scrub the place out a bit". This recalls Lenny's story earlier about the virtual rape of the girls in the rubble of a bomb site, which he said was "near the Scrubs", referring to the prison, Wormwood Scrubs, in West London.

It's at this point that Sam steps forward to say that Max's friend Mac had sex with Jessie in the back of his taxi cab, after which he croaks and collapses. Joey establishes that he's not dead, although Lenny suggests that he probably was dead for thirty seconds or so, long enough to make his revelation, in other words, meaning that such truths have no place in a world of lies.

Max's comment that Sam has "a diseased imagination", echoing his demand at the end of Act I that Teddy remove Ruth's "stinking pox-ridden slut" from his house: "Take that disease away from me," is followed by a pause after which Ruth, continuing on from her earlier musing about "a workable arrangement", adds: "Yes, it sounds a very attractive idea."

This episode underlines one theme of the play, which is that of the reality underlying the illusion of the idea of "happy families". As we saw in Act I, there are intimations of Jessie's adultery with Mac and of the legitimacy of Max's boys. Max's reminiscing that "she wasn't such a bad bitch" is countered by his saying that it made him "sick just to look at her rotten stinking face". Again, in that confrontation with Teddy at the end of Act I, he says that he's never had a whore in the house before, adding, "Ever since your mother died," a typical Pinter ambiguity. Similarly, his rosy memory of family life in Act II, "it was like Christmas", is contrasted with his "three bastard sons, a slutbitch of a wife".

Teddy also tells Ruth on their arrival in the house that the family had knocked a wall down in the living room to make an open living area. The "structure", he said, "wasn't affected", adding: "My mother was dead." Where the meaning of the play is concerned, the metaphorical significance of this is clearly that the structure of the "home" or family, rather than of the house of bricks and mortar, wouldn't be affected by making an "open", living area, i.e. one with no secrets suddenly revealing themselves, since Jessie was dead. But Sam's revelation, which he makes in an effort to prevent what he considers the scandalous situation with Jessie from repeating itself with Ruth, reveals the reality, just as Max's response shows that self-delusion has no limits.

Interestingly, Harold Pinter would later write an Oscar and BAFTA-nominated screen adaptation of John Fowles' 1969 novel *The French Lieutenant's Woman* for a 1981 feature film of the same name in which he refers to William Acton's 1857 book *Prostitution, Considered in its Moral, Social, and Sanitary Aspects.* This mentions that there were 80,000 prostitutes working in the rigidly "moral" society of Victorian London, where one house in 60 functioned as a brothel. Considering the law of supply and demand, with so many sex workers, the number of male clients from that supposedly upright society must have been enormous!

This doesn't, however, mean that Ruth necessarily has any intention of working as a sex worker. Indeed, the hard bargain she drives with Lenny concludes with his complete agreement to her demand that all aspects of their agreement and conditions of employment would be clarified "to our mutual satisfaction". From what we see of Ruth on stage and the comparisons made with Jessie's role in the family, it seems far more likely that she'll do exactly what she wants. Max's final question on the subject, in response to her "attractive idea", as to whether she wants to "shake on it now" or "to leave it till later", suggests just such an outcome as he elicits her casual reply in favour of the latter, which proves to be Teddy's cue to take his leave.

Unemotionally lamenting Sam's prone form in terms of a lost opportunity for a lift to London Airport, Teddy is equally detached in telling Ruth that he'll leave her suitcase. Mention of the *Underground* and Piccadilly *Circus* pass ironic comment on the reality of family life, before we're offered one more absurd exchange on the subject of "happy families" involving "Dad" and "son". Max asks Teddy whether his boys would like to see a photo of their grandfather. Teddy knows they would. Conveniently, Max has one handy in his wallet and offers it to Teddy, who says that his sons will be "thrilled". Cue handshake with Lenny, which represents a certain rapprochement between them as brothers in truth, and a more detached farewell to Joey, who, jealously possessive of Ruth, merely offers a distant "Ta-ta".

As Teddy leaves, Ruth addresses her farewell to him as "Eddie". He turns and, after a pregnant pause, she says: "Don't become a stranger."

This belongs to those famous enigmatic lines that almost have a separate life from their literary or dramatic context. Of course, as Teddy's wife, Ruth has her own relationship with him. She knows him in a way that's different from that of his London family, which is characterised here by an alternative name as in *The Birthday Party*.

Yes, but how does Ruth know Eddie, and what does she mean by "Don't become a stranger"? From the evidence in the play, it's clear that Ruth, with an acute sensitivity to the reality of a situation, specifically that relating to desire in her case, must have recognised Teddy as similarly sensitive, although she didn't realise that this related to truth where he was concerned, rather than desire. On the basis of their parallel sensitivity, however, they married and left the Old World for the New.

But, after six years' experience, if Ruth had ever believed in the American Dream, we know that she's now totally disillusioned. Not only does she see the New World as a desert, with those who believe in it as "insects", and clearly resents the fact that childbearing has disqualified her as a glamour model, she can't even find the shoes there that she wants, as she tells Lenny, particularly as she's "very fond of clothes" and needs "an awful lot" in her "wardrobe" to be "content".

Similarly, from the evidence, she clearly feels disconnected from her husband's inner life. Apart from Teddy's self-conscious and unconvincing assurances to her in this respect, she also tells Lenny that her connection with his brother is: "I'm his wife." In short, it's clear that her new life in America was lived on Teddy's terms. This isn't something that could be expected to continue, considering her strong character, which is another way of saying her determination, her drive to power.

This led Teddy to take her to Venice in an effort to provide the stimulation that was clearly lacking in her life. On the way home, he, also increasingly dissatisfied, if not totally disillusioned, like her, with the American Dream, decided to stop off in London to seek some stimulation for himself in his "home" environment. He certainly found it, if not in the way he expected. Ruth, too, found stimulation from the trip, but not as Teddy had intended.

At first, she clearly wasn't too keen on the homecoming, even suggesting they leave almost as soon as they arrived. But that changed after the confrontation with Lenny, which most certainly did stimulate her, beyond anything she could have dreamed of, in fact.

So, what does Ruth mean by "Don't become a stranger"? From the above, it seems clear that Ruth hasn't given up on Eddie because "Don't become a stranger" means "remain as someone I can relate to in the future." And, from what we know of Teddy, he can, at the conclusion of the play, move forward in his life in one of three different ways. He can reconnect unconditionally with his commitment to truth, which he rediscovers in the play, or he can abandon that commitment entirely for the attachment to the desire for power, either in New or Old World terms. The third of these options is clearly Ruth's hope, because only in that way could she relate to him comfortably. Just as she has now come home, so does she hope for *him* to come home, too, if he's to remain familiar to her, to be again the man she married.

Of course, as noted earlier, Teddy's future is impossible to predict from the actions of the play, so we're left with Ruth, harbouring a lingering attachment to Eddie, but, brutal pragmatist that she is, facing up to her own future in London as Teddy shuts the front door. What this will involve is now suggested by the final scene, which corresponds to the final scene in Act I, when Teddy squared up to Max with his "Come on, then."

As Ruth sits relaxed on her chair and Sam lies still, Joey kneels at her feet and puts his head in her lap as she touches his head, lightly, in a maternal gesture. This reminds us that in the final stages of her confrontation with Lenny in Act I, as he'd tried to relieve her of the glass of water to establish his power over her, Ruth had seriously disturbed him, indeed, disarmed him, by calling him "Leonard". Lenny had been disturbed because, as he told her, "Leonard" was the name his mother gave him.

Now, Lenny, knowing Ruth's quasi-maternal power over him and having promised her "everything you need" in order to keep her, stands and watches as Max tries to assert his authority as patriarch by attempting to bully Ruth, telling her that he's not too old for her and that she will have to work, "to take them on", which recalls Teddy's "Come on, then". As with Teddy's earlier attempts to persuade her to return to America, however, and Lenny's in Act I to browbeat her, Max's threats find her imperturbable. He's reduced to stammering and voicing his suspicions to Lenny that

Ruth will "do the dirty on us", that she'll use them for her own ends. He can smell it, he says. "You want to bet?"

This is highly significant because it relates to a discussion between Max and Lenny at the very outset of the play, which means that this scene is intended to bring the play full circle. As Max was talking about Jessie, Lenny asked his opinion about the chances of a horse called "Second Wind". This led Max to reminisce about a love of horseracing and his "smell of a good horse", particularly the fillies, who, he said, were "more highly strung" than the colts and "more unreliable". He could, however, tell a winner simply by looking her in the eye.

Pinter clearly intends the "highly strung" and "more unreliable" here to relate to Ruth. "Highly strung" and "sensitive" are synonyms, for instance, and we saw how Ruth relates to "sensitive" in her confrontation with Lenny. Joey's inability to "go the whole hog" with Ruth also led Lenny to call her "a tease", i.e. someone who is "unreliable" and does "the dirty" on men, telling Max that she'd had Joey "on a string", providing a perfect connection between the "highly strung" and "unreliable".

Now, Max's conviction in his earlier discussion with Lenny that "Second Wind" didn't "stand a chance" and Lenny's that the horse was "the winner" suddenly has a strong whiff of relevance. For Ruth surely represents a second wind as "the backbone to this family" as Jessie once was. And, true enough, Max's fear that Ruth won't "be adaptable" is followed by his groaning and falling to his knees by the side of Ruth's chair. Amusingly, this recalls Max earlier complaining about "the pain of childbirth" over his "three bastard sons" and his "slutbitch of a wife". He'd "still got the pangs", he said; when he gives "a little cough" his "back collapses", suggesting his humiliation over his suspicions of Jessie's infidelity with Mac, suspicions confirmed earlier with

Sam's revelation, followed by *his* croaking and collapsing.

However, Max makes a final effort to straighten up and to look at Ruth, as he would with those unreliable fillies. But, now, he's kneeling before this particular filly as he insists that he's not an old man, raises his face to her and demands that she kiss him. Ruth continues to touch Joey's head lightly as Lenny stands watching. Max's histrionics merely confirm his impotence. This family is again a matriarchy.

Old Times

The Homecoming is a work of art and, as such, its meaning is universal and timeless. What it says about the human condition is just as relevant at any other time or place as it was in London in 1965. Its particular relevance to that time and place, however, was judicious because it came out at a time of enormous change in Western society, change which liberalised family values and human relations generally. Of course, London itself is famous for the "swinging sixties" when many girls no longer expected or accepted a life as wife and mother to the exclusion of other possibilities. As for the United States, the play opened in New York in early 1967, the year of the "summer of love", when so-called free love replaced conventional morality. As a result, the play appeared amazingly prescient both then and subsequently as society appeared to accommodate itself to its theme of looser ties.

As we've seen, however, the artist Harold Pinter was certainly no friend to progress. Indeed, the overarching theme of *The Homecoming* is not family values, which is merely a constituent, but how ideas of progress can seriously interfere with an individual's attempt to answer the question *why*. Nevertheless, the play's apparent sympathy with unfastening the marital corset certainly enhanced Pinter's popularity with the theatregoing public, just as his way with words and dramatic situations attracted film producers, ensuring his wider recognition as a writer. In this respect, Pinter's early success with *The Servant* was swiftly followed by further adaptations, most notably *The Go-Between* (1971), which won many awards, especially for Pinter himself as screenwriter.

But it was as playwright that his reputation had been established, a fact recognised by the award of the prestigious German Shakespeare Prize in 1970. Receiving the prize in Hamburg, Pinter made a speech in which he commented on the irony of the occasion, considering that he was writing nothing and could write nothing, by which he meant anything original. "I don't know why," he said. "When you can't write, you feel you've been banished from yourself."

This recalls the empty chair that belongs to Teddy in *The Homecoming*. Appropriately, that play would be the last in what turned out to be Harold Pinter's early trilogy of masterpieces. Henceforth, he would no longer write from the inspiration of an artist travelling along the road of truth, which explains both his inability to write and his ignorance as to why. Rather, new plays would come from his memory of being an artist in the past, although he would still be inspired from time to time. This patchwork of memory and episodic inspiration characterises all three of his so-called "memory plays", *Old Times*, *No Man's Land* and *Betrayal*.

Old Times, which premiered in London in June 1971, and in New York in November of that same year, was both a commercial and critical success, and has been produced many times since. It is, however, a relatively slight play, a country cottage in comparison to the stately home of art that is *The Homecoming*.

The play hinges on the fact that the desire for power, for happiness, looks backward, "mixing memory and desire", as T. S. Eliot put it in *The Waste Land*, just as it looks forward with hope.

A married couple, Deeley and Kate, are visited in their coastal converted farmhouse by Anna, who shared a flat in London with Kate 20 years earlier. Reminiscences about Kate from Deeley and Anna lead the latter to say that it's possible to remember some things "even though they may never have happened"; as she recalls them, "so they take place". *"What?"* replies Deeley, thus flagging the importance of the statement to the meaning of the play.

Apart from T. S. Eliot, another possible influence on *Old Times* is Oscar Wilde's *The Importance of Being Earnest*, in which Cecily states: "Memory usually chronicles the things that have never happened, and couldn't possibly have happened," happiness, in a word.

Old Times also looks back to *The Homecoming*, with its rubbishing of the sacredness of marriage: "What God has joined together let no man put asunder." Deeley recalls meeting Kate as they both exited a viewing of the 1947 film *Odd Man Out* and he commented to her that the actor Robert Newton was "fantastic" and she replied that she thought he was "remarkable". Deeley concludes that it was Robert Newton who brought them together and only he who could tear them apart.

Old Times is also reliant on *The Homecoming* for Ruth's farewell to Teddy: "Don't become a stranger," because Kate is clearly a "stranger" to both Deeley and Anna, with "stranger" meaning "odd man out", "outsider" or "alien" in the sense of the novella, *L'Étranger*, by that writer of the absurd, Albert Camus, who defined the protagonist as someone "who doesn't play the game", the game, that is, of seeking the illusion of happiness.

Significantly for the meaning of the play, Deeley sees Kate as "compliant only to the shifting winds, with which she went, but not *the* winds...winds that only she understood, and that of course with no understanding whatsoever..." The "winds" here suggest the wind of truth, the wind of Bob Dylan's "Blowin' in the Wind". Similarly, "winds that only she understood" relates to Teddy's "You wouldn't understand my works," while "with no understanding whatsoever" relates, in turn, to Teddy's "It's nothing to do with the question of intelligence."

Kate, then, is a truth seeker, and Deeley and Anna's increasingly competitive imagined memories of closeness *to* her are absurd attempts to give their lives meaning through a corresponding or collateral closeness to truth *through* her. Pinter makes clear that both of them are at loss without Kate. Deeley, for instance, goes to see *Odd Man Out* after "walking in no direction" and describes their initial love-making as touching her "profoundly all over". Indeed, Kate's aura for Deeley, and this is just how absurd this play gets, stretches even to her underwear.

Anna's leaving her supposedly glamorous lifestyle in her "rather fine" Sicilian villa with her "gourmet" husband to visit Kate and revisit the supposed happiness of their past together, one she'd clearly like to resurrect, conveys the same message.

There's a definite feeling here that Pinter himself was seeking to find a way to reconnect with the spirit of truth in order to escape a feeling of emptiness and futility, his increasing celebrity having perhaps distanced him from the humility necessary for its reception, something of which he'd already been unusually aware as far back as *The Birthday Party* when he showed the catastrophic effect of a perceived celebrity status, particularly on Goldberg with his "gift of the gab".

Naturally, where *Old Times* is concerned, Deeley and Anna's sense of futility could hardly end well – note that the first word spoken in the play is "Dark" – nor, indeed, would it end well for Pinter himself, whose next play, *No Man's Land*, is about as bleak as existentialism gets.

Thus, while, at first, it looks as if Anna is stealing a march on Deeley and winning Kate away from him, her triumph, like any prospect of lasting happiness, is ultimately dashed. For while Kate, at the outset of the play, isn't looking forward to seeing Anna again, indeed, hardly remembers her, and is finally prompted by Anna to recall their friendship, she only remembers her as a "dead" person.

Just as Petey turns the tables on Goldberg in *The Birthday Party*, so does Kate turn the tables on Anna. For while Anna admits to watching Kate unobtrusively in an effort to pierce her secrecy and discover her soul, so does Kate admit that she, too, had watched Anna to puncture her self-confidence and reveal her absence of soul. Anna had tried to prove Kate wrong in this by adopting superficial mannerisms based on hers but merely confirmed the profound truth that her "pupils" were missing from her eyes, i.e. that she can't *see*, as Teddy expresses it in *The Homecoming*.

Kate's pause after her dismissal of Anna is barely long enough for Deeley to register his triumph in their rivalry for her soul before he suffers a similar fate. Kate makes fun of his pretence of self-confidence on their first acquaintance, similarly of his conviction that being a man made him more likely to win her from Anna.

To express her true feelings, she had scooped up handfuls of soil from the window-box in which Anna had planted "our pretty daisies", no doubt to represent herself and Kate as "charming", and plastered his face with it. Deeley, infuriated at his come-uppance, forcefully resisted in an effort to preserve his mask of superiority, before suggesting a wedding and a change of environment in order to try to seduce her to join him in gambling on happiness. Just as Anna pretended that all she wanted for Kate "was her happiness", so, too, does Deeley. This, however, is the last thing the truth-seeking Kate wants, proving how little they know her.

Thus, she responded to their courtship rituals with "a little trick" of her own, which was to pretend to co-operate when, in reality, "neither mattered". To her, they're "no one".

The play ends with a mime as a final expression of its meaning. Anna attempts to leave as Deeley starts to sob. Anna returns, switches off the lamps and lies down to mimic the truth of Kate's contention that she lives in the darkness of ignorance and is effectively dead as a soul. Deeley then stands and looks down at Anna as if considering an alternative to his hopeless pursuit of Kate. He, too, then attempts to leave but is forced to return and prostrate himself before Kate, before accepting that he's nothing to her and sits slumped in defeat in a separate armchair.

The set is then sharply lit up to reveal the truth of their reality, and, by implication, that of the human condition, which is that of a willed separation from ultimate reality. We are, that is, "banished from ourselves", as Pinter himself felt when he wasn't inspired to write. The scene was set for Pinter's next full-length play.

No Man's Land

No Man's Land was premiered in April 1975 by the National Theatre at the Old Vic in London before transferring to the West End, then to the new National Theatre building on the South

Bank, following its opening in 1976, the same year it also had a run in New York.

The play features Hirst, a highly-successful alcoholic writer in his sixties, who has invited Spooner, a down-at-heel poet of the same age, to his grand house in North West London for a drink after meeting him in a Hampstead pub on a summer evening. The action takes place in a large room with a wall of bookshelves, an antique drinks cabinet and heavy curtains across the windows.

The first line, spoken by Hirst as he pours whisky for Spooner, is: "As it is?" This is something of an iconic opening. On one level, of course, Hirst is simply asking Spooner if he wants his drink neat. But the phrase "as it is" can also mean "in the present condition or current situation" and, as a question, therefore, written by Harold Pinter, means: "Do you want to know the bare truth?" Spooner's reply, that he wants it "absolutely as it is", ups the ante by suggesting that we're talking philosophical absolutes here, no less than the reality of the human condition.

This is followed by Spooner's repeated comment that Hirst is "very kind", which, in turn, suggests that the two are of a kind, i.e. that that the human condition in question applies to them both, the equivalent of Bob Dylan's "my friend" in "Blowin' in the Wind". Indeed, when the relationship between them has developed significantly, Hirst will call Spooner "my friend". The nature of the human condition to be expounded in the play is then further suggested by Spooner's "Terribly kind of you," in response to Hirst's offer that he help himself to more drinks. As we shall see, this flags up the nature of the human condition as nothing less than "terrible", although Pinter also shows exactly why.

This is compounded by Spooner's subsequent speech, which recalls the ending of *Old Times* as Kate punctured the self-confident pretence of both Anna and Deeley to reveal the neediness beneath. *No Man's Land*, then, follows on directly from *Old Times* in its meaning. Spooner explains that some people's perceived strength is merely "a calculated posture" through which a man of "intelligence and perception" can see the flabbiness. "I am such a man" he says. Hirst then asks whether he means that he's a person who maintains such a posture or one who punctures it in others. Spooner insists that he's the man of "intelligence and perception", certainly not one of the former. The truth of this claim is one of the questions the play sets out to answer.

In writing *No Man's Land* after the relatively slight *Old Times*, there's little doubt that Harold Pinter was seeking to write a masterpiece in the same mould as the plays of his great early trilogy. True to form, therefore, whether consciously or not, he incorporates many of the themes of those classics in *No Man's Land*, which, as a result, has something of a summary quality.

Thus, Spooner's claim to see through people's masks recalls Teddy's sensitivity and ability to *see*. Similarly, Spooner's subsequent insistence on observing others with detachment, keeping a "proper distance" so as to maintain what he calls "an objective relation to matter" recalls Teddy's refusal to be "lost" in what people do so that he can "maintain intellectual equilibrium". All this is gradually building up a picture of Spooner, certainly in his own estimation, as an artist.

Spooner makes the same point when he says that he's "a free man" by living in an eternal present, i.e. not looking forward to a hoped-for happiness in the future or backward to an imagined happiness in the past. He then confirms this through a crucial passage in which he recollects sharing a drink with a Hungarian émigré on a midsummer night, a meeting which changed his life and made him the man he is. Formerly, he says, he had "expectations" and was "a captive to memories".

The fact that the émigré was "bald" suggests that he, in contrast, was pure soul, which Spooner then confirms by saying that the man possessed a "serenity" which provided him, Spooner, that is, with a template for living. This also harks back to the truth-seekers of Pinter's previous great plays. The émigré's teaching him "how quiet life can be", for instance, recalls Aston's "quiet", while his "serenity" recalls that of Petey and Kate.

Spooner concludes the story by telling Hirst that he'd met him in the same pub as the émigré although, significantly, "at a different table". This is significant because Spooner expresses the émigré's eternally present fixedness in terms of his "unmoving table". The coincidence of the meeting place, however, now leads him to wonder about Hirst as he'd once wondered about the Hungarian. But will he, he asks, still wonder about Hirst tomorrow as he still wonders about the émigré today. This is another question that the play sets out to answer.

Spooner now introduces himself as a poet and guide to the young, his vocation one of "art" leading to "virtue", which, in the context of the previous praise for detachment and serenity, can only mean that art, true art, art guided by the spirit of truth, leads to a proper relationship towards reality, which is the only virtue. This prompts Hirst's first significant contribution to the conversation, one which also leads to a dramatic change. He recalls garlands being hung in his village church in honour of all those who died "unmarried", having lived "a blameless life". The "married" here, as we saw with Teddy in *The Homecoming*, could mean to a partner or to desire. And, indeed, the latter appears to be the case since it would explain the "blameless life" in response to Spooner's "virtue".

Spooner, however, misunderstands as a result of what appears to be some heavyweight emotional baggage that he carries. He first asks Hirst to tell him more about the garlands, which he labels "quaint little perversions". When Hirst says there is no more, Spooner questions Hirst about his wife, ignoring his "What wife?" (an echo of Stanley in *The Birthday Party*) to ask, absurdly, how "true" she was in terms related to the bowling of a cricket ball. His ironic description of his own wife then reveals that this is the likely source of his emotional baggage. He persists in questioning Hirst about his wife before appearing to suggest that his alcoholism is related to that wife.

Hirst, however, responds with one of his iconic pronouncements. This is that Spooner, whom he now calls "my friend", finds him in "the last lap" of a race that he'd long "forgotten to run". What this means is that he's coming to the end of a life in which he'd long given up on the pursuit of happiness.

Spooner responds by suggesting that, in his impotence, Hirst is avoiding facing up to some emotional baggage and, significantly, like Goldberg in *The Birthday Party*, suddenly uses slang to show that he's revealing another side of himself as he tells Hirst that he has "a long hike, my lad" up which he's slogging unfriended. He then, equally uncharacteristically, mixes his metaphors, as he offers himself as Hirst's friend, his "boatman" on the "deep and dank architecture" of the river he's navigating. He is, in other words, adopting a "calculated posture" of strength to what he perceives to be Hirst's weakness. Spooner then taunts Hirst about losing his wife, absurdly bursting into folk song in the process.

So much for Spooner's living in the eternal present! The down-at-heel poet's visit to a rich man's mansion with unlimited booze on offer has properly turned his head, that "my friend" from his host giving him an idea for some great expectations, as, indeed, we might recall was also the case with both Stanley and Goldberg with their public appearances. What's more, as well as that "quiet" recalling Aston in *The Caretaker*, we may also now recall that Spooner had earlier exclaimed to Hirst: "My Christ" at a meeting of minds, recalling Davies and a similar prospect of exploiting another's generosity.

What we are dealing with in this play, then, is the temptation of a man away from the road of truth towards a perceived gravy train of happiness. *No Man's Land*, in short, is concerned with the fall of an artist as he changes from "a man of intelligence and perception" to one with "a calculated posture" aimed at persuading Hirst to employ him. And that seduction, as with Davies, will involve his adopting the pretence of altruism to get what he wants, hence "My Christ".

This, of course, provides an interim answer to the question asked at the outset of the play about Spooner's nature: is he a man of perception or of pretence? But we are now also offered an interim answer to the second question about Hirst's nature: will Spooner still wonder about him tomorrow as he does today about the serene émigré?

This question, about Hirst's nature, is now revealed to be essential to the meaning of *No Man's Land* because he now replies to Spooner's offer to steer him through the "deep and dark architecture" of his life's journey by rejecting the offer. What's more, and crucially, he explains that rejection by quoting the play's title, which he says, neither moves nor changes but remains forever icy and silent.

Hirst, in short, is caught in the no man's land between truth and desire, aware of the former and its passport to freedom for the soul, but with his self still clinging to the latter and so unable to move. Thus, by effectively abandoning what the émigré taught him, Spooner is to find himself in this same neither-nor world as the price of his betrayal of soul. He will, that is, pay the price for his own flabbiness.

Pinter, moreover, makes it clear that this outcome is inevitable, considering the nature of the human condition.

Spooner's fall is first suggested by a mime or dumb show on the part of Hirst, who, dead drunk, staggers across the room before falling, getting to his feet, falling again, and crawling to the door and out of the room as Spooner watches.

Spooner then comments on what he's observed by quoting from T. S. Eliot's "The Love Song of J. Alfred Prufrock", a poem about a truth seeker who abandons a commitment to truth because he's afraid of the consequences. The poem makes much of the protagonist's experience of life in terms of the repeated phrase: "I have known…" And now Spooner says of Hirst's fall and crawl: "I have known this before."

This is significant because, when insisting to Hirst earlier about the need for detachment in order to be a free man living in the eternal present, he'd dismissed experience as "a paltry thing… the wetdream world". For experience of life is merely experience of the attachment to desire and its consequences; so that when Hirst told Spooner that he spoke with "the weight of experience behind him", he replied that such experience was "beneath me". Well, yes, perhaps it was then, but not anymore. Now, it's to be his destiny: it's before him.

This theme is continued into the next scene, which introduces the play's other two characters, Foster, a budding poet in his 30s, and Briggs, a brute in his 40s, who together look after Hirst's needs and who have returned after their night off.

The theme of inevitability, of having been here before, is introduced almost immediately by Foster, who, unable to find a taxi, has had to walk back and says he thought he'd never make it: "What a hike." This echoes Spooner's "You have a long hike, my lad," in the previous scene. Foster then welcomes the availability of "a nice lighthouse like this one", which is precisely what the house represents to Spooner. As for his pretence of altruism towards Hirst, Foster addresses a "Christ, I'm thirsty" to him on arrival. Another factor in the inevitability of Spooner's downfall and its consequences for him is that Foster and Briggs will be his tormentors, the devils in his chosen hell.

In his efforts to ingratiate himself, Spooner tells them a story about a man sitting very still, in shadow, at a café table beside a canal in Amsterdam, whistling under his breath, oblivious to the bustle and noise around him. The story echoes Spooner's earlier tale about the Hungarian émigré. He tells the duo that he intended to paint a picture of the scene and to call it "The Whistler", regretting that he hasn't yet done so.

Foster warns him that if he leaves it too long, he might lose the inspiration. Pinter could hardly be clearer: Spooner is in serious danger of ceasing to be an artist. This is compounded moments later when he begins to paint a fantastic picture of an apocryphal lifestyle: "a calculated posture" recalling Stanley's "world tour".

Foster then tells a story intended to dispel any alternative spiritual mumbo jumbo from the East to the simple inspiration of the spirit of truth, which is available to everyone and which Spooner is renouncing. This is the equivalent of Lenny's rubbishing academic philosophy in *The Homecoming*.

It's at this point that Hirst returns in dressing gown, having slept briefly and dreamt of a waterfall, no, a lake. This appears to be related to Spooner's "fall" (as in Adam's "fall") in the previous scene – "just recently" – and his destiny as a result, which is to end up in an icy no man's land, all seen in terms of Spooner's "wetdream world" of human experience, the world of illusion. Hirst says that he saw someone drowning in his dream. That person would appear to be Spooner.

It was Hirst, however, who spoke of being in "no man's land" and now, for the first time in the play, he begins to reveal why he's trapped there.

He speaks of a photograph album which recalls his youth, when the sun shone, the girls were lovely, and tenderness towards others reigned. He sees happiness in terms of memory, in the shape of the album, and also of making plans for the future, but it's the album that predominates for this old man. He looks back on the world of his photo album as "solid" even though, as an artist, he wonders whether it ever existed or, if it did, whether it could survive the inevitability of change. And, as he looks back, so does the memory of a particular girl cause him to lose all dignity as he drinks directly from the whisky bottle.

Now, he makes clear the roots of his "no man's land" as, remembering this "happy" world of his imagination, he veers from a commitment to truth: "It never existed," to an attachment to desire: "It remains," which is why he's "sitting here forever". As for his staff, his guest, his generosity with his booze, this is revealed to stem from his fear of living – and drinking to forget his predicament – in this hell alone.

He becomes confused as his recent dream and memories of his youth merge into one another, just as Spooner's destiny and his own merge into no man's land, where truth and desire clash. Thus, recalling a perfumed muff and an incomparably beautiful girl looking at him overwhelms his self, only for his soul to dismiss them as "all poison".

He returns to the dream, the fall of water, and it's at this point that Spooner gate-crashes Hirst's rambling monologue to claim that it was he who was drowning in his host's wetdream. This may be true, but, as Hirst's dream is proving something of a harbinger of doom in the sun-kissed azure skies of his recollections of youth, Spooner is setting out to gain his gratitude by reassuring him that, personally, he has nothing to worry about from the dream. This is one aspect of his perceived altruism towards Hirst, while another reveals itself when Hirst, blind drunk from guzzling whisky straight from the bottle, falls to the floor and Spooner rushes to his assistance, dismissing Foster and Briggs as pitiless and promoting himself as Hirst's "true friend" like those in his photograph album.

This prompts Foster to react with "Christ", before himself and Briggs respond to Spooner's attack on their continued employment by scorning his pathetic stratagems. On the one hand, Foster cautions him against falling "into a quicksand", which, in this instance, is a synonym for "no man's land", and on the other, he warns him against trying to disrupt the "happy family life" that exists in the Hirst household, Pinter's ironic glance back towards *The Homecoming*.

Foster then bemoans his lot of "looking after a pisshound", before dreaming of finding "the right niche" for happiness. Briggs, meanwhile, who has no such illusions, offers Hirst precisely the kind of tough love he needs. He commands him to stand before leading him from the room with some truly profound advice where his happy dreams of youth are concerned: "Don't look back."

Act I ends with Foster's dual revenge on Spooner's pretence. The first is metaphorical as he tells him an absurd story about seeing a man in the Australian desert carrying two umbrellas. The umbrellas represent Spooner's twin attempts at hypocritical altruism towards Hirst, supposedly shielding him from harm.

Spooner asks Foster if it was raining. Foster replies that it was a beautiful day, passing comment on Spooner's hypocrisy. He says that he nearly asked the man what he was up to but changed his mind. Spooner's resulting question: "Why?" flags up his abandonment of a commitment to truth, which is the result of choosing to answer the question *why*. Foster comments on this by saying that he decided that the man with the umbrellas was "some kind of lunatic".

This metaphorical revenge is then followed by a more practical one, which also passes comment on Spooner's abandonment of the light of truth for imprisonment in the darkness of illusion. This is to show him what he's done by turning the lights off and locking him in the room for the night.

Act II begins with morning and Spooner's renewed perception of his destiny with another: "I have known this before," which introduces the scene that follows. Briggs enters to announce that Hirst's financial adviser, who was due to visit, has cancelled because of "a vast aboriginal financial calamity", with the "aboriginal" recalling Foster's story of the man with the two umbrellas in the Australian desert. Spooner's reply that the adviser "clearly needs an adviser" again passes comment on his own hypocritical claim to be Hirst's best adviser and the impossibility of insuring against impediments to the fulfilment of happiness.

Briggs serves Spooner with the adviser's breakfast and tells him an absurdly apocryphal story about how he met Foster. This involves Foster asking him the way to Bolsover Street, which Briggs tells him is in the middle of an intricate one-way system easy enough to enter but impossible to exit. The people who live there, he says are in a state of despair. He describes it as "Life at a Dead End". Aside from being a highly amusing story, this is also clearly a fable for Spooner's benefit as to where his posturing will lead him: into "no man's land".

Briggs tells Spooner, on "doctor's orders", to finish the "freezing" bottle of champagne he served him for breakfast, freezing like the "icy" no man's land to which he's destined, upon which Spooner asks why he was locked in the room overnight. "Doctor's orders", replies Briggs. This is Pinter's ironic comment on Foster and Briggs' role in unleashing nemesis on Spooner for his hubris in trying to con Hirst. For Briggs now reveals that Hirst is also a writer, which provides Spooner with what he'll see as his golden opportunity to exploit him.

Briggs is then called away, leading Spooner to introduce the next scene with yet another reminder of his destiny: "I have known this before." This scene, which involves a dialogue between Hirst and Spooner, is probably the funniest ever written by Harold Pinter. Like *Old Times*, the scene deals with the role of memory in creating an absurd fiction in which we achieve glorious fulfilment for our self, happiness assured. But Pinter grossly exaggerates the fiction to the point of making it caricature, a role play, a farce within a play. At its conclusion, however, this farce merges with the play to reveal how what we consider to be memory is nothing of the kind; reveals how it separates us from reality to live in an illusionary world of our own making.

That this is farce is signalled at the outset as Hirst enters, immaculately attired and sober as a judge, to welcome Spooner in an impeccably upper-class accent as his old friend, "Charles Wetherby". He then orders Briggs, as "Denson", to bring coffee.

Hirst begins by complimenting the exhausted and probably already quite drunk and disreputable-looking poet on how "remarkably well" he looks, before trying to recall their last meeting, whether at "the club" in '38 or the "Pavilion at Lord's" in '39.

With great relish, he then confesses to cuckolding "Charles" with his wife, Emily, whose ardour he recalls as unparalleled. All this is Hirst's delicious revenge for Spooner's taunting him in the previous act over his supposed impotence by twisting the knife into Spooner's wound over his wife's fidelity. He subsequently taunts the cuckold with being a "natural athlete". Once a winner, always a winner he tells the wretch before him.

Hirst then pretends regret that they saw so little of each other after coming down from Oxford. But perhaps that was because of their literary careers. They'd occasionally met, but had never been close. He wonders why, adding that, of course, he was successful "awfully early", with the inference that his guest wasn't.

Having skewered Spooner good and proper, to his obvious delight, he then questions him directly about his war record and literary career after the war. Spooner now begins his counter-attack in this fabulous clash of egos. He first sets out to disarm Hirst by acknowledging that he has done "rather well" in his career, before turning to the subject of Hirst's supposedly magnificent sex-life.

Hirst amorally and imperturbably bats away Spooner's barbs in the tone of a lord who can do exactly as he pleases, while Spooner adopts the tone of a knight in shining armour facing up to a cad. Spooner then changes roles with Hirst as he reveals that he was something of an amoral sex-god himself, while Hirst adopts the moral tone, until, scandalised, he accuses Spooner of being a scoundrel.

Spooner counters with the accusation that it's Hirst who's the scoundrel, for, among other things, having an affair with his wife, who was joined to him in God. This provides no little confirmation that the emotional baggage Spooner revealed earlier in his scene with Hirst involved his wife's infidelity, although it's unlikely that it was with Hirst since there seems little doubt from the evidence in the play that they were strangers when they met. No, what happened was that the game-playing went too far to be acceptable to Spooner's pride, who revealed this by calling his wife "Emily Spooner", when in the role-play he's supposed to be Charles Wetherby.

Now, just as Spooner stopped playing the game because he no longer found the farce funny since it offended his amour propre, so, too, does Hirst, and for the same reason. This occurs because, after the bitter exchange over Spooner's cuckolding, Spooner makes a crack about Hirst's limitations as a poet. This is too much for Hirst, the fact that Spooner, a down-at-heel poet, has the gall to criticise him, a highly successful writer, in his own house. This prompts Hurst to call for Denson to serve him whisky. The first whisky downed, he regrets how the most sensitive and cultivated of men can change, almost overnight, into a brigand. There's an element of truth here, which means that we're now segueing from farce to play.

At this point, Hirst attempts to re-establish his dominance over Spooner by offering to show him the tools of his trade as a writer, concluding with his willingness to show him his "footstool". This harks back to Meg in *The Birthday Party* and the stool her important father gave her as a sign of her inferiority and dependence. And this is precisely what Hirst is suggesting to Spooner, i.e. that he was willing to treat Spooner as an equal in a game between them in order to humour him, ignoring the fact that he was humiliating him in the process, but that Spooner hadn't played by the rules, rather, had grossly flouted the rules to hit him below the belt, or, more appropriately, below the water-line, by acting as if he actually *was* his equal. It's more appropriate because Spooner had earlier told Hirst that he'd served in "torpedo boats" during the war, a typical Pinter detail to make a point.

In a crucial monologue, Hirst now extends his magnanimity to Spooner over his footstool to showing him his photograph album. Where he's concerned, there's absolutely nothing farcical about memories such as these; this is serious, certainly for him, although, in the light of reality, just as farcical. The monologue ends with Hirst's plea to Spooner to "tender the dead" as he would like to be tendered. The verb "tender" here means to cherish, to value, to respect the dead, which Hirst claims will give those dead "unbounded joy". This smacks very much of Goldberg's imperative in *The Birthday Party* to respect tradition, whose roots, absurdly, go all the way back to "your great-gran-granny".

Hirst's imperative in *No Man's Land* receives short shrift from Briggs, who represents a kind of rough-hewn Petey. Thus, as Hirst drinks whisky at the rousing conclusion of his paean to the "good ghost", Briggs comments: "They're blank, mate, blank. The blank dead."

Hirst's response is to demand Briggs give him the bottle of whisky, the consequence of his being "lost" in his memories when, as an artist, he should know better, just as Teddy should know better than to follow the American Dream or Aston the mirage of altruism. Briggs' refusal hands Spooner his opportunity: he puts himself forward as Hirst's secretary and even offers to help him with his photograph album, which prompts Hirst to comment that certain places in his heart are forever closed to any "living soul", which is a pity, because that's why he's in no man's land. Hirst signals this killing of the light in his soul by closing the curtains on the rapidly fading light outside and replacing it with artificial light.

Spooner persists in trying to persuade Hirst to let him live with him and be his secretary, which Hirst hears as a buzzing fly. This prompts Spooner to launch into the first of two monologues. This has precisely the same tone and meaning as that made by J. Alfred Prufrock once he's resigned himself to insignificance on giving up his commitment to truth. It also reveals more about Spooner's emotional baggage. He was, he says, one of his generation's chosen ones only for something to happen which stymied his potential. He has, however, survived "insult and deprivation". This recalls his story to Hirst about meeting the émigré when he was, he recalled, a prey to memories of a particularly "pronounced grisliness". It appears, then, that, as with Hirst, Spooner has also been wounded by memory, but if Hirst's are memories of happiness, Spooner's are memories of misery. Either way, they're both victims of desire.

Spooner's second monologue is a return to farce as he sets out to seduce Hirst with the prospect of a poetry reading in the upstairs room of The Bull's Head pub in Chalk Farm. Free drinks and a meal in a local Indian restaurant would be thrown in on top of the fee or a substantial share of the profits. He could, also, only if he liked, of course, use the occasion to speak through the press to the world.

Hirst responds to this generous offer of a stadium concert in a broom cupboard by changing the subject for the last time: anything to bring this drivel to an end! Egged on by Foster and Briggs, he now agrees simply to sit there forever in an eternal winter night. The one pity is that he can hear the sound of birds, which must have sounded when he was young, only he never heard them then. There is, in other words, life out there.

He then returns to his dream. This now takes on a whole new meaning. Hirst is walking towards a lake; in his wake, a pursuer that he loses easily. He sees a body in the water, floating, but, on closer inspection realises that he was wrong. He thought he saw a body drowning, but there's nothing there.

As a parting gift from a great writer, this is, as usual with Harold Pinter, highly ambiguous, but also potentially uplifting. What it means is this: the "I" walking towards the lake is the artist or truth seeker's soul, the pursuer his self. The soul can easily lose the self through detachment, but that's not enough to find freedom. For that, it's necessary for the self to die, which is why the onlooker, the soul, is excited in the dream to see the body in the water. But he was mistaken. There's nothing there, which is to say that the self is still alive. And, in that case, the soul remains in no man's land, an intermediate state between truth and desire, which requires a final commitment from the soul to dispense with the self. This explains Hirst's statement after the curtains are closed that he'll resolve certain matters today; he'll come to a decision. But he doesn't.

In turn, this explains the play's ending, spoken by Spooner, quoting Hirst from Act I, about no man's land. Hirst's "I'll drink to that" signifies resignation to his fate.

Betrayal

That wasn't the outcome Harold Pinter ultimately chose. Although clearly familiar from his own experience with Hirst's philosophical dilemma, he effectively elected to distance himself entirely from his life as an artist by unmistakeably identifying with his self, i.e. to choose the pursuit of happiness, although he probably still considered himself an artist. This accounts for the nature of his later career. Of course, from an artist's point of view, this was a betrayal of his commitment to truth, to answering the question *why*, and, in turn, a total rejection of the meaning of his great plays. It's appropriate, then, that Pinter's last great play is called *Betrayal*.

The play's overriding theme, and something of its construction, is indebted to British writer Ford Madox Ford's 1915 novel, *The Good Soldier*, originally called *The Saddest Story*, a tale of multiple betrayals told by an unreliable narrator. Pinter acknowledges this indebtedness in the pivotal central scene, of its nine, when a publisher, Robert, tells his wife, Emma, who is engrossed in a new novel, that there isn't much more to say on that book's subject, which, he says, is betrayal. Later in the scene, as Emma is trembling when she realises that Robert has discovered her affair with Jerry, a literary agent, his oldest friend and the best man at his wedding, Robert recalls how Jerry used to write him long letters about Ford Madox Ford when, close friends, they were both bright young editors of poetry magazines.

From the above, it's no surprise that *Betrayal* is also a tale of multiple betrayals. One theme, for instance, is that both Robert and Jerry betray their youthful literary idealism as commercial considerations gradually take over. But the play is largely concerned with Jerry's seven-year affair with Emma, details of which Pinter admitted were based on a similar extramarital affair of his own in the 1960s when he was married to his first wife, actress Vivien Merchant, who starred as Ruth and Anna, respectively, in the premieres of *The Homecoming* and *Old Times*.

But why, then, does Robert tell Emma that there's not much more to say on the subject of betrayal? Is Pinter, through Robert, adopting the role of an unreliable narrator? In fact, Robert's comment is a typical Pinter touch, a kind of literary wink to the audience, nudging them away from first impressions towards a deeper meaning to the play. Considering that it's called *Betrayal* and is manifestly concerned with betrayals, this might seem strange. But "betrayal" can mean "discovery", as in "revelation", as well as "deceit", as in selling out or infidelity. And we know from the analysis of his previous plays how often Harold Pinter loves to play with words to reveal different meanings and, thereby, direct the audience towards the truth. Indeed, this is fundamental to his genius.

Where *Betrayal* is concerned, this is effectively confirmed immediately after Robert's comment that there's not much more to say on the subject of betrayal when Emma disagrees with him that the subject *is* betrayal. When Robert responds by asking her what, then, is the subject, she replies that she'll tell him when she's finished it, but, actually, she, and Jerry, especially Jerry, will only know the subject of their own drama when it's finished. Uniquely, this doesn't mean at the end of the play, since, in a nod to *The Good Soldier*'s construction, based as it is on a series of flashbacks, *Betrayal* is told in generally reverse order so that, while Emma's discovery or, rather, self-revelation, comes in the first scene, and Jerry's in the second, *we* don't appreciate the full meaning of those revelations until we reach the last scene and the start of the affair.

The play actually begins two years after the end of the affair before moving on to that end, on to the year before and then to the discovery of the affair by Robert and its immediate aftermath, before going on to its early days, until it arrives back at its beginning. This final scene reveals Jerry's motivation for propositioning Emma as twofold, firstly, his wanting to "have" her, to "blacken" her in her "bridal dress" before her wedding, and, secondly, that without her consent to his advances, he'd be condemned to a state of desolation and emptiness.

This dual motivation is central to the meaning of the play, although isn't its essential meaning. In the first instance, Jerry's description of this state of desolation and emptiness, made, as he admits to Emma, when he is drunk, recalls Hirst's drunken description of "no man's land" as unchanging, icy and silent, a state where, as Foster says, he'll "be sitting here forever", or "Life At A Dead End", as Briggs calls it. Jerry, too, uses similar terms such as "total paralysis" and "catatonia".

Jerry, then, like Hirst, is in the no man's land between truth and desire. And he's seeking a way out, but not through a more absolute commitment to the spirit of truth, and, hence, towards a deeper reality, but, on the contrary, towards an attachment to a more naked desire for power and, hence, a more frenzied illusion, in the shape of Emma. Thus, he talks about being "crazy" about her, about being in "a whirlwind", about being "overwhelmed", "knocked out", "dazzled", "madly in love", and, most revealing of all, that he'll never be able to sleep again, i.e. dream again, without her. He concludes by saying that he's "lost", which recalls Teddy's "I won't be lost in it" in *The Homecoming*.

But that's not why he wants Emma, that's not the focus of his desire. *That* is a macho rite of passage which involves cuckolding Robert, his oldest friend. This will make the cuckolding so much more satisfying because fulfilling a naked desire for power means triumphing over all constraints, particularly any kind of conventional morality such as the absolute trust of close friendship. This recalls Hirst's amoral delight in the idea of seducing Spooner's wife, whose ardour he recalls as unparalleled, and explains Jerry wanting to "blacken" Emma in her "bridal dress" before ushering her into her wedding as her "best man". When she corrects him that he was her husband's best man, Jerry counters with "No. Your best man," meaning that Robert would merely have been her second best man as her husband if he'd already "had" her.

Significantly in this respect, Jerry's propositioning Emma occurs as he surprises her during a party at her house in the bedroom she shares with her husband. Equally significant is the fact that Robert enters the room shortly after their first kisses, when Jerry explains their being there by saying that, as Robert is his best and oldest friend, as well as his host, he decided to compliment his wife on her beauty, i.e. that it's *because* Emma is his best friend's wife that he prizes her.

Robert's "Quite right" pointedly introduces the theme of conventional morality. Jerry replies by saying that it's "quite right" to "face up to the facts", which clearly trump conventional morality here, and to "offer a token" without shame of his "unalloyed appreciation", that "token" suggesting that his pursuit of Emma is merely a by-product of something else, which is "unalloyed" i.e. unfettered by any morality. Jerry suggests the nature of that "something else" in his final words: "no holds barred", recalling Lenny's "the land of no holds barred", and meaning, in this case, an amoral macho rite of passage by putting one over Robert by seducing his wife. Robert's reply: "Absolutely", suggests that, once again, we're talking absolutes here, the human condition.

Going forward in time, but back in the play, to the previous scene, which occurs a year-and-a-half into the affair, we find the now adulterous couple – Jerry is also a married man, to Judith, a hospital doctor, with two children – meeting at the flat he rents for their trysts. Jerry arrives after Emma and talks of walking through a beautiful, empty Hyde Park, sitting down under a tree and appreciating the quiet while looking at the Serpentine. There's more than a hint here of Aston's "quiet", which Jerry has left behind him and may be missing. The "quiet" is quickly dispelled however, as Jerry admits his irritation at Judith meeting a fellow doctor for drinks.

This prompts Emma to suggest his leaving his wife for her, which Jerry promptly dismisses on the grounds that Judith loves him and their children, all of which "means something", with which Emma agrees, before Jerry tells her that he adores her. Jerry, in short, wants a wife and a mistress, for different reasons, and Emma, as we saw above, fulfils the role of the latter, while Judith clearly fulfils the role of the former. At this point, Emma tells Jerry that she conceived with her husband while he was away in America. This whole passage introduces the theme of security, initially for the female of the human species, Emma clearly being concerned with nest-building, although Jerry, too, wants the security of a wife and children, only not with her.

The previous three scenes, 5-7, which occur two years later, and follow one another in time, deal with Robert's discovery of the affair while on holiday with Emma and their two children in Venice and the aftermath of that discovery. The scene following the discovery deals with Jerry and Emma's reunion in their flat, when she fails to tell him that Robert knows about their affair, which is a betrayal that will prove crucial in Jerry's downfall, and her alarm that Jerry and Robert are soon to meet for lunch, when she supposes he'll find out, prompting the end of the affair. This clearly matters to her because, aside from her security, she also loves to be adored, which passes comment on the nature of the desire for power, maternity or no maternity, recalling Ruth in *The Homecoming*.

More nest-building by Emma follows as she places a tablecloth she bought in Venice "for the house" on the table of their rented flat. This is succeeded by Jerry's admission of panic over two episodes that could have alerted his wife to his adultery, but which proved to be false alarms, to his enormous relief. Again, this passes comment on the conflicted nature of his desire for power, revealing an element that will provide the ultimate meaning of the play.

It's important to note here that there's no sense of guilt at the adultery, the flouting of conventional morals, on the part of either Jerry or Emma. This is most definitely not where the play's meaning is heading. Harold Pinter's previous plays consistently scorned conventional morality as hypocrisy, mere game-playing in the desire for power. *Betrayal* is no different in this respect. On Robert's discovery of the affair in the previous scene, for instance, Emma trembled as she realised that her affair with his best friend had been discovered, but this was simply fear at being unmasked and at the prospect of losing her security. The most she was able to offer her husband in terms of regret was a limp "I'm sorry," his *"Sorry?"* in reply passing comment on the inadequacy of this excuse for regret. Neither did she seek to end the affair on its discovery, even buying a lovely tablecloth for her love nest.

Jerry, too, clearly has no sense of guilt at his adultery, hypocritically being irritated at his wife's meeting a colleague for drinks when he's established a love nest after swearing fidelity at their marriage ceremony. He does, however, pay a price for his adultery. This is revealed by his remembering a time years before in Emma's kitchen when he picked up her eldest child, Charlotte, and lifted her up high as she laughed. Jerry remembers how light she was, amidst general laughter, a memory he can't escape. He "can't get rid of it" because the memory represents the innocence he's lost and which he clearly misses. His recalling how light she was suggests how heavy he is, weighed down by his experience of life, which is to say, his experience of the desire for power. But, as we'll see, this has nothing to do with guilt but something more universal, more generic to the desire for power.

Emma, too, has some instinctive understanding of this as she promptly corrects Jerry over the fact that the episode occurred in *his* kitchen, thereby reminding him that it was he who initiated the affair which led to them betraying the partners and children who trusted them. But, as Jerry takes her to bed, she relents, renewing her faith in the importance to her happiness of her adultery by assuring Jerry that he had every right to throw her daughter up.

The following scene involves the lunch meeting between Jerry and Robert in which the latter gets drunk, bemoans his job as a publisher of modern novels, which he hates, and recalls reading Yeats, his greatest influence as a young poetry editor, while on holiday in Venice. This was the morning after he discovered his wife's adultery with Jerry, although he doesn't tell Jerry that, which is another betrayal that will have enormous consequences for him. He does, however, say that he was so happy walking about alone in the early morning, by which he clearly means not only of that day in Venice but also through its recalling his youth as a poetry editor, a feeling with which Jerry concurs.

This reminds Robert of their early friendship, based on a shared passion for serious literature, and he responds by suggesting that Jerry come round for a drink as Emma would love to see him. This effectively amounts to Robert's acceptance of his wife's adultery with Jerry, to which he's clearly resigned himself.

That visit occurs a year later and makes up scene 4 of the play. This is an interesting scene because it passes comment on the fact that, although Robert is clearly the victim in his wife's adultery, in which he's cuckolded by his best friend, nevertheless he's an accessory after the fact, not only because of his acceptance of it, but because he had, in a sense, initiated it, which, in turn, is why he's resigned to it. This is shown in two different ways.

In the first instance, Robert and Jerry discuss parenting, specifically the fact that boys are more anxious than girls about facing the world, which suggests that they have more to prove in order to justify their pride in themselves. This is later confirmed when Robert asks Jerry when they are to resume playing squash, admitting that he's playing regularly with Casey, Jerry's client, a modern novelist Robert's firm publishes.

He comments that Casey is a "brutally honest" squash player while urging Jerry to play again as, he says, he was "rather good", with which Jerry agrees. This equates "brutally honest" with "rather good", making a moral case for brutal honesty, and relates to Jerry's "no holds barred" that signals the start of his affair with Emma, just as "the land of no holds barred" was where Teddy's marriage to Ruth foundered in *The Homecoming*.

The rest of the scene prepares the ground for *Betrayal's* denouement as Jerry and Robert discuss making "a date" for the game and subsequent lunch as if it were a love match. Thus it is that when Emma asks if she can watch the game and accompany them to lunch, Robert rejects her suggestion in a "brutally honest" manner, which relates to the "brutally honest" nature of Casey's squash playing and introduces the idea of an exclusively male conspiracy where macho interactions are concerned. And this is precisely what Robert goes on to describe: the fact that men don't want women around for their "battle" and subsequent deserved refreshments for "fear of improper interruption", with the "improper" here underlying that we're dealing with a morality which dispenses with conventional politeness towards women. We're talking men's talk.

Jerry's response: that he hasn't played squash for years, suggests that he's not involved any more in such macho rituals, except, of course, that he is. For, as we've seen, his seduction of Emma is just such a macho ritual. And this is precisely why he doesn't need to play squash, because he's proving his manhood in a far more satisfying way. This is why Robert is complicit in Jerry's affair with his wife, because he shares the same macho desire for power and, indeed, encourages it in Jerry. Thus, when Jerry tells Robert that they can't play squash because he'll be on a trip to New York with Casey to discuss a film of his novel that Emma considers "bloody dishonest", a trip that he says Casey thinks he deserves, Emma asks him: "Do you deserve the trip?" She is, in other words, questioning Jerry's macho triumph over Robert through their affair because she hopes it's deeper than that, something more in tune with her nest building.

This is confirmed in the previous scene, which deals with the end of that affair, when, having not met in their flat for months, Emma says that she can't bear to think of it standing empty, "an empty home". Jerry counters that it's not a home, adding that he knows what she wanted, i.e. to build a home with him, but that it could never "actually" be a home as they both already had homes. In turn, Emma points out that the flat was never intended to be the same kind of home, indeed, that Jerry never saw it as a home in any sense. He agrees that it he saw it "as a flat...you know". And now it's Emma's turn to be "brutally honest", as she specifies: "for fucking". Jerry's lame reply, "No, for loving" equates to her lame "I'm sorry" to Robert when he discovers her adultery.

The exchange that signals the end of their affair reveals that Emma's original naivety about the nature of their relationship has now changed through "brutal" experience from initial romanticism to a deeper understanding of the desire for power in "the land of no holds barred", as Lenny once put it, to "something approaching the naked truth". And just as Aston's disillusionment from his naïve altruism prompted a creative response, so is Emma's disillusionment about the nature of relationships revealed to have prompted a creative response, as we learn that she's now running an art gallery. This relative movement towards reality and away from illusion explains her parting remark to Jerry that they've made "absolutely" the right decision. But that doesn't mean that her learning from experience is over. She's still got a little way to go. Jerry, on the other hand, has a long way to go in a very short time.

The first two scenes of the play deal with the meeting between Emma and Jerry in a pub two years later and its immediate aftermath. Emma has called Jerry following a crisis in her marriage, although she doesn't reveal this for some time. She merely says that she thought of him "the other day", but as she later repeats this and persists in trying to find out whether he still thinks of her, the meeting obviously has a hidden agenda.

Jerry affirms that he doesn't need to *"think"* of her, which, as he also answers "Absolutely" to her asking whether he agrees that it's nice to think back sometimes, clearly means that Emma is imprinted on his memory, but not nostalgically, as an illusion of happiness, but, on the contrary, as a pointed reality check, "nice" for him, if not for her, meaning precise rather than pleasant.

Jerry mentions seeing Emma's daughter, Charlotte, in the street, whom he recognised because of her similarity to her mother, commenting that he thought her "lovely" when Emma asks him what he thought of her "really". Emma concurs, describing the now 13-year-old Charlotte as "smashing", a highly ambiguous word, and typical of Harold Pinter, as it could mean either "wonderful" or "shattering", and, as we'll see, in this case, actually means both.

Mention of Charlotte reminds Emma of the time Jerry threw her up and caught her as a child. Emma tells him that Charlotte remembers the episode, to which Jerry replies: "Really?" As with that "Absolutely" earlier, this flags up reality again, and Emma's affirmative to Jerry's question, adding "Being thrown up", suggests the idea of deeply-buried memory being forced to the surface of consciousness to reveal something fundamental, something universal and generic to the desire for power, as was mentioned earlier, with Jerry's "What a memory" confirming this.

What's being thrown up is immediately suggested by Jerry questioning Emma about whether Charlotte knows about their relationship, to which Emma replies that she simply remembers him as an old friend. Jerry's "That's right" has the conventionally moral connotation that this is as it should be, which is confirmed by him remembering the episode as a happy family occasion, for both their families, when he threw her up in Emma's kitchen. Emma corrects him that it was in *his* kitchen, which, out of the blue, as it seems, after a silence rather than the more typical Pinter pause, prompts Jerry to call her "Darling".

This seems strangely out of step in the circumstances of the meeting and is the kind of planted detail that, after the events on stage have been seen and assimilated, has the potential to flower to its full bloom to reveal the play's meaning. Needless to say, this isn't, as in a romantic comedy, that Jerry has always loved Emma and was only waiting for her to contact him again after their break-up to confess his undying love. Indeed, after Emma tells him not to say such a thing, as if prompting him to go further, he interrupts by saying that, for him, anyway, it all seems such a long time ago, prompting *her* to question whether it really does, because it sure as hell doesn't to her. In the circumstances, his "Same again?" over their drinks seems like a calculated insult.

Unfazed – she's a very determined woman, or desperate, or both – Emma returns to her theme of the happy old days, telling him again that she thought of him the other day. This time, it's to recall their love nest after driving through Kilburn and suddenly realising that she was in the vicinity of the house where they had their flat. Naturally, she couldn't find their name "on the bells". That's because they haven't been there for years, Jerry explains matter-of-factly.

That "bells", though, rings a bell in Jerry's memory, not the one Emma hopes, but one that reminds him about hearing that Emma is seeing a bit of Casey. This alarms the secretive Emma, with Jerry commenting that all he felt at the gossip was irritation that nobody gossiped about them "in the old days". He was irritated because, while she might be having the occasional drink with Casey, "who cares", they had a seven-year affair and none of the gossiping bastards knew anything about it. This suggests that, on one level, he would have liked people to acknowledge his, to him, heroic cuckolding of Robert; but only on one level, and, as we'll see, not the essential level where he's concerned.

His subsequently questioning the nature of her relationship with Casey prompts Emma, hopefully, to ask Jerry if he's jealous. Imperturbably, he brushes off her angling for a catch by pointing out that he's Casey's "agent", a weighted word here as it implies that Jerry is both Casey's literary agent and promoter, i.e. that he left Emma free for Casey after dispensing with her, and, consequently, couldn't be jealous of him, particularly as their own affair was over years ago. He's happy if she's happy. As she's still married, however, he then goes on to ask about Robert.

It's at this point that, having failed, despite all her efforts, to produce any spark of their former relationship in Jerry, she reveals the point of their meeting. This is that she and Robert are to separate as she's discovered that he'd betrayed her for years with other women. Jerry promptly quashes any potential moral outrage on her part by brutally pointing out that *they* had betrayed *him* for years, before asking whether Casey, her new lover, knows about this, suggesting that, if Casey knows about Robert's infidelities, he might be willing to marry her if she and Robert divorce as a result. But Emma brings the situation back to the reason for their meeting, which is that in her moment of crisis it was *he*, Jerry, she phoned, not Casey, although, disappointed with his response to her emotional overtures, she adds that she doesn't know why.

Jerry, meanwhile, continues indifferently on his course of brutal honesty by pointing out that, throughout all his drinks and lunches with Robert, there had never been even the slightest evidence that he was being unfaithful to his wife, while it had been he, Jerry, who'd been calling Emma while leaving Robert boozing at the bar.

Jerry is suggesting, in other words, that, in his experience, Robert had always been totally faithful in his marriage, while she had not. Naturally, this leads Jerry to ask himself why Robert had told Emma that he'd been unfaithful to her for years, which prompts him to question Emma further. She replies that they'd talked all night.

This sets off an alarm in Jerry's head about whether Emma told Robert about their affair, so he asks her whether he came into their conversation. She evades the question by saying that she phoned him because they were old friends, which is to say former-lovers, and that she suddenly felt that she wanted to see him with her marriage "finished". This "finished", of course, chimes with Emma rejecting betrayal as the subject of the book she's reading in Scene 5 and whose subject she will only know when it's "finished". We are, in other words, approaching the subject of the play.

Returning to Scene 1, however, Emma's not saying that she told Robert about their affair assuages Jerry's alarm so that he's willing to at least appear sympathetic to her predicament. Encouraged by his reply, Emma now drops all pretence and cuts to the chase, which, without her actually spelling it out, is that she'll shortly be single and free to marry him.

Thus, she reminds him of the passion of their former affair, in which he'd constantly reiterated his adoration of her, phrasing the reminder in terms of "Do you remember? I mean, do you remember?" He does. She reminds him that he couldn't afford their love-nest when he took it, to which he replies that "love finds a way". She then reminds him that she'd always wanted the flat to be a home by pointing out that she'd bought the curtains, a pathetically vulnerable admission in the circumstances, although, typically with Pinter, it also flags the fact that "curtains" keep things hidden, things which are about to be revealed. Yet Jerry doesn't know this yet so he merely replies that she'd found a way.

Now, Emma makes her final pitch, asking Jerry to listen, to her deeper meaning, that is, by telling him that she didn't want to see him for nostalgia, which, in the circumstances, is pointless, but because she wanted to see how he was, "truly". So she asks: "How are you?" This is as true, as honest, as far as she's willing to go to propose.

All this recalls Teddy's lingering illusion in *The Homecoming*, after he's brutally rejected by Ruth, that if he makes it sufficiently clear that she can always return to him, even though she seems adamant on pursuing a life apart, she *will* eventually return to him. But Jerry brutally destroys Emma's own lingering illusion that he would ever marry her by dismissing her question with a brutal one of his own: "Oh, what does it matter?"

Now, just as Emma has revealed her deepest desire to him, so does Jerry reveal his deepest desire to her. This is that no one important to him should know about his affair with her. The reason for this is that, for all his macho posturing, or, more precisely, his macho posturing *in secret*, Jerry also wants to be well thought of by those he believes love him as a trusted friend, husband and father: Robert, as his oldest friend, his wife, Judith, his children, and Robert and Emma's children, too. He wants, that is, his cake and to eat it, too.

This is, in fact, the meaning of the play, the fact that every human being wants to be well thought of. It's their deepest desire. And it explains the "Darling" to Emma that fell from Jerry's lips, even though, throughout the rest of the scene, he shows himself to be completely indifferent to her, she having served her purpose as far as he's concerned. His "Darling", in fact, was an involuntary reaction of gratitude towards her for reminding him of his moment – it's in *his* kitchen – of triumphant popularity with both their families when he threw Charlotte into the air. It's this that's the essential betrayal of the play, Jerry's betrayal of his false image of his self, his self-esteem, by exposing its "calculated posture" of trustworthiness to discovery as a result of his macho rite of passage. He can't, that is, have his cake and eat it, too, as he's about to find out.

This explains his concern that Charlotte might have discovered his affair with her mother. And now he expands this concern to Robert, asking Emma whether she told *him* about their affair. Her admission that she did prompts Jerry to point out that Robert is his oldest friend, that he picked Charlotte up in his arms, threw her up and caught her as Robert watched.

Emma, however, who has finally reached her Waterloo with Jerry's terminal rejection, echoes him in saying that it doesn't matter. It doesn't matter because, as far as she's concerned, all those illusions about their being nice people, trustworthy and, hence, worthy of love and respect, are gone. The desire for power isn't nice, conventional morality is a charade. It still remains, however, for Jerry to reach his own Waterloo.

This occurs in the next scene, which takes place later the same day. Jerry has asked Robert to come round. Robert admits that he knows all about Emma's affair with Jerry but dismisses it as unimportant, having been over for years. Jerry counters with the fact that he considers it important, to which Robert replies: "Really? Why?" This, by involving reality and the question *why* means that we have finally arrived at a central question of the human condition, with which Harold Pinter as an artist and, by implication, the play deals.

Jerry tells Robert that he thought he was going to go mad, with Robert, detached and indifferent, asking him what exactly he wants to say. Jerry says that he doesn't know why Emma had to tell him about their affair, in other words, why she had to betray his "calculated posture", in Spooner's words, about his being a fine fellow, the kind who throws a young girl into the air and catches her, revealing his dependability. He tells Robert that he knows about his marital situation and he's sorry, trying, in the process, to win back some sympathy from Robert about his decency, but also persists in questioning why Emma unmasked him after all these years.

But Robert sees no reason for him to be sorry, at which point he reveals that Emma told him about her affair with Jerry four years earlier. Where Jerry's concerned, this is a bolt from the blue. He's shattered. He can't believe that, since Robert's discovery, they'd seen each other and Robert hadn't revealed his discovery. Robert's reply that, even if they had seen each other, they'd never played squash reveals that he understands Jerry's reason for cuckolding him, his desire to be Emma's "best man", and that he hadn't let on because *he* was putting one over on *him* by pretending that he didn't know about the affair, when he did, effectively besting him in a macho contest as if it were a squash match.

Jerry, however, is still pining for the loss of his good name with Robert, pointing out that he was his best friend, with which Robert agrees. At this, Jerry holds his head in his hands in despair at losing his good name when he believes that it could have been avoided. But Robert simply echoes Emma's dismissal of Jerry's concern at the loss of his good name as not mattering by telling him that there's no point in getting upset at such a thing.

But Jerry is fixated on Robert's not telling him that he knew about the affair when he did, eventually calling Robert a "bastard" for his secrecy, to which Robert replies by questioning how Jerry, who had betrayed *him* for years could call him a bastard. But it appears that Jerry still hasn't reached his Waterloo because, moments after his realisation that his pretence of being a good friend is finally gone, he panics over the fact that his charade of being a good husband might also be exposed and asks Robert if he'd thought of telling his wife about the affair.

Robert, however, reassures him that he couldn't care less about "any of this". He admits that he hit Emma once or twice, but not to defend a principle, not from any "moral standpoint", only from "the old itch" to give her "a good bashing", i.e. from a macho point of view, adding "you understand", referring to their games of squash and Jerry's reason for his affair. This reveals how Robert has changed as a result of his wife's adultery with his best friend, because the moral outrage he expresses later in the play at her lame "I'm sorry" at his discovery of the affair has now been replaced by an acceptance of who he is, which explains his echoing Emma earlier about none of this mattering.

Thus, Jerry's pointing out Robert's perceived hypocrisy in his beating his wife for her betrayal when he had betrayed *her* is airily dismissed by Robert's readily admitting that he had, indeed, betrayed her, too. Of course, this explains why Jerry never saw any evidence of Robert's infidelities when they spent so much time together because his infidelities only occurred as a result of his discovery of Emma's adultery, which, like his giving her "a good bashing", amounted to revenge for his humiliation at her betrayal by betraying her in turn.

Similarly, when Jerry points out that Emma hadn't known about Robert's infidelities for years, this prompts Robert to question whether she hadn't known, because his discovery of her adultery had destroyed any pretence of their happy marriage, which was bound to have a profound effect on him, an effect which would make it perfectly understandable, in light of the desire for power which is the human condition, that he would be adulterous in return.

Now, when Jerry points out that he hadn't known about Robert's infidelities, Robert finally gets his revenge on Jerry for cuckolding him by pointing out that he didn't know much about anything "really", meaning that Jerry had been the fool when he thought he was being so clever in betraying him, with which a chastened Jerry agrees.

Seeing his advantage, Robert now points out to Jerry that Jerry did know about something that he, Robert, didn't, i.e. his seven years of trysts with Emma. This echoes Jerry's pointing out to Emma in the previous scene that, while Robert might have betrayed her for years with other women, so had they betrayed him for years. In turn, it shows that, while it's easy to point out hypocrisy in others, it's not so easy to admit it in ourselves.

So, finally, Jerry has reached his Waterloo, just as Emma and Robert had before him. To be specific, their Waterloo is the realisation, that "really" of Robert's, that none of them is in a position to be morally outraged at the amoral actions of others, because they're all in the same boat together. Whenever it's in our perceived self-interest, in other words, we're all prepared to betray others. The desire for power, for happiness, is a merciless master. Incidentally, this explains why Jerry doesn't have to *think* of Emma, as he tells her in Scene 1, because he's subliminally aware that their affair provides a perennial threat to his reputation as a "nice" person; it's a sword of Damocles hanging over him, a car crash waiting to happen.

At this point, Jerry points out to Robert that they used to like each other, but Robert says that they still do, because, where macho rites of passage are concerned, whether on the squash court or in the bedroom, Robert and Jerry are of a kind. This prompts Robert to say that he believes Casey is having an affair with his wife, when they used to have "a damn good game of squash", Casey's affair with Emma replacing the squash, just as it did for Jerry.

Now, Robert and Jerry's shared complicity in their amorality towards relationships is extended to include their self-interest in the book sales of their writers, as Jerry says that he thinks Casey is over the hill as a writer, to which Robert responds by pointing out that he still sells very well, which is "very good" for them both, that "good" making clear that morality, what's good, is what people think gives them more power, greater happiness, rather than more truth, greater reality.

As for Jerry's current reading, he says that he's been reading Yeats, reminding Robert that he, too, once read Yeats in Venice. This followed his discovery of his betrayal by Emma and Jerry. Similarly, Jerry's mentioning Yeats follows his learning of his betrayal by Emma for not telling him of Robert's discovery of their affair and Robert's by also keeping quiet about this. These round robin betrayals have now reached their conclusion, with all three having learned from the experience that they're not as nice as they once thought they were. They've all been apprised of "something approaching the naked truth", where human nature is concerned, leaving them all suitably chastened. Where Jerry's concerned, this is expressed in his telling Robert that his family's summer holiday will be spent in the Lake District, the lakes providing a perfect metaphor for his tears at learning that his pretence of being a fine fellow has been punctured good and proper, as, indeed, was Spooner's for his own "calculated posture" in *No Man's Land*.

Betrayal, then, is a play about the fact that we're not as nice as we think we are, that our self-esteem is never justified, but also how, as well as being shattering, our discovery of this can be wonderful, too, wonderful as in revelatory, just as the "really lovely" Charlotte is "smashing", in that by shattering our illusions it provides us with a "lovely" opportunity to learn how the desire for power separates us from reality, from a true perception of who we are. None of us are "nice". That's only a game we play.

As this study contends, *Betrayal* was Harold Pinter's last serious full-length play, after which he spent much of the rest of his career acting as a moral chorus to mankind. That he wrote nothing of consequence, certainly where truth is concerned, perhaps tells its own story about how much *he* learned from his own plays. Whatever, he was a man, but, as an artist, he did leave the world with several of the greatest plays ever written. And *we* can all learn from those.

Bob Dylan

SOONER OR LATER

Bob Dylan is arguably the most complete artist of the age for the distance he's travelled along the road of truth. In that respect, certainly, he's one of the outstanding artists of all time, irrespective of his considerable talent with words and music. Inevitably, his work has elements in common with any artist, yet it's also defined by a relatively rare focus on an overriding theme, indeed, one which is unique where the artists featured in this book are concerned. This theme is that of authenticity between religion and spirituality. In which can truth most surely be found? The strength of Bob Dylan's feelings on both sides of this argument is such that the clash between them accounts for many of his greatest songs, including, for instance, "Visions of Johanna", the "best song lyric ever written", according to former UK poet laureate Andrew Motion, and an abiding favourite with Dylan fans.

Dylan first explores the theme in the album many consider to be his best, 1966's *Blonde on Blonde,* then again in his outstanding album of the 1970s, *Blood on the Tracks,* and it was still on his mind almost half a century later in 2020's *Rough and Rowdy Ways.* In the last track, for instance, "Key West (Philosopher Pirate)", which he may have intended, at least when he wrote it, as a final farewell to his song-writing career, Dylan takes himself back to the very beginning of his lifelong questioning of truth by remembering his coming-of-age bar mitzvah as a Jewish boy: his wedding to Judaism, as he characterises it.

He was just two days away from his 13th birthday at the time, and so, technically, still 12-years-old as he recalls being "put in a suit" and "forced" to marry "a prostitute" with "gold fringes on her wedding dress", a reference to the religious trappings of the ceremony. Of course, where the incipient life of the artist Bob Dylan was concerned, that might have been it. Before the ceremony he'd been seen as a "goody-goody" boy by his contemporaries, "kind of nerdy" with his smart clothes and neatly-combed hair, and, as for the event itself, the rabbi was extremely pleased with his progress as he chanted Hebrew scripture. Indeed, Dylan says in "Key West", "that's my story", adding, however, as a nod to his future as an artist, "but not where it ends". He might still find his adolescent bride "cute", and they're "still friends", yet the fact that he sees her as a "prostitute", cute or not, suggests that religion, Judaism at that time, mostly not later, was always a synthetic temptation to him, yet no match for the real thing in the spirit of truth, merely a self-satisfying substitute.

As for the start of his story, that was in the city of Duluth, Minnesota, on Highway 61, in the cold far north of the United States. And for someone who once said that peace is just the time it takes to reload, Bob Dylan certainly picked an appropriate moment to be born. His birth date of the 24th of May, 1941, occurred in the relatively brief pause between two of the bloodiest phases of World War II: a mere three days *after* the official end of "the Blitz", the German bombing campaign of civilian and industrial targets in Britain, and four weeks *before* the launch of Operation Barbarossa, Nazi Germany's invasion of the Soviet Union, the largest military campaign in history, noted for its ferocious battles, horrific atrocities and enormous casualties. None of these events, however, impinged upon Robert Allen Zimmerman, as the infant was named, since the US didn't enter the war until six months later, following the Japanese attack on Pearl Harbour, when the conflict actually did become a *World War*.

Dylan's parents, Abe and Beatty, (Abram and Beatrice), were Jews whose families had emigrated from the pre-revolution Russian Empire at the beginning of the 20th Century to escape anti-Semitism. Both families were large and Bobby, as he was generally known – he was always "Robert" to his father – spent his early years surrounded by relatives, although he remained an only child, a small asthmatic introvert, as he recalled, for the first five years of his life, after which he had a brother.

In 1947, however, around the time of Bobby's sixth birthday, the family moved to the remote mining town of Hibbing, quintessential small-town America, 75 miles to the north-west of Duluth, where Abe joined his brothers' electrical retail business after contracting polio and losing his job in the accounts department of Standard Oil.

The business prospered and the Zimmermans were soon enjoying a comfortable lifestyle, which later included one of Hibbing's first television sets, as well as a piano. Abe and Beatty had both played musical instruments, a violin and piano, respectively, in their early years, Abe even performing at some high school concerts with his brothers, and Bobby also played the piano and acoustic guitar as a boy.

Until he reached adolescence, Bobby seems to have been an obedient child, something of a loner, in common with many incipient artists, but loving towards his mother and striving to please his rather authoritarian father. Although his parents were not strictly Orthodox Jews, they were both consciously Jewish, Bobby attending a Jewish summer camp from the age of 12 and learning Hebrew and studying the Scriptures for his bar mitzvah.

In retrospect, however, that confirmation of his Jewishness can be seen as the high tide of his role as a dutiful son. Dylan certainly sees it that way in "Key West (Philosopher Pirate)". For, as he attained adolescence, two events in particular suddenly triggered open rebellion in him.

The first was the James Dean film *Rebel Without a Cause*, released in October 1955, which Bobby went to see again and again, ironically at Hibbing's Lybba Theater, which was owned by his mother's family and named after his maternal great-grandmother. Dylan seems to be recalling this event in "Key West" when he writes that he never wasted his time with an "unworthy cause", suggesting again that he wrote the song to bring his life as an artist full circle. Bobby was so influenced by Dean that he soon started wearing a red leather jacket like him and, when he reached 16, persuaded his father to buy him a motorcycle, like Marlon Brando in the film *The Wild One*, another adolescent favourite of Bobby's. Here, then, is the philosopher pirate beginning to express himself.

The transformation from Abe and Beatty's "good boy" into Minnesota's equivalent of a prototype English "teddy boy" or "rocker" of the 1950s can be seen in the fact that while Robert Zimmerman regularly appeared on Hibbing High School's "honour roll" for exceptional students from 1952 to 1955, his name is absent for the following three years. This newly aggressive attitude from the previously rather passive boy also expressed itself in the form of new friends, teenagers from "the wrong side of the tracks," including his first serious girlfriend, Echo Helstrom, who, like himself, sported a leather jacket. Tellingly, when she asked him, at their first meeting, whether he was Jewish, he stubbornly refused to reply.

At the time, this mute denial of his religious background might well have arisen from nothing more than a rebellious adolescent's bid for independence, something that would soon become so common in the West that it hardly merits much comment. With Bob Dylan, however, the denial of his childhood Judaism went much deeper. Thus, when, in Britain, in 1965, *The Jewish Chronicle* asked him: "Are you Jewish?" he categorically denied it: "No, I'm not."

Thirteen years later, in 1978, he still stubbornly maintained his denial, telling an interviewer for *Playboy* magazine: "I've never felt Jewish. I don't really consider myself Jewish or non-Jewish. I don't have much of a Jewish background." This is in spite of his bar mitzvah and, more pertinently, the fact that he'd actually prayed at Judaism's sacred "Wailing Wall" in Jerusalem on his 30th birthday seven years earlier.

Again, in an interview with *Rolling Stone* magazine six years later in 1984, Dylan employed all his formidable powers of irony not only to deny that he'd ever suffered from anti-Semitism as a child, but also that he was even Jewish: "Nothing really mattered to me except learning another song or a new chord or finding a new place to play, you know? Years later, when I'd recorded a few albums, then I started seeing in places: 'Bob Dylan's a Jew,' stuff like that. I said: 'Jesus, I never knew that.' But they kept harping on it; it seemed like it was important for people to say that, like they'd say 'the one-legged street singer' or something. So, after a period of time, I thought; 'Well, gee, maybe I'll look into that.'"

It's obvious from such vehement denials that the issue is one of considerable significance for Bob Dylan. Clearly, the point of the denials is that, as an artist, he doesn't want to be identified with any religion, indeed, with partiality of any kind, whether religious, political, social, or whatever, since partiality muddies the meaning of songs that advocate an absolute commitment to the spirit of truth.

The second transformative event of Bobby's teenage years after seeing *Rebel Without a Cause* was to prove even more momentous than the first, certainly in the creation of Bob Dylan. Little Richard's raucous rock 'n' roll classic, "Tutti Frutti", which Bobby heard soon after its release in November 1955, has influenced many musicians, and particularly Bobby Zimmerman. In 2010, the US Library of Congress actually added the recording to its National Recording Registry, a list of sound recordings deemed "culturally, historically, or aesthetically important", on the basis that the "unique vocalizing over the irresistible beat announced a new era in music".

That's exactly what Bobby thought at the time. Now, suddenly, he took to playing on the family piano with the same passion as his musical idol, banging away like a demented dervish. This isn't to say that he hadn't been widely influenced by music before first hearing Little Richard. His favourite singer had previously been Hank Williams and, to this day, Dylan considers the country artist, with songs like "Your Cheatin' Heart", "You Win Again", and "I'm So Lonesome I Could Cry" to be the greatest American songwriter. It was, however, "Pictures from Life's Other Side", a largely traditional song portraying the fate of desperate gamblers, a suicidal single mother and a hapless GI, performed by Williams' alter ego "Luke the Drifter", that influenced Bobby the most.

He also listened to that other Hank, singer-songwriter Hank Snow, who, as well as selling 80 million albums in a career spanning six decades, performed in lavish and sequin-studded suits and even managed Elvis Presley for a short time. This combination of abundant creativity and a certain drama of life and performance, "attitude", in a word, appealed enormously to Bobby and explains why Johnnie Ray, "Mr Emotion" or "The Cry Guy", was another 1950s singer who made a big impact on him, not only as a singer and songwriter, but even in the way he dressed, as Dylan told him when they met in a lift in Sydney, Australia, many years later.

It was, however, so-called "black music" from the Deep South, blues and rhythm and blues, to which the adolescent Bobby seems to have listened most frequently. "Late at night, I used to listen to Muddy Waters, John Lee Hooker, Jimmy Reed and Howlin' Wolf blastin' in from Shreveport," he told *Rolling Stone* magazine in 1984. Shreveport, incredibly, is in Louisiana, around 1,200 miles at the other end of America from Hibbing, down towards the southern delta of the Mississippi River that connects Minnesota to Louisiana and not far from the terminus of the parallel Route 61, later given global status by Bob Dylan as *Highway 61 Revisited* in the song and album of that name. "It was a radio show that lasted all night," he said. "I used to stay up till two, three o'clock in the morning, listened to all those songs, then tried to figure them out. I started playing myself."

Again, in 1997, he recalled: "The reason I can stay so single-minded about my music is because it affected me at an early age in a very, very powerful way and it's all that affected me. It's all that ever remained true for me."

This provides yet more evidence that Bob Dylan intended "Key West (Philosopher Pirate)" to bring his creative life full-circle, back to a beginning that he only now fully understands for the first time, since one meaning of the "Pirate" in the song is that of what he saw as a "pirate radio station", one that he first heard in

Hibbing, Minnesota, which is in America's Midwest, and which provided one of the keys to his artistic vocation as a songwriter. Thus, the "boondocks" or middle-of-nowhere in the song where he heard the "wireless radio" is Hibbing rather than Key West in Florida in this instance, as are "the flatlands" of the song, which apply equally to Minnesota and the Florida Keys; similarly the fact that he recalls the radio signal being "clear as can be" refers to the fact of his amazement at that clarity, considering that it was coming from so far away.

Whatever his musical influences in blues or in country, however, it was Little Richard who decided Bobby on a career in music. Certainly, it was hearing "Tutti Frutti" that led him to form the first of a number of bands specifically to cover Little Richard songs, along with songs from other rock 'n' roll "greats" of the time such as Buddy Holly, Chuck Berry, Gene Vincent, Jerry Lee Lewis, Eddie Cochran, and, of course, Elvis Presley, whose early 1954-55 Sun recordings Bobby greatly admired, particularly "Mystery Train", an image that would play a significant role in his own lyrics. The bands tended to be dominated by this formerly quiet and shy boy as he pounded the piano and sang "Rock 'n' Roll is Here to Stay". Thus it was that his stated ambition in the school's yearbook on graduating from Hibbing High in 1959 was "to join Little Richard," this alongside a photo of himself sporting a passable imitation of his idol's outrageous pompadour.

Earlier that same year of 1959, Bobby had received a further incentive to pursue a musical career. This was seeing Buddy Holly on stage in Duluth on the 31st of January in the singer's penultimate concert before his death in a plane crash. Bobby would remember that concert for many years to come, particularly the fact that Holly had looked down at him, in his place on the front row, and caught his eye, which he seems to have taken as a fateful sign of his own musical destiny. It was in 1998, in fact, almost 40 years later, when collecting a Grammy Award for "Album of the Year" for *Time Out of Mind*, his 30th studio album, that Dylan recalled: "And I just want to say that when I was 16 or 17 years old, I went to see Buddy Holly at Duluth National Guard Armory and I was three feet away from him…and he looked at me. And I just have some sort of feeling that he was – I don't know how or why – but I know he was with us all the time we were making this record in some kind of way."

Many interviews attest to the fact that Bob Dylan is highly sensitive to what he sees as the role of destiny in his life, which he has defined as a feeling that he knows something about himself that no one else does, allied to a certainty that this innate potential will be fulfilled. There are certainly many felicitous coincidences that can be related to him. Most significant of all, perhaps, Sinclair Lewis (1885-1951), the first US writer to win the Nobel Prize in Literature in 1930 – Bob Dylan, of course, being the last, in 2016 – was born in Sauk Centre, Minnesota, 150 miles south of Hibbing, and was actually living in Duluth when Dylan was a child there. He was famous, among other books, for *Main Street*, published in 1920, a satirical novel about American small-town life that could just as easily apply to Hibbing as it does to Lewis's fictional Minnesota "village nothingness" of Gopher Prairie.

But for all Bob Dylan's claims to be considered a writer rather than just a songwriter, "poet first, musician second" in his own words, his perceived receipt of the baton from Buddy Holly in the cultural relay of civilization related most specifically to a career in music. In that respect, he was evidently right. But it wouldn't be with rock 'n' roll, or not exactly. In fact, although Bobby Zimmerman had begun his own musical career by singing "Rock 'n' Roll Is Here To Stay", the genre was already coming to a premature end at the time of Holly's death in the first hour of the 3rd of February 1959, the closure of a musical era, according to American singer-songwriter Don McLean's 1971 hit song "American Pie", recorded two days after Dylan's 30th birthday and which included a reference to him as a "Jester" wearing James Dean's coat.

The fact is that rock 'n' roll ran out of steam just as it seemed to be establishing itself as the dominant pop music medium, with all its principal exponents leaving the stage within months of one another. Little Richard, for instance, had already become a born-again Christian and trained for the ministry by the time Buddy Holly died, while Bob Dylan's fellow-Minnesotan singer-songwriter, Eddie Cochran, died in a road accident in April 1960 at the end of a British tour; as for Elvis, he started two years' military service in March 1958 and changed his repertoire on his return. Until The Beatles renewed rock 'n' roll in the early 1960s, spearheading "the British invasion" of America, and Bob Dylan invented rock music, transforming popular music into an art form by adding poetical lyrics to rock 'n' roll, the pop charts were dominated by sentimental teen idols such as Fabian, Frankie Avalon, Bobby Rydell, Bobby Vinton, and Bobby Vee, whose "Take Good Care of My Baby" was No.1 in both the US and UK singles charts in 1961. The parallel renaissance in youth counterculture of folk music was a reaction to this kind of popular music, so that, when Bob Dylan moved on from rock 'n' roll, it was to folk that he turned, a folk movement that, as with rock music, he helped to define.

"The thing about rock 'n' roll is that for me anyway it wasn't enough," Dylan remembered later. "'Tutti Frutti' and 'Blue Suede Shoes' were great catch phrases and driving pulse rhythms and you could get high on the energy but they weren't serious or didn't reflect life in a realistic way. I knew when I got into folk music it was a more serious type of thing. The songs are filled with more despair, more sadness, more triumph, more faith in the supernatural, much deeper feelings…There is more real life in one line than there was in all the rock 'n' roll themes. I needed that. Life is full of complexities and rock 'n' roll didn't reflect that."

This relates to a more fundamental aspect of "Key West". For the "signal clear as can be" in the song, as well as the "Philosopher Pirate", also relates to Bob Dylan's first contact with the spirit of truth, which, along with the music, is the reason for his philosophical or spiritual vocation as a singer-songwriter, as an artist, in direct contrast to the "that's my story" of his religion. As a teenager, in fact, Bobby wrote poems, which, according to his father, were "about the wind", and in "Key West" he specifically refers to "the healing virtues of the wind". This, of course, is the wind of truth, which, he says, enabled him to find his mind, along with a love or spiritual commitment so deep that he "can hardly see" because, henceforth, as an artist, he would only see the world *through* the spirit of truth. Incidentally, this explains Bob Dylan's intuitive confidence in his destiny as an artist, because what he knows is that the spirit of truth is with him and that it's the ultimate source of creative inspiration and spiritual fulfilment.

This, in fact, is the subject of his first masterpiece, "Blowin' in the Wind", written in April 1962 when he was still only 20 years old and a year after his move to Greenwich Village in New York City to pursue a career in music as "Bob Dylan". Released on Warner Brothers as a single in June 1963 by folk trio Peter, Paul and Mary, it sold 320,000 copies within little more than a week, thereby becoming the fastest-selling disc in the record label's history at that time. Many radio disc jockeys called it "the record of the year" as it went on to sell more than a million copies and to reach No. 2 in the US pop singles chart. It was subsequently recorded by scores of artists to become one of the pre-eminent "standards" of the early '60s.

The song's subsequent adoption by the civil rights movement as its anthem, alongside "We Shall Overcome", meant that Dylan was provided with a platform in the fields of both popular music and civil rights at a time when the latter was fast becoming a major factor in American politics. While the song may have provided the civil rights and also the anti-nuclear peace movements with a theme song, however, "Blowin' in the Wind" is, in fact, a major work of art.

Dylan pulled this off by universalising the nine questions asked in the song so that they applied to the human condition per se rather than to a cause at any particular time and place. Perhaps the three verses could be said to deal, firstly, with why men feel the need to prove their manhood through war and is this inevitable; secondly, is intolerance and despotism inevitable; and, finally, why are so many people blind to beauty and indifferent to human suffering. Yet so unspecific are the questions that any reader of the lyrics or listener to the song could justifiably have their own interpretation as to what exactly Bob Dylan is saying.

The questions Dylan asks, however, all relate to mankind's attachment to the desire for power, with the force of that desire, "the prince of this world" in Christ's words, arguably the "mountain" in the song that dominates the human skyline and blocks the way to the open sea of reality. It wouldn't be until Dylan wrote "She Belongs to Me" on his fifth album, 1965's *Bringing It All Back Home*, that he would reveal his awareness of the existence of that force, which is the "she" of the song and whose title means that desire "belongs" or is related to the "me" of the self or ego. There's no doubt, however, that Dylan was aware of desire's *effect* on humanity earlier since that's what the questions in "Blowin' in the Wind" deal with. On that reading, then, the "some people" in the song who are not "free" could just as easily apply to all those in the grip of the desire for power as it could to the Afro-Americans suffering discrimination in the United States.

But the committed, whether politically or socially or whatever, are bound to see everything in terms of their commitment. And Bob Dylan had already provided evidence of his partiality to their causes with several rather minor but unquestionably "protest" songs. In this context, the fact that "Blowin' in the Wind" is so universal in its expression, so unspecific, meant that it was hardly surprising that the civil rights and peace movements *assumed* that Bob Dylan was singing about their causes in the song.

Dylan's answer to the questions he posed in "Blowin' in the Wind", however, prove categorically that, as an artist, he was most definitely NOT committed in any way, *at least where this song is concerned*, indeed, was absolutely uncommitted or detached. This is because his inspired reply states that the answers to the questions can only come through the "wind", which is to say through an absolute commitment to the spirit of truth, thereby effectively dismissing so-called "protest" as a distraction or diversion from what's really important, which is to answer the question *why*. In fact, "Blowin' in the Wind" is Bob Dylan's first and perhaps most pointed philosophical statement as an artist, one on which his entire subsequent career has been based. And it follows, therefore, that the "my friend" to whom he directs the song can only be another soul, whether truth seeker or artist. Similarly, Dylan's next masterpiece, "A Hard Rain's A-Gonna Fall", is directed at "all souls". The song, moreover, states that humanity's pride, "where souls are forgotten", is bound to lead to a fall, hubris to nemesis.

The point of "Blowin' in the Wind" is that we all have the free will to be directly inspired by the spirit of truth, enabling us to answer any question about the human condition and thereby extricate ourselves from the desire for power in order to discover ultimate reality: to "find God" in popular parlance. Bob Dylan makes precisely this point in "Crossing the Rubicon" on *Rough and Rowdy Ways* at the other end of his life's journey along the road of truth:

> "I feel the Holy Spirit and see the light that freedom gives
> I believe it's within the reach of everyman who lives."

And if that's the case, what's the point of religion? Who needs intermediaries to guide us, *any* human intermediaries, when we have the spirit of truth, God's own intermediary, as our personal guide?

In his song-writing career, Bob Dylan came to use the image of a railroad track or train line as a metaphor for the religious alternative to spirituality. The image comes from *Matthew* (7:14): "...strait is the gate, and narrow is the way, which leadeth unto life..." This is Dylan's straight and narrow railway line. It first appears in "Stuck Inside of Mobile with the Memphis Blues Again" on *Blonde on Blonde*, where "Mona", i.e. Leonardo's "Mona Lisa", which Dylan uses to express truth through her smile of Buddha-like enlightenment, counsels him to stay away from "the train line". Then, in "Absolutely Sweet Marie" on the same album, he tells us that he "can't jump" your "railroad gate", i.e. can't make the necessary leap of faith to accept religion. So it is that, looking back to the very start of his commitment to truth in "Key West", Dylan sees himself as being "born on the wrong side of the railroad track", which he equates with the spiritual Beat writers of the 1950s such as Allen Ginsberg and Jack Kerouac, as well as singer-songwriters such as Buddy Holly. All this, in other words, relates to his choosing the unorthodoxy, where religion is concerned, of being a philosophical or spiritual pirate, so that, as he tells us in the song, while "it might not be the thing to do", i.e. not religious orthodoxy, he intends sticking with "you", which is to say the spirit of truth, "through and through", which, incidentally, explains the title of Dylan's 33rd album, 2009's *Together Through Life*. Similarly, in "Crossing the Rubicon", he tells us that "Mona" is "still in my mind" as nobody else could have stayed with him for so long.

Although, as we've seen, "Blowin' in the Wind" is most definitely not a protest song, yet there's no doubt that Bob Dylan was a protest singer, or, more precisely, did write a number of major protest songs with which he's been associated throughout his career, songs such as "The Times They Are A-Changin'" and "Masters of War". His principal reason for writing these songs was his desire to please his first serious love, Suze Rotolo, who *was* politically and socially committed, principally to the cause of civil rights for Afro-Americans and to the anti-nuclear movement. Previously, while many of his friends were fiercely anti-establishment, sometimes in an overtly political way, Dylan had always stood out through his noticeably apolitical nature as an incipient artist.

It's worth expanding on this point a little because it's fundamental to understanding the artist Bob Dylan. As we saw in the Introduction, for an artist to be an artist, it's absolutely essential that they're detached from the desire for power in order to receive the inspiration of truth and, thereby, come to understand the nature of the human condition. And politics, any kind of social or political commitment, or, indeed, any kind of religious commitment, is all about the desire for power, or the pursuit of happiness. It makes absolutely no difference whether this relates to those who appear to have the power or those who don't but are attempting to obtain it because they hope to change things for themselves and those with whom they identify.

Bob Dylan would comment on this many times in his songs, but he also spelled it out as plain as day in a couple of interviews he gave to *Playboy* magazine in 1966 and 1978. In the first, he says: "Things are going to happen whether I know why they happen or not. It just gets more complicated when you stick *yourself* into it. You don't find out why things move." (As we've seen, Harold Pinter also made this very point, most notably with Teddy in *The Homecoming*, who refused to be "lost" in the happiness-seeking hurly burly of daily life). Again, in his second *Playboy* interview, speaking with a hard-earned and profound understanding of the years of political protest in America in the 1960s, Dylan reiterated the importance of detachment for the artist: "…there were people who were trying to change things. They were involved in the political game because that is how they had to change things. But I have always considered politics part of the illusion. I don't get involved much in politics."

The upshot of this dichotomy was that, even as Bob Dylan launched his relatively-brief folk-protest phase in the early 1960s, it was always in conflict with his rapid development as an artist. As a result, even unquestionably topical or protest songs from this period benefited enormously from Dylan's artistic bent in that he couldn't help but reveal their timeless significance. Nudging topical lyrics as near to universality as they could go meant that many reached a literary standard rarely, if ever, surpassed.

One such song that, conveniently, has a decidedly religious bent is "With God on Our Side". This sits firmly in the anti-nuclear camp with its verses about the Cold War between the US and the Soviet Union and the possibility of nuclear annihilation. Bob Dylan, however, gives the song a philosophical framework, one in which he questions the very nature of religion. More precisely, he questions humanity's interpretation of God's will, on which many religious organisations claim to have a unique insight.

Arguably, the most significant question in this respect occurs in the song's penultimate verse, where Dylan admits that he has agonised over whether Judas Iscariot, who "betrayed" Jesus Christ "by a kiss", had God on his side. The question was to prove particularly relevant to Bob Dylan himself because, in one of the most famous episodes in rock music history, he was heckled as "Judas" by an audience member during a concert at Manchester's Free Trade Hall on the 17th of May, 1966. This occurred on a world tour to introduce his apolitical – and unquestionably artistic – rock music to fans, many of whom were bitter about his abandonment of folk-protest.

Throughout the ages, Judas's betrayal of Jesus was regarded as so heinous that "Judas" has become a generic term for "traitor". Yet, according to Jesus himself, the betrayal was part of the fulfilment of God's will for him to die upon the cross. It was certainly the perfect conclusion to Christ's mission to introduce the spirit of truth to humanity. This is because the nature of his death proved a conclusive relinquishment of his own will and acceptance of God's, which, in turn, amounts to a final confirmation of the soul's absolute commitment to the spirit of truth. Dylan makes this very point in "Crossing the Rubicon" on *Rough and Rowdy Ways*, which is a song about accepting religion as an alternative to spirituality. Thus, Dylan writes that, in doing so, he "poured the cup and passed it along", i.e. *away* from him. This is a reference to Christ's agony in the garden of Gethsemane as he faced the prospect of death on the cross: ""O my Father, if it be possible, let this cup pass from me: nevertheless not as I will, but as thou wilt," *Matthew* (26:39). Christ later explained his agony in terms of "the spirit indeed is willing, but the flesh is weak," *Matthew* (26:41).

So, if Christ's death on the cross was God's will, did Judas, then, have God on his side in facilitating this sacrifice? Who are we to say? Dylan's point is that it's not for the artist or truth seeker to question destiny, merely to follow the spirit of truth wherever it leads. This is the meaning of faith in its true sense: as absolute trust in that particular supernatural guide and no other.

The fact that such meditations had nothing to do with Dylan's protest phase, indeed, were on a higher plane than the jostling for power of the political/social/religious scrum, was made post-protest when Dylan returned to the theme in "Love Minus Zero/ No Limit" on *Bringing It All Back Home*. This song is arguably his first love song, and certainly one of his most beautiful, to the spirit of truth. And in the third verse Dylan reveals the depth of his own commitment to the spirit by dismissing man's questioning of the supernatural, its "grudge" over human suffering, by referring to the spirit's indifference to such matters through its superior knowledge.

Indeed, this theme is so fundamental to the artist or truth seeker's journey that Bob Dylan can't even forget it during his aberrant Christian fundamentalist phase in the late '70s/early '80s. In "When You Gonna Wake Up?" on 1979's *Slow Train Coming*, he brings up the question of God's will yet again, dismissing the self's view of God as merely "an errand boy" to satisfy its "wandering desires": "With God on Our Side" revisited.

"Highway 61 Revisited" on the 1965 album of the same name also deals with self-centred interpretations of God's will. The song is a re-visitation twice over. In the first instance, it goes over the same ground as "With God on Our Side", beginning, as does that earlier song, with upbringing and ending, like its predecessor, with the prospect of a Third World War. This time, though, Dylan doesn't wring his hands with liberal anguish but merely laughs at the whole absurdity of mankind's hubris, suggesting that it gets what it deserves, an echo of "A Hard Rain's A-Gonna Fall".

However, more significant than Dylan's application of his greater understanding of the human condition to world affairs is that to family affairs, specifically his own, proving, as was suggested in the Introduction, that the philosophical begins and ends with the personal. This explains his revisiting Highway 61 because, as we've seen, Dylan's birthplace, Duluth, was situated on that route. What's more, Dylan uses the image of "the highway" as a metaphor for the wide way of desire in contrast to "the road less travelled" of truth. Thus, the song begins with Bobby Zimmerman's Jewish conditioning, based on the *Old Testament*, as opposed to the conventional Midwest upbringing based on American values of "With God on Our Side". The *Old Testament* in question comes from *Genesis* (22:1-2), which deals with God's tempting Abraham by telling him to offer his son Isaac as "a burnt offering". Dylan has this as God saying to Abraham: "Kill me a son". What's significant about this is that Bobby Zimmerman's own father was also called Abraham or Abram, who, in bringing him up as a good Jewish boy, was effectively killing him as a truth seeker or artist. Highway 61 is also significant because it provides a direct link to the South. And Bob Dylan uses "the South" in his songs as a metaphor for the warmth of illusions, here specifically religious, in contrast to the cold light of reality delivered by the spirit of truth. Bob Dylan's "south" metaphor for illusion first occurs in "To Ramona" on Dylan's fourth album, *Another Side of Bob Dylan*, where a timorous sister-soul is poised between persisting in her commitment to truth and returning south.

The introduction of the image announced a recurring theme in Bob Dylan's work, one varied by the use of different Southern towns to convey the same idea. What's more, the metaphor soon came to represent the Roman Catholic Church rather than illusion, Judaism or religion in general in his songs. For, in spite of his momentary Christian fundamentalism, an aberration that echoed his earlier years of protest, religion has largely meant Catholicism to Bob Dylan throughout his song-writing career.

Appropriately for such a definitive song, "Visions of Johanna", which appears on *Blonde on Blonde*, is the first lyric Bob Dylan wrote in which he contrasts the claims to truth of the Church with those of a spirituality represented by Joan of Arc, whose visions provide a dramatic stand-in for the inspiration of the spirit of truth. The Church, in turn, is symbolised by Louise, the female of Louis, gentile version of Levi, the Israeli tribe designated as the priestly class with religious duties. The difficulty for Dylan in separating the two is that Louise is "so entwined" with "her lover" in his mind. This "lover" is unquestionably the spirit of truth, which explains why Dylan considered the Church as an alternative, since she, (the Church is always "she", seeing herself as "Mother Church", as does Dylan in "Tough Mama" on his 1974 *Planet Waves* album), claims to represent that spirit in the world, with the Pope its ultimate interpreter.

She certainly has some ancient claims in this respect. According to the *New Testament*, Jesus Christ's final words to the Apostles were: "...ye shall receive power, after the Holy Ghost is come upon you: and ye shall be witnesses unto me...unto the uttermost part of the earth," *Acts* (1:8).

Sure enough, as Christ predicted, soon after, and as was quoted in the Introduction:

> "And suddenly there came a sound from heaven as of a rushing mighty wind, and it filled all the house where they were sitting...And they were all filled with the Holy Ghost, and began to speak with other tongues, as the Spirit gave them utterance."
>
> *Acts* (2:2-4)

Yes, but that was a long time ago and much has changed since then. And in the very next song on *Blonde on Blonde*, "One of Us Must Know (Sooner or Later)", whose title means that either the Church or the artist will eventually find out conclusively where the truth lies, Dylan claims that the Church has said "goodbye" to her friend, which can only be the spirit of truth, "for good".

As often with Bob Dylan, this has a dual meaning. In the first place, it means that Christ's mission was to preach the availability of the spirit of truth to every individual soul, a mission that he passed on to his apostles. But this is most definitely not what the Catholic Church, which took over from the apostles, teaches; hasn't been teaching for centuries, in fact. Indeed, throughout those centuries, the Church has been consistently hostile to any interpretation of the *Bible* at odds with her own, which she considers heresy. In other words, she said "goodbye" to her spiritual mission "for good" or forever.

Dylan's second meaning of the Church saying "goodbye for good" is that she has replaced Christ's original message about the spirit with another based on her members reaching paradise by being "good", i.e. by practising a morality based on altruism. As we've seen in the interpretation of Harold Pinter's *The Caretaker*, the claim that altruism provides mankind with a higher purpose than mere self-interest is false. And this is also the fundamental theme of "Visions of Johanna".

In his 2004 memoir, *Chronicles: Volume One*, Bob Dylan reveals the roots of his songwriting, particularly with respect to the songs of the blues singer-songwriter Robert Johnson. These, he says, are elemental in both their expression and meaning, incorporating profound truths while smacking of absolute absurdity, precisely what his own songs became. Dylan was as impressed with the form of Johnson's songs as he was by their content, a methodology he saw as highly sophisticated, just a few words conjuring fathoms of meaning. No surprise, then, that he subsequently adopted Johnson's methodology hook, line and sinker, notably in "Visions of Johanna".

Thus, in the final verse of the song, Dylan creates a picture of the Church's replacement of Christ's message of truth with one based on being "good" that incorporates a cast of characters and seemingly absurd imagery, yet whose meaning, however dramatically expressed, points in only one direction. Beginning as he means to go on, Dylan categorically dismisses altruism as "pretending to care", as hypocrisy. This is because the soul is the mind turned exclusively towards the spirit of truth and, as such, has no truck with any alternative, any "ism". Altruism, therefore, is an action of the self, the mind turned towards the desire for power. In this respect, altruism might be termed an attempt to obtain "soft" power over others, power based not on control or fear, and, hence, "hard", but on obligation or gratitude, and, hence "soft", but power nevertheless.

But, as we saw in the Introduction and with Harold Pinter's great plays, any attempt to obtain any kind of power is merely a response to the prompting of the force of the desire for power. Dylan refers to this in the next line of "Visions of Johanna" by calling anyone who claims to care for others "a parasite", i.e. of the force of desire.

As for the Church's attempt to replace an individual soul's adherence to the spirit of truth with her own theology, one on which she, naturally, has the exclusive power to decide the terms, Dylan dismisses it as a magic trick: the flowing of "her cape of the stage". The trick is in magically liberating the self from the "cage" of desire by inventing the so-called selflessness of altruism, putting others before ourselves. And it's by this means that the Church claims that we can earn our entrance to a heavenly paradise after our death. Dylan expresses this fact through an arresting image in Visions of Johanna: "jewels and binoculars", which represent a distant prospect of rich reward in heaven for being selfless. These "jewels and binoculars" are said, however, to "hang from the head of the mule" on which Christ rode into Jerusalem prior to his death on the cross, which is the reality of "selflessness", prompting Dylan to comment that the Church's magic trick is a "cruel" deception.

With respect to orthodox religion's desire to change his message to mankind about the spirit of truth or "Holy Ghost", Jesus has this to say in *Matthew* (12:30-31), specifically about the Pharisees of his own day, but his comments apply equally to all religious who don't accept the direct inspiration of the spirit of truth as the only source of truth in the world:

"He that is not with me is against me; and he that gathereth not with me scattereth abroad. Wherefore I say unto you, all

manner of sin and blasphemy shall be forgiven unto men: but
the blasphemy against the Holy Ghost shall not be forgiven
unto men."

Christ, as a prophet of the spirit of truth, is not speaking
threateningly here, not speaking as a bully, as a righteous
martinet. He's simply making a statement of fact. And what he's
saying is that mankind's being a slave or "parasite" of the force
of desire, "the prince of this world", is the human condition; it's
the way things are. But that condition isn't hopeless because
the spirit of truth or Holy Ghost offers a means of escape. If,
however, man discounts, misinterprets or turns against the Holy
Ghost, then his condition *will* become hopeless because he'll be
condemning himself to perpetual slavery. It wouldn't be fanciful
to say that Bob Dylan is referring to this prognosis of the human
condition when he comments in "Visions of Johanna" that when
the musician artist, or "fiddler", takes "to the road" of truth,
everything has "been returned which was owed" or, in Christ's
words "forgiven unto" him. The fiddler does this, moreover,
on "the back of the fish truck that loads", a reference to Christ's
telling the apostles "I will make you fishers of men," *Matthew*
(4:19), implying that the Church adopted its ersatz theology of
altruism in order to make itself a mass movement and maximise
its worldly power.

Dylan follows this up by saying that his "conscience
explodes", which amounts to a total rejection of a morality based
on altruism as an alternative to an absolute commitment to the
spirit of truth, a morality, it must be said, that's shared by other
religious and humanist organisations the world over, by every
sort of "ism", in fact. Other songs on *Blonde on Blonde* echo
"Johanna" in this rejection, notably "Just Like a Woman", where

Dylan states categorically that he "just can't fit" in a Church that fakes.

In other songs, however, he's not so sure. The title of "Most Likely You Go Your Way (and I'll Go Mine)", for instance, suggests that the decision is not cut and dried, Dylan saying that the Church tells "stories/That you know I believe are true" yet "Sometimes it gets so hard to care," which echoes the "pretending to care" of "Visions of Johanna".

"One of Us Must Know (Sooner or Later)", meanwhile, sets a trend that still resonated in "Key West" on *Rough and Rowdy Ways*, where Dylan sees himself as "still friends" with Judaism. His implied tolerance of Catholicism, on the other hand, is expressed in terms of the Church just doing "what you're supposed to do", with Dylan denying that he ever "really meant to do you any harm".

Similarly, in his extended tribute to the Catholic Church in "Sad-Eyed Lady of the Lowlands", he leaves the question of his conversion open, asking whether he should leave his self, or selves, by its railway "gate", or wait. Indeed, he wouldn't offer a definitive answer to the religion versus spirituality question until his follow-up album, *John Wesley Harding*, although even that didn't turn out to be his last word on the subject, far from it.

Considering that Bob Dylan skewered religion good and proper on *Blonde on Blonde*, or, up to a point, even earlier with "With God on Our Side" and "Highway 61 Revisited", an urgent question arises: why keep returning to it like a dog to its vomit?

Several answers present themselves. The one that appears the least likely, however, is almost certainly the true one. This is that, throughout much of the 1960s and '70s, Bob Dylan often felt that the spirit of truth was absent, leaving him in a quandary as to how to progress along the road of truth. At first sight, this conviction of Dylan's appears frankly incredible, considering that few artists have been so inspired.

From "Blowin' in the Wind" onwards, he produced a string of amazing songs elemental in their expression and meaning, a meaning incorporating profound truths, as he said of Robert Johnson's songs. These were songs, as Dylan put it memorably in *Chronicles*, "that floated in a luminous haze", songs of "the kind where you hear an awful roaring in your head", songs that indicated a songwriter who was "feeling the full force of the wind", songs that were like "stellar explosions", songs, finally, that, in subsequent years, left even Bob Dylan wondering at their genius: Did I really write that? How did I write that? Through the inspiration of the spirit of truth, that's how.

Yet from "I Don't Believe You (She Acts Like We Never Have Met)" on *Another Side of Bob Dylan*, he complained again and again that the spirit was missing, until, shortly before his dramatic conversion to Christian fundamentalism, he wrote perhaps his most anguished song of spiritual abandonment, "Where Are You Tonight? (Journey Through Dark Heat)", on 1978's *Street Legal* album.

The title of "I Don't Believe You" isn't about incredulity but the fact that a relationship with the spirit of truth is based on experience, on understanding, not belief. Thus, the song begins "I can't understand/She let go of my hand/An' left me here facing the wall." The "she" here is the spirit of truth, while the "wall" signifies a separation from reality. The "tonight" and "dark" of "Where Are You Tonight? (Journey Through Dark Heat)", meanwhile, signify the dark night of the soul in which Dylan feels that his guide has left him alone and lost.

A degree of incomprehension and soul solitude is usual on the road of truth because the force of the desire for power is a formidable foe and doesn't give up its hold on the self easily. As a consequence, this self is constantly interfering in the soul's progress and preventing its contact with the spirit of truth. In Bob Dylan's case, however, this interference is chronic. And its expression is in his expectation, indeed, his obsession, with receiving visions or mystical revelations; in short, with proof that he's on the right road. Dylan explained this "doubting Thomas syndrome" in "Dear Landlord" on 1967's *John Wesley Harding* as: "All of us, at times, we might work too hard/To have it too fast and too much."

It was no accident that he characterised the supernatural inspiration of the spirit of truth on *Blonde on Blonde* in terms of "visions of Johanna", visions that he himself hankered for. That this obsession was a product of the self can be seen in the fact that when Dylan did finally feel in late 1978 that he'd received a vision in terms of a presence that was unmistakeably Jesus Christ, who, he said, had actually put his hand on him, the upshot was that he abandoned the direct inspiration of truth for the rabid self-righteousness of Christian fundamentalism.

Bob Dylan's recurring sense of spiritual abandonment explains his fascination with the Catholic Church because it's when he feels that the spirit of truth is distant that he becomes aware that the Church, in contrast, is close: "Louise, she's all right, she's just near," as he says in "Visions of Johanna", and, again, in "One of Us Must Know": "You just happened to be there, that's all."

But if the Church is always there for him, unlike his perception of the spirit of truth, she's only there for his self, not his soul. The Church, in other words, like all worldly organisations, is predicated on satisfying the self's desire for power, for happiness, whether in this world or in another. Thus, in "The Ballad of Frankie Lee and Judas Priest", which, like "Visions of Johanna", pits a pirate philosopher against the Church, characterised as a significantly-named "Judas Priest", while the Church might promise "Eternity" or "Paradise", what it actually delivers is more self-satisfying and, hence, soul-destroying. Indeed, just as Dylan sees Judaism as a "prostitute" in "Key West", so does he see Catholicism as a bordello in "The Ballad of Frankie Lee and Judas Priest".

The song appears on *John Wesley Harding*, in which Dylan felt that he'd said his final word on the subject of the Catholic Church, or religion in general. The album concludes with "I'll Be Your Baby Tonight", in which he assures the spirit that, henceforth, in the "tonight" of the dark night, he'll be "your baby", i.e. as pliant as a trusting child.

More than half a century later, with a droll irony directed entirely at himself, Dylan tells us: "I thought I could resist her but I was so wrong," as he bids a "final farewell" to religion in "Goodbye Jimmy Reed" on *Rough and Rowdy Ways*, "Jimmy Reed" being Dylan's rhyming slang for "creed", just as "Frankie Lee" is for "me".

The stubbornness of Dylan's addiction to religion can be seen in the fact that no sooner had he kicked Catholicism into touch with *John Wesley Harding* and testified to his absolute commitment to the spirit of truth than he returned to his childhood allegiance to Judaism as an alternative. If it's not one religion, then it's another. This was part of a new role that he adopted at the time as a husband and father. "Having children changed my life and segregated me from just about everybody and everything that was going on," Dylan remembered in *Chronicles*. "Outside of my family, nothing held any real interest for me…Truth was the last thing on my mind…"

It wasn't until 1974's *Planet Waves* that truth became, once again, the first thing on his mind. And with the return of truth, inevitably came a more truth-inspired consideration of religion, specifically Catholicism. In "Tough Mama", this is relatively light-hearted, Dylan referring to the Pope in the Vatican as "Papa's in the big house, his workin' days are through," "Pope" coming from the Latin word "papa". "Dirge", on the other hand, is one of Bob Dylan's most depressing songs, testimony to his anguished perception of the soul-destroying power religion has over him: "I hate myself for lovin' you and the weakness that it showed/ You were just a painted face on a trip down Suicide Road." This appears to quote French existentialist and absurdist writer Albert Camus, who said that religion is "philosophical suicide".

Religion, specifically Catholicism, however, was merely an afterthought on *Planet Waves*, Dylan being so deliriously joyful to have returned to the spirit of truth that nothing else mattered much. With his next album, 1975's *Blood on the Tracks*, considered one of his greatest for the consistently high quality of the songs, it was the main topic of conversation.

Dylan may have intended the album to be a tranquil reflection on his former passion for the Church, characterised as the railway "tracks" of the album's title, but that wasn't the way it turned out, at least not on "Idiot Wind", one of his most passionate songs. Yet again, he tells us that this is his final farewell where the Church is concerned: "I been double-crossed now for the very last time and now I'm finally free;" but that's only what he'd like to think. Like every addict, he never stops promising that this is his last fix.

As with Judaism, the Church might be a prostitute, as Dylan tells us in "You're a Big Girl Now", "I know where I can find you… In somebody's room," but that doesn't stop him pining, "going out of my mind…Ever since we've been apart."

The upshot of his feeling for the Church, and religion in general, seems to be that it's his natural partner, the perfect companion for his self. All his other relationships, he tells us in "You're Gonna Make Me Lonesome When You Go" have been bad, full of "scenes" that can't be compared "to this affair". But it *is* only an affair and not like his marriage to the spirit of truth. *That* is the meaning of "Wedding Song" on *Planet Waves*, where Dylan tells us that he loves the spirit "more than blood", the "blood" that is spilled on the tracks in the title of the next album.

In contrast to his self's relationship with the Church, *this* relationship with the spirit is with his soul. Thus, just as the overriding impression left by *Blonde on Blonde* is that he "just can't fit" in the Church, in any religious organisation, so, too, is it that of *Blood on the Tracks*. Dylan expresses this rejection in "You're Gonna Make Me Lonesome When You Go", even if reluctantly, with "When somethin's not right, it's wrong." This echoes Christ's "He that is not with me is against me," *Matthew* (12:30).

The fact that answering the question *why* is confined exclusively to a human mind's direct relationship to truth makes the process incontrovertible, beyond doubt or dispute to each individual who experiences it, irrespective of their philosophical sophistication. And that's its beauty, its purity and simplicity. This is the exact opposite of any process involving questions of morality or ethics, which are based on the often-conflicting desires of the mind's self and, hence, subject to infinite nuance and dispute, requiring great acumen to untangle.

So clear is the nature of true spirituality, in fact, that, just as Bob Dylan couldn't entirely forget truth when he was in the throes of his protest mania, neither could he entirely escape it when the balance of his mind was deranged with Christian fundamentalism. Thus, just as we have "With God on Our Side", a protest song that's not entirely blind to truth, so, too, do we have "Gotta Serve Somebody" on 1979's *Slow Train Coming* album, a fundamentalist lyric whose categorical statement that we all "have to serve somebody" is true up to a point. The point is that we all have to serve either the desire for power or the spirit of truth, rather than "the devil or the Lord" of the song. In both cases, however, it's a simple either/or choice at any one moment.

Dylan discovered as much when he tried to reconcile the two by dreaming of returning the Church to its pioneering early days as an advocate for the spirit of truth. He makes the point in "Shelter from the Storm" on *Blood on the Tracks:* "If I could only turn back the clock to when God and her were born." But the supernatural link having long been severed and the Church having become something else entirely in the meantime, he eventually accepted that this was merely wishful thinking. The upshot was that he would have to take the advocacy on himself, as he tells us in "Up to Me", an outtake from *Blood on the Tracks* long considered a lost classic by Dylan fans. Dylan sums up the situation in the first verse: "I know you're long gone, I guess it must be up to me."

In the song, Dylan imaginatively sees the Church as having disappeared "into the officers' club" of worldly power. He maintains that stance in 1978's *Street Legal*, whose title refers to the nature of that power, which is both "streetwise", as in worldly, in opposition to the road of truth, and purveyor of religious "legality", as opposed to God's "Law" of reality in "She Belongs to Me". Both images: "street" and "legal", come from "Where Are You Tonight? (Journey Through Dark Heat)". But it's in the songs "Changing of the Guards" and "Señor (Tales of Yankee Power)" that Dylan makes his most definitive statements in relation to the Church.

In the former, the religious are the "Gentlemen", whose "organization" Dylan says he no longer needs, as he tells the Church to "brace yourself for elimination" if she no longer has the "courage for the changing of the guards", the "guards" referring to defenders or protectors of Christ's mission to bring the spirit of truth to individual souls. In "Señor (Tales of Yankee Power)", the Church is now Spanish, suggesting the Spanish Inquisition, which persecuted as heretics any individual who questioned the Church's absolute authority. Dylan ends the song by saying "let's disconnect these cables", suggesting lines of attachment to the desire for power, and "overturn these tables", a reference to Christ overturning the tables of the moneychangers in the temple, *Matthew* (21:12-13), in both cases a rejection of the Church's worldly power.

Emerging in the mid-1970s from his role as a paterfamilias, in which he'd re-adopted his own father's Jewish religion, Bob Dylan then returned to his commitment to the spirit of truth, which explains *Planet Waves*, before seeking material for a new album. This brought him back to his last major subject of the 1960s, which was religion, or, specifically, Roman Catholicism. The result was *Blood on the Tracks*. This process of aural nostalgia was so creatively satisfying and commercially successful that Dylan maintained it. This had the unintended consequence of taking him back to the overriding trope of the 1960s, which was his despair at being unable to commit himself absolutely to the spirit of truth, to choose once and for all between self and soul, whatever the consequences. As we've seen, this was also Harold Pinter's dilemma, a dilemma that surfaces in different ways throughout his great plays, with the resulting despair accounting for their drama. It's also the hidden agenda of *Street Legal,* a despair that led to Bob Dylan overdosing on Christian fundamentalism as an intended escape. Mercifully emerging from this after two or three years, Dylan was bound to compare his feeling for fundamentalism with that for the religious orthodoxy of Catholicism. This accounted for songs such as "The Groom's Still Waiting at the Altar" on 1981's *Shot of Love,* "Caribbean Wind", an outtake from that album, and "Jokerman" on 1983's *Infidels.* In spite of the imaginative quality of those songs, however, Dylan had nothing new to say on the subject. There was definitely a feeling that the Catholic Church was merely a handy topic for new songs.

As for songs of genuine inspiration in the 1980s and early 1990s, those were few and far between. In one such, "Dark Eyes" on 1985's *Empire Burlesque* album, Dylan reached back to the truth-Church dichotomy of "Visions of Johanna": "Oh, the French girl, she's in paradise and a drunken man is at the wheel." But the fact is that Dylan's profound disenchantment with fundamentalism, to which he'd committed so much energy, believing, as he did at the time, that he'd found a clear route forward, led him to abandon any sort of commitment, including that of artist, and to replace it with the role of rock star. In the August 1986 press conference in London for the 1987 film flop *Hearts of Fire,* for instance, in which Dylan plays a retired musician, a journalist suggested that his last tour had been made exclusively "for the money" and asked whether this was his "new philosophy". "I'm always doing tours for the money," Dylan replied. "What's so new about that?" Again, in *Chronicles,* he recalls the year 1987 as a time when: "There was a missing person inside of myself…I felt done for, an empty burned-out wreck…Wherever I am, I'm a '60s troubadour, a folk-rock relic, a wordsmith from bygone days…I'm in the bottomless pit of cultural oblivion."

It wasn't until 1997, in fact, that he rediscovered his inspiration and his relevance – truth is timeless – with *Time Out of Mind,* an album title that summed up Dylan's two previous decades of spiritual amnesia. At the time, naturally, his principal concern was with the spirit of truth. Of course, that had also been the case in 1974 with *Planet Waves*. But, this time, he wouldn't let anything distract him, indeed, hasn't ever since where his songs are concerned. As for religion, his newly-detached summary of the issue was brilliantly expressed in "Mississippi" on 2001's *"Love and Theft"* album, "Mississippi" being the latest of Dylan's synonyms for the "South" of Catholicism's comforting illusions. Employing his most pointed understatement, Dylan ironically says that he "stayed in Mississippi a day too long". This is the equivalent of his dismissal of Suze and the related protest phase as "You just kind of wasted my precious time" in "Don't Think Twice, It's All Right" on 1963's *The Freewheelin' Bob Dylan*. The difference is that, now, with the benefit of spiritual experience, he's a little less precious and more humble about his own importance.

Bob Dylan's more measured attitude to the road of truth, minus the hope of mystical visions and the related credulity to religious promises, characterises all his new-millennium albums. They catalogue his progress along the road of truth and its consequences, which might be summed up as increasing distance from a world under the total control of the desire for power. Once the illusion of altruism with its ethics of good and evil is dismissed, it becomes clear that the world can't be changed or improved in any meaningful way, as Harold Pinter stated categorically. The reality of the human condition is that our planet is a prison controlled by the force of the desire for power and the only hope of escape is the spirit of truth. There is no other. We're all prisoners of the absurd illusion of happiness.

Of course, Bob Dylan has told us this before, not least in "Visions of Johanna". But his experience of truth is that, as the full implications of the reality of the world become more established, so they become more accepted by the soul, and the self less encumbered by illusions. Dylan's new-millennium songs are still full of profound truths smacking of absolute absurdity except that now it's the other way round: it's the absolute absurdity of the world that is the profound truth. And, as the absolute nature of its absurdity becomes established in the soul, so does any idea of the world's reality *fade*, the mind's place in it less and less assured, and its only purpose revealed as the natural way *through* to a supernatural reality; and not necessarily *after* death. This is to say that the soul doesn't hope for a life in a heavenly paradise after death because it doesn't hope. It simply follows the spirit of truth. Bob Dylan had earlier expressed this in "Wedding Song": "And if there is eternity I'd love you there again." Note the "if" rather than "when" and the "I would" rather than "I will".

Perhaps the Bob Dylan song which best expresses the fact that the world has no reality other than as a passageway for the soul to find its ultimate destination is "Things Have Changed", the song that might be said to announce the ultimate stage of his journey along the road of truth, just as "Blowin' in the Wind" announced the initial stage.

"Things Have Changed" was used in the 2000 film "Wonder Boys", winning both the Academy and Golden Globe Awards for "Best Original Song". The nature of the change in this ultimate stage of Dylan's career is specified in the chorus as: "I used to care…" with the implication: but not anymore. What he no longer cares about is the state of the world, which is beyond redemption. A spiritual leaving is the only option, both for oneself and for others, which is why Dylan tells us that he's "locked in tight" to the spirit of truth and "out of range" of the "prince of this world", the desire for power, to ensure that he's "only passing through".

The song is full of the absurdity of the pursuit of happiness, whose implications are enlarged upon in "Mississippi", where the hopelessness of the human condition without the spirit of truth is reiterated throughout, from the "all boxed in" of the first verse to "the emptiness is endless" of the final verse. Dylan's considered awareness of the "Long and Wasted Years" of religious distraction, as he expresses it in the song of that name on 2012's *Tempest* album, means that he's now absolutely focused on his vocation as an artist. The result is that he again benefits from "the full force of the wind", as he did in the 1960s.

The song that most recalls the high point album of that decade, however, *Blonde on Blonde,* isn't obviously overflowing with creativity à la Bob Dylan, although it is highly sophisticated, paradoxically combining vulgarity with subtlety. This is *Rough and Rowdy Ways*' "Black Rider", which features a development on the earlier album title. *That* referred to the so-called "Horsemen of the Apocalypse" from *Revelations*: chapter 6, where two of the horsemen rode on a white horse and a pale horse respectively, hence *Blonde on Blonde*, which Dylan employs to represent mysticism and religious orthodoxy on the album. One of the other horsemen, meanwhile, sat on a black horse and "had a pair of balances in his hand", *Revelations* (6:5). This suggests that the song, like "Key West (Philosopher Pirate)" and, indeed, the album as a whole, represents something of a final judgement or summation for Dylan.

"Black Rider" also suggests Stephen Crane's existential horror-poems *The Black Riders and Other Lines* and J.R.R. Tolkien's "Black Riders" in *The Lord of the Rings*, both of whom are associated with death; spiritual death, where Dylan's concerned. The song, as with many of his new-millennium lyrics, is also full of self-references as Dylan clearly sees his oeuvre as the tale of a soul's progress towards ultimate reality.

Dylan's "black rider" is clearly the Catholic Church, with references to "Changing of the Guards" in the first and final verses and the same message: it's time to go. The final verse also references the avalanche of cases over the sexual abuse of children, particularly boys, in which Church religious have been caught out over recent decades and senior prelates pilloried for cover-ups. Thus, Dylan first dismisses the size of the black rider's "cock" in the spirituality stakes before imagining suffering in silence as he's sodomised. He jokes that he might take the "high moral ground" adopted by the Church as his own response to the buggery before opting instead to sing her a song "some enchanted evening", i.e. one inspired by the magical spirit of truth. This is also a reference to the song "Some Enchanted Evening" from the Rodgers and Hammerstein musical *South Pacific*, "South", of course, being Dylan-speak for the Church. *Rough and Rowdy Ways*, all Bob Dylan's new-millennium albums, in fact, are packed full of such cultural references as he seeks to bring all culture, all human life, within the scope of art.

The song begins with Dylan telling the Church that her railway line is "too narrow to walk" as she constantly tries to remain relevant by adapting her message to changing morality, when, as he says in the second verse, she'd do better to let all her "earthly thoughts be a prayer", i.e. to the spirit of truth. In the third verse, in contrast, he counsels her to return to her own "wife" of altruism instead of cheating with "mine", i.e. pretending to represent the spirit. He then refers to Christ's "Think not that I come to send peace on earth: I came not to send peace, but a sword," *Matthew* (10:34) as he threatens to "hack off your arm" if she continues to distress his soul.

In "Goodbye Jimmy Reed", meanwhile, Dylan widens his scope to condemn all religions as expressions of human power play in contrast to the worldly detachment of spirituality. But, to return to the start of this chapter, it's in "Key West (Philosopher Pirate)" that he brings his song-writing career full-circle, ending where he began, with an absolute commitment to the spiritual because there's simply no alternative.

"Key West (Philosopher Pirate)" begins with news of the death agony of US President William McKinley after he was fatally shot by an anarchist on the 6th of September, 1901, that the song's chronicler says he heard "on the wireless radio", which, as we saw earlier, is an image for the spirit of truth which, at the same time, suggests detachment from the desire for power, as in the "disconnect these cables" of "Señor". The chronicler, moreover, is said to hear the news as he is "searchin' for love and inspiration/On that pirate radio station". And, as the song reaches its climax, Dylan returns to President McKinley's final moments as the chronicler hears the news of his "last request". This is clearly meant to evoke Christ's agony in the garden of Gethsemane since McKinley's last words, in reply to his wife's "I want to go, too," were: "We are all going, God's will be done, not ours." Dylan then rounds off the song, and his musical vocation, by commenting that this is where to be if you're looking for "immortality", for "paradise divine".

Ian Curtis

Wounded Genius

While Bob Dylan's conversion to Christian fundamentalism in 1978-79 was ushering in a near 20-year interruption in his cultural and spiritual significance, a parallel development was taking place on the other side of the Atlantic, one that offered an illuminating contrast to his own. Appropriately, perhaps, this development took place in Manchester, England, where, in May 1966, Dylan had been berated as "Judas" for a previous change of direction. It involved another artist whose musical career, although it lasted barely three years, provides a concentrated replay of Dylan's own creativity, but with a different direction, proving Spanish poet and mystic John of the Cross's dictum that, while the road of truth is always the same, universal and timeless, each artist's journey along that road is unique.

The artist in question was Ian Curtis, singer and lyricist with the post-punk rock band Joy Division, who, like any artist whose work is recognised as significant, continues to fascinate and perplex to this day. Expressed truth always acts as a beacon to anyone who asks the question *why*. And, indeed, as if to underline this point, one of Curtis's first songs, "At a Later Date", actually asks the question, as he states boldly that the only thing he's thinking about is why we're all here.

There were many striking similarities between Ian Curtis and Bob Dylan. Like Dylan, for instance, Curtis was death-obsessed from an early age. Again like Dylan, he actually bought a red jacket to match the one that James Dean wore in *Rebel Without a Cause*. Unlike Bob Dylan, however, who expressed profound relief in 1978 in the song "Where Are You Tonight?" that he was still alive, Curtis didn't survive, committing suicide in May 1980, aged just 23, on the very cusp of stardom.

In the circumstances, it would be no surprise to find that Curtis was a Bob Dylan fan who followed in the footsteps of his mentor. But that wasn't the case. Curtis *was* a music aficionado, particularly of lyrics, but he was more interested in English singer-songwriter David Bowie, notably his electronic avant garde album *Low,* released in 1977, likewise in American "Godfather of Punk" Iggy Pop's solo albums *The Idiot* and *Lust for Life,* written and produced in collaboration with Bowie in the same year. Another influence was The Doors' lyricist and celebrity martyr Jim Morrison, who died aged 27 in 1971. Like Bob Dylan and, indeed, Jim Morrison, however, Curtis was profoundly influenced by French Symbolist poet Rimbaud, whose "I is someone else" he references in one of his last songs, "Something Must Break", included on Joy Division "greatest hits" album *Permanent*, where he writes that the life he was living "isn't mine".

So what was that life? Ian Curtis was born in Manchester on the 15th of July, 1956, to a close-knit working class family, his father Kevin being a detective officer in the British Transport Police, a special force for the rail and light-rail network. A bright boy, Ian won a scholarship to the prestigious King's College in the small market town of Macclesfield, just south of Manchester, where he excelled in History and Divinity, although, Christian confirmation apart, he was never a church-goer, nor does he seem to have been overtly political.

Dropping out of school aged 17, he qualified as a civil servant, eventually being appointed a disablement resettlement officer in Macclesfield, where he helped those with illness or disablement to find work. Married at just 19 years old, he and his young bride Deborah settled in the town in 1977, where his first priority was to set up a room specifically for writing song lyrics. This was for a band named Warsaw, whose founding members, guitarist Bernard Sumner and bassist Peter Hook, had been inspired to start playing by seeing UK punk pathfinders The Sex Pistols, whose June 1976 gig at Manchester's Lesser Free Trade Hall also played a significant role in launching the careers of other local bands such as The Buzzcocks, The Smiths, and Simply Red.

Initially a punk band, although its members swiftly adopted a smart look more suited to their day-jobs than to punk, the band recorded their first release, an EP entitled *Ideal for Living*, at the end of 1977. The record coincided with a change of name to Joy Division, a name Curtis adopted from a 1955 novella, *House of Dolls*, which deals with young Jewish women kept as sex slaves in Nazi concentration camps during the Second World War. The record sleeve, featuring a graphic of a Hitler Youth drummer-boy, raised the question over whether the band had Nazi sympathies. And, indeed, one of the songs on the EP, "Leaders of Men", testifies to a possible fleeting adolescent infatuation with leaders "promising a new life". In an echo of Bob Dylan's injunction in "Subterranean Homesick Blues" not to follow leaders, however, Curtis then goes on to reject such promises as "self-induced manipulation" leading to imprisonment in a hate mentality. Another song, "Failures", also dismisses "false Messiahs".

These rather trite lyrics, which wouldn't be out of place in a university student's essay, were swiftly followed, just as Dylan's adolescent efforts seemingly metamorphosed into masterpieces in the blink of an eye, by songs of a remarkable maturity. "Walked in Line", for instance, while initially adopting a moral attitude to totalitarian brutality, hardly surprising for a young man, suddenly switches to a clear-eyed perception of the force of the desire for power that holds its victims in a "hypnotic trance", one that blinds them to any understanding of their condition. The song echoes Bob Dylan's masterpiece about the desire for power, "She Belongs to Me", in which he brands the malevolent force a "hypnotist collector".

Indeed, the explanation for Curtis's rapid development from novice to master-songwriter lies, as it did for Bob Dylan before him, with his discovery and subsequent commitment to the spirit of truth. This is first hinted at in an early song, "The Kill", in which Curtis initially sees himself as trapped by the desire for power, "in a hired car" (an oblique reference to Rimbaud's "I is someone else"?) with "no way to run", only then to spot an escape route by keeping "my eyes on you", the "you" here being the spirit of truth, as subsequent songs gradually reveal. Thus, in "Digital", Curtis feels the presence of the spirit "closing in" while "patterns" of understanding "seem to form", "shadows start to fall", causing him to plead with his muse never to fade away, always to answer his need for understanding.

By this time, Joy Division had moved on from their early efforts to post-punk rock music of remarkable sophistication and maturity, as witnessed by their first album, *Unknown Pleasures*, a title encapsulating the joys of understanding arising from a journey along a road of truth whose direction is unknown: "Where I'm bound, I can't tell," as Dylan put it in "Don't Think

Twice, It's All Right". The album was recorded in Manchester in March and April 1979, the latter coinciding with the birth of Curtis's daughter, Natalie.

The first song, "Disorder", sets the context of the entire album in its first line, in which Curtis tells us that he's been waiting "for a guide" to take him "by the hand" before going on to say that he's "got the spirit" but must now "lose the feeling", i.e. that his commitment to truth involves a detachment from desire. Curtis places himself, that is, squarely in Dylan Thomas's "half-way house" between truth and desire, Harold Pinter's "no man's land", which is precisely the phrase Curtis uses. In the excitement of his requited quest for understanding, he dismisses the world's interpretation of what's right and wrong as "who can tell". Only when "the spirit" provides the answers, he says, will "you know".

The final revelation that it's the spirit of truth he's writing about comes, appropriately, in one of Joy Division's first undoubted masterpieces, "Shadowplay", where Curtis dispenses with suggestion to state baldly that he "found truth" in a room "with a window in the corner". This is the "window of opportunity" that is free will, the window that appears in several Bob Dylan songs, from "It Ain't Me, Babe" to "It Takes a Lot to Laugh", to Ophelia "beneath the window" in "Desolation Row" to "Can You Please Crawl out Your Window?"

"Shadowplay" is just 11 lines long, but those lines incorporate a whole world of meaning, introducing new themes and developing old ones, and all to a thrilling beat that drives home the profound significance of the lyrics.

The song's introduction states clearly that what we're dealing with here is something that is central to the human condition, Curtis taking us with him as he journeys "to the centre of the city", which is "where all roads meet", as he "waits for you".

Curtis, a prize-winning divinity student at King's College, cannot have been unaware of St. Augustine's mammoth work, *The City of God*, a city which is contrasted with the Earthly City, the former dedicated to eternal truths, the latter to mankind's worldly desires.

"Shadowplay" then reveals in no uncertain terms that we're heading for the heart of light, to the "depths of the ocean" of reality of the second line, "where all hopes sank", i.e. all hopes of happiness, prompting Curtis to "search for you". The third line then makes clear that what's at issue is an inner, spiritual journey as Curtis describes "moving through the silence" without there actually being any motion, as he waits for truth to arrive. Bob Dylan makes the same point in "Not Dark Yet" on 1997's *Time Out of Mind* album: "I know it looks like I'm moving, but I'm standing still."

"Moving through the silence" and "standing still" are rather beautiful ways of expressing French philosopher Simone Weil's "attention" or "waiting on God", the Buddhist's meditation, or Aston's "quiet" in Harold Pinter's play *The Caretaker*, i.e. the artist's detached questioning of the world around them before waiting for answers to arrive. It's at this point in "Shadowplay" that Curtis makes his great reveal about the spirit of truth being his muse.

The second verse provides us with the meaning of the song's title in its first line, while also quoting from the "shadows start to fall" of "Digital". "Shadowplay", we're told, is the "acting out" of "your own death", the doing to death of the many selves or "shadows" that make up the ego, self-extinction, in short, disillusionment, in a word. The extinction of our different selves in tune to the inspiration of truth is then expressed in a remarkably original and dramatic way in terms of lines of dancing "assassins", a pointed reference to what is probably Joy Division's first "good" or successfully-realised song, "Transmission".

Like "Shadowplay", "Transmission" recreates the process of disillusionment in terms of "silence" and "destruction" in "waiting for our sight" as the soul responds to the "live transmission" or inspiration of the spirit of truth, a radio-related metaphor also used by Bob Dylan in "Key West (Philosopher Pirate)" on the 2020 *Rough and Rowdy Ways* album, as we've seen. In the song, human attachments are memorably characterised as "touching from a distance", as we never actually grasp them, however hard we try, and, as they fade away during the process of disillusionment, so are they "further all the time". The former phrase is understandably famous with Joy Division fans as it's the title of Deborah Curtis's memoir of her husband, *Touching from a Distance: Ian Curtis & Joy Division*.

"Transmission" then goes on to characterise the process of truth-transmission and soul-reception as a "dance to the radio", which, as a description of inspiration is really quite something, while, conveniently, also providing a "dance, dance, dance" pop song to bring Joy Division to the attention of the record-buying public. As Deborah Curtis recalls, Ian was always "thoughtfully sincere, generous to a fault", and perhaps uniquely, towards the spirit of truth and to his bandmates at the same time.

Returning to "Shadowplay", after introducing the process of disillusionment, Curtis then conjures the "cold steel" required to cut human attachments, echoing Bob Dylan's "hand on the sabre" of "Something There Is About You" on 1974's *Planet Waves* or the "King and Queen of Swords" in "Changing of the Guards" on 1978's *Street Legal*. The painful strenuousness of the process of disillusionment is then brought to life by referring to the dancing assassins having "odour on their bodies", before suggesting that the pain is well worth it in the end as it makes "a move to connect" to reality, recalling Bob Dylan's "lookin' to connect" in the song "If You Gotta Go, Go Now". The "further all the time" of detachment, however, inevitably distances the artist from their society, alienation, in a word, which is brilliantly characterised by Curtis in the song as himself staring "in disbelief as the crowds all left".

The greatness of "Shadowplay" as a work of art is only confirmed in the final verse where the intimate portrait view of the soul suddenly opens up to the landscape view of the wider world, the world of the self, the Earthly City, in St. Augustine's phrase. In this verse, in contrast to his depiction of others being the slaves of desire in "Walk the Line", Curtis now places himself squarely alongside them to make the point not only that we're all part of the same human condition, artist and non-artist alike, but, more importantly, more graphically, that the alternative to a commitment to truth, power-enslavement, is utterly horrible, "The horror, the horror" of Joseph Conrad's protagonist Kurtz in his 1899 novella *The Heart of Darkness*.

Curtis recreates this horror in just 16 words, seven to conjure what passes for selfish behaviour, nine for a truly disgusting depiction of what qualifies as unselfish behaviour, altruism. According to his description, however, the two are shown to amount to the same thing, echoing both Harold Pinter's *The Caretaker* and Bob Dylan's "Visions of Johanna", in that both are a response to the same desire for power. Thus, in the first line, Curtis tells us that he did everything he wanted to, a line that seems entirely innocuous on its own, even innocent, but when joined to the next line takes on a nightmarish quality. This second line tells us that he let them "use you" for "their own ends", implying, but not specifying, that he did the same as "them" to "you" in the first line. The vagueness of the two lines, their shadowy quality, is intentional, just as horror movies set out to frighten the audience by leaving the nature of the threat unspecific: fear makes merry in the dark. The song's final line is Curtis's reaction to "The horror, the horror" of the Earthly City, a return to "the centre of the city" of God, with himself firmly "in the night" of disillusionment, and waiting for truth, his guide, to take him by the hand and lead him away.

"Day of the lords" is another of the album's masterpieces, as well as being a musical tour-de-force. The song is Curtis's *Ā la recherche du temps perdu*, his retrospective song; "I do it all the time," said Bob Dylan, referring to French writer Marcel Proust's novel about redeeming lost time, so, naturally, does Ian Curtis. For, as the roots of our attachments lie mostly in our childhood, when we're most susceptible to conditioning, so must we return to find that lost time and regain it for our soul's sake.

"Day of the lords" is also full of the ambiguities that make Ian Curtis songs so rich and powerful, both deeply disturbing as a song and profoundly reassuring as a work of art. The first verse, for instance, seems to begin at the beginning, with Ian's birth in the Memorial Hospital, Stretford, Manchester, in "the room" that saw "the start of it all", the "no portrait so fine" comment that follows referring to his mother's gazing in wonder at his beloved little face, while the "bloodsport and pain" could be her birth pangs. As for the recurring phrase "the bodies obtained", an extremely ominous expression whatever its meaning, this probably refers to the babies born in the maternity ward, the "lords" of the title, where their swooning parents are concerned. The even more ominous chorus of "Where will it end?" could simply be musing about what kind of life the infants can expect. Then, again, the "bodies obtained" smacks of a nightmarish science fiction fantasy where children are kidnapped by an alien force, which, of course, Curtis knew that they were, by the desire for power and the colluding parents, teachers, friends and influencers.

The second verse makes clear that "Day of the lords" is about childhood conditioning, the "friends who goaded you on" demanding "more proof", of the assertive pride, that is, which underlies all desires for power, also a focus of Harold Pinter's *Betrayal*. Curtis then switches abruptly to the antidote for this conditioning, detachment, "withdrawal pain", which he tells us, "is hard", adding a rare glimmer of humour by punning that the withdrawal "can do you right in", which might mean that it can drive you to despair or refer to the self-extinction that the process of disillusionment involves, or, most likely, both. Now, the same chorus that asks where all this will end has a totally contrary meaning to its first incarnation. Then, it meant whither the self; now, it means whither the soul?

The third verse takes us back to that "hired car" in "The Kill" that substitutes a stand-in life as a puppet of power for a real life of the soul. And, sure enough, the car described is off-the-road, of truth, one presumes, with all its windows closed, no exercise of free will, then, to call up the spirit, hence the desire for power's rule is not "disturbed". The world of power described here is that of "the heat" of battle, "the survival of the fittest" in English philosopher Herbert Spencer's memorable alternative phrase for Charles Darwin's "natural selection" in *On the Origin of Species*. Curtis tells an interlocutor in the song that he guesses they were right when they said that there was "no room for the weak". This verse is particularly disturbing when we learn that Curtis told a close friend shortly before his suicide: "There's no room for the weak or emotive."

The final verse returns to the beginning, only this time in retrospect, as time regained, now the "nights of bloodsport and pain" are no longer the pains of childbirth but the nightmarish power-play of human life, now "the bodies obtained" could be corpses collected from the battlefield or the extinguished selves of freed souls. The final chorus, then, asking where will it end, could mean whither mankind in its poisonous climate of power or whither the freed soul. The crucial phrase, however, is Curtis's "I remember it all."

It may seem strange for a 22-year-old man to go back over his life, but just as it's never too late to ask the question *why*, so is it never too early. Ian Curtis had this quality of starting early very much in common with Bob Dylan, not to speak of Rimbaud, whose own creativity was coming to an end around the same age as the young Mancunian's was beginning.

"Insight" echoes "Day of the lords" in that its operative idea is remembering, specifically remembering "when we were young". Ambiguous, as ever, this might be Dylan's "younger than that now" of "My Back Pages" on the 1964 *Another Side of Bob Dylan* album, childhood innocence as the condition of a commitment to truth, or it could mean nostalgia for a happier time; probably the latter, at least momentarily, before Curtis's artistic soul imposes itself. Thus, one minute, he seems to be saying to his wife that difficulties in their marriage were causing "sadness and upheaval for you" and that they had wasted time together, before adding that they didn't *really* have time, meaning that the dream of a happy-ever-after marriage has no basis in reality, an echo of Harold Pinter's *The Homecoming*.

Personal insights apart, the song is a solid artistic statement, remembering as part of the process of disillusionment, starting off with the reality that "dreams always end" and that Curtis no longer cares, indeed, is unafraid to face the dreams down, to watch them dispassionately as they disappear. He has, he says, got over his initial fear of the consequences of a commitment to truth and is "not afraid anymore".

The crucial importance of remembering the past is underlined in one of Joy Division's most famous songs, "She's Lost Control", which was apparently prompted by an epileptic girl Curtis was trying to help in his civil service job. Epileptics were an important part of his work and he would regularly attend a specialist centre to learn more about the most severe cases. Unfortunately, this led to a profound pessimism about his own epilepsy when it was diagnosed shortly before *Unknown Pleasures* was recorded.

Although it may have been prompted by an epileptic, however, "She's Lost Control" is not about epilepsy. Curtis, like Harold Pinter with *Betrayal*, for instance, and, indeed, any artist, simply uses personal experience as a starting point to make statements about the nature of reality, which is the purpose of art. The song is actually about the fact that we all allow the desire for power to control us, indeed, conspire to work with it in order to ensure that we remain its slaves. Thus, the girl in the song responds to a control from outside, something that we can all confirm for ourselves, being shown to collaborate with her gaoler, "upon the edge of no escape", and laughing as she admits to her loss of control. Most significantly in terms of the "remembering" theme of *Unknown Pleasures*, however, is that she is said to have "given away the secrets of her past" instead of keeping them close to examine their meaning, as Curtis himself was doing, confirming, in the final verse, the absolute necessity of exposing "the myths and the lies" of one's personal history in order to gradually open up one's world and ultimately find freedom. The alternative, as Curtis tells us in the album's concluding song, "I remember nothing", amounts to just doing "time" in the desire for power's illusionary confined world, "trapped in a cage", along with violence and despair.

Ian Curtis and Joy Division had an unusual and interesting creative relationship. Lead guitarist Bernard Sumner explains: "Ian was a catalyst for the rest of us. He would cement our ideas together. We would write all the music, but Ian would direct us. He'd say, 'I like that bit of guitar, I like that bass line, I like that drum riff.' And then I would arrange it, mostly I would arrange it, with additional suggestions from the other members of the band. He'd put the lyrics in later, but he always had some ready. He had a big box with lyrics in. He brought our ideas together in his own way, really." Curtis very quickly developed an unerring instinct about the kind of music he wanted for each song. As Sumner remembered, once the music was completed, Ian "would just pull some words out and start singing them, so it was pretty quick."

Curtis himself told a journalist: "I've got this little book here, full of lyrics it is. I just pull it out and see if I can fit something in. I have loads of lyrics in reserve…all waiting in there. I'll use them when the right time comes along. Sometimes it's a line from one song mixed with a line from another. Sometimes the original lyric gets completely changed…it just gets used as a guide lyric and leads to something else. You never know. But I have to have this reserve, this lyric bank."

Like Harold Pinter and Bob Dylan before him, Ian Curtis may have left conventional education behind quite early on, but he never stopped learning, reading widely in a highly focused way. His wife remembers him reading Dostoevsky, Nietzsche, Jean-Paul Sartre, Herman Hesse and JG Ballard and he also loved Albert Camus of *The Outsider* fame and the Beats, particularly

Jack Kerouac and William Burroughs. What's more, when he read the books, it was always in his song-writing room; the books weren't entertainment but work. There are obvious references to writers in title tracks, for instance, including "Atrocity Exhibition" (Ballard), "Colony" (Franz Kafka), and "Dead Souls" (Nikolai Gogol). With other songs, he seems to quote favourite writers. In "New Dawn Fades" on *Unknown Pleasures*, for instance, a song that describes the emptiness of his life before he discovered truth, Curtis speculates whether "a loaded gun" can set the self free from its bondage. It just so happens that the 19th century American poet Emily Dickinson also broached the subject of her life before the appearance of the spirit of truth in a poem identified by its first line:

"My Life had stood – a Loaded Gun -
In corners – till a Day
The Owner passed – identified –
And carried Me away."

It's perhaps significant that when Curtis names his muse as the spirit of truth in "Shadowplay", he finds it "in the corner".

As we've seen with "Shadowplay" and St. Augustine's *The City of God*, Curtis was also familiar with religious literature and understood the language. In "Wilderness" on *Unknown Pleasures*, for instance, a song that echoes Dylan's "A Hard Rain's A-Gonna Fall" with its question-and-answer scheme, he writes of "the power and glory of sin" and "the blood of Christ on their skins". The "wilderness" of the song's title, however, is not that of Armageddon's "end times"; there are no thunderbolts from heaven, only humanity's power-driven destruction of knowledge, which Curtis clearly considers our most precious commodity.

Ian Curtis had first considered the relevance or otherwise of religion to an artist's life early in his writing career in a short song entitled "The Drawback". The song begins liturgically enough with Curtis describing having seen "the evils of this world" and "the stretches between godliness and sin". But it then scotches the adoption of even the faintest hint of a religious, as opposed to spiritual, attitude to life. Thus, the song broaches "the promise of truth faith" before firmly and decisively slamming the door on any religious outcome by writing of "the hypocrisy that always lies within" any religious creed.

It's in this respect that Ian Curtis is entirely different from Bob Dylan. Of course, Dylan himself rejected religion's claims to truth in many different songs, a fair few of which are masterpieces. But he did eventually succumb to the claims of one expression of religious dogma, albeit temporarily. Not so Ian Curtis. What's more, Curtis and Joy Division wrote one of their greatest songs, an irrefutable masterpiece and a composition of operatic beauty, at least partly about the essential hypocrisy of all expressions of religious faith, certainly where truth is concerned.

This song is "Dead Souls", a lyric that, in the light of Curtis's subsequent suicide, is often seen as a harbinger of that suicide, a prediction of his approaching end, particularly with its chorus proclaiming that the dead souls of the title "keep calling me". Yet this would only be the case if, by the "dead souls" in question, Curtis means "the dead", as, for instance, James Joyce clearly does in his short story "The Dead". But, judging by the content of the song's two verses, Curtis clearly doesn't mean "the dead" when he writes of "dead souls". He actually means people whose souls are dead, people who've never asked the question *why* and live exclusively for their dreams of power, for happiness.

The song begins with a long musical introduction that sounds like an outtake from Richard Wagner's *Ring* cycle of operas as it builds to the first of a number of climaxes. The lyrics are a relatively late introduction, but certainly worth the wait. Curtis first pleads for "these dreams" to be taken away, dreams that "point" him "to another day". The plea echoes that towards the end of *The Lord's Prayer* given to his apostles by Jesus, a plea not to be led into temptation, to be delivered from the evil of desire, of attachments, of dreams. Curtis explains in the next two lines that the dreams are part of a "duel of personalities", a duel, that is, between the self and the soul, a duel, what's more, that stretches "all true realities". In other words, as it's the self that blocks the way to reality, Curtis is effectively asking his muse to help him remain soul-focused rather than self-distracted by dreams that keep calling him, by attachments that keep him tied down.

The dilemma is also stated in another song of this period, "Something Must Break", the one that includes the "I is someone else" phrase, "this life isn't mine". "Something Must Break" is Curtis's equivalent of the Robert Frost poem, "The Road Not Taken", which begins: "Two roads diverged…" while the song begins: "Two ways to choose…" Curtis sees himself as being "on a razor's edge" which is a confounding of two images to express his choices, one the "cold steel" of "Shadowplay", the other "upon the edge of no escape" of "She's Lost Control". The echo of "Dead Souls" occurs in the third verse, where Curtis asks the spirit of truth to "decide for me" so, as he tells us in the next verse, he can "get back to where I belong", his soul-life, that is.

Returning to "Dead Souls", the second verse deals with political and religious faiths, condemning their leaders' claims to truth, to any sort of answer to mankind's spiritual aspirations on the irrefutable grounds that they all belong to the world of power, the world of hopes and ambitions, the world of self-salvation, the world of dreams. Thus, Curtis begins by referring to one of his earliest songs, "Leaders of Men", as he writes of "figures from the past" standing tall, all the so-called great men of power and influence from past ages, and responds with "mocking voices ring the halls", mocking because they're all dead, their dreams of power extinguished.

He then considers the aspiration to world-wide domination of the major religions, which he summarises in four words: "imperialistic house of prayer". This speaks for itself, but for the sake of the song and to drive the point home in a cinematic way, he imagines "conquistadors" who "took their share". This amounts to Curtis's perception that religion is a philosophical weakening or softening-up process that leaves its believers ripe for exploitation by the men-of-power who follow in the wake of the ideas, just as, for instance, the French Revolution exploited the philosophical ideas of Jean-Jacques Rousseau, with his "Man is born free and everywhere is in chains," while the Spanish conquistadors enslaved the bodies of their victims in the Americas while the Catholic Church enslaved their minds. In short, Curtis is making the point that religion is simply one aspect of a conspiracy of power, the ideas part, while others provide "the muscle", in Mafia parlance.

To say that "Dead Souls" is a masterpiece is the least that can be claimed for the song. Written sometime in 1979, when Bob Dylan was launching himself into his evangelistic phase, one that would, at least in the mind of many fans, negate all the good he'd ever achieved in freeing people from illusion, "Dead Souls" provides a devastating counterweight to the vast majority of the songs on Dylan's three Christian fundamentalist albums. Irrespective of its relationship to Bob Dylan, however, it is, quite simply, one of the greatest expressions of truth ever written, short and simple as it is. And, where the music is concerned, it must be said that Joy Division rose to the challenge of creating a sound sufficiently cataclysmic to satisfy Curtis that it matched the ideas expressed.

Ian Curtis himself responded to the devastating impact of the song by rewriting a song he'd written several months earlier, "Chance", in a newer version entitled "Atmosphere", another masterpiece, but one that, this time, in contrast to the "avoid at all costs" advice of "Dead Souls", counselled a "try this for size". It was no accident that the songs made up the two sides of a Joy Division single. The song counsels facing life's illusions squarely on the grounds that attack is the best form of defence. The alternative, he tells us, is "confusion". If confronted, however, illusions die.

The song begins with a pointed reference to the "moving through the silence" of "Shadowplay", which is now "walk in silence", a metaphor for humility, detachment, acceptance of truth's guidance. "Chance" then asked whether this meant walking *away* in silence, but "Atmosphere" pointedly changes this to "*Don't* walk away in silence". The two versions then agree about the absolute necessity of seeing "the danger", i.e. understanding where the impediments to freeing the soul lie. But the song also counsels that there is "always danger" because, as illusions disappear, they're replaced by others, "life rebuilding", as Curtis characterises it. Bob Dylan's religious mania is a case in point.

"Atmosphere" makes clear that the artist's journey along the road of truth is rarely an easy one, a crucial phrase in the song being "due care". But the artist is also a person who generally has to act out their life in society. As we've seen, Ian Curtis and Bob Dylan had much in common as artists, with the one fundamental difference of religion; likewise in their daily lives there were many similarities, as we shall see. But there was one fundamental difference in their personal lives. This one thing they didn't have in common was Ian Curtis's epilepsy, which may well have proved the crucial factor in his suicide as it was a severe disability in the "front man" of an increasingly successful rock band, a disability that compares to composer Ludwig van Beethoven's deafness, which also conjured the spectre of suicide in its victim.

Ian Curtis's epilepsy was of the so-called "grand mal" kind where he would lose consciousness before having violent muscle contractions. His first recorded epileptic fit occurred when Joy Division were driving back to Manchester in the early hours of the 28th of December, 1978, following their first London gig. Thereafter, the fits occurred relatively frequently and were often associated with concert performances. Curtis was famous for the coiled intensity of his singing and for his extraordinary stage "dance", a kind of robotic series of marionette movements that mimicked an epileptic's muscle contractions, one, moreover, that he performed with staring eyes as if hypnotised, and, initially, months before his first actual seizure, as if rehearsing it. Subsequently, the dance would sometimes degenerate into a full fit on stage, increasingly often, in fact. Indeed, the stress of his performances and his role as band leader on whom the other members depended, not to speak of the record company, management, and fans, could have been a major factor in his epilepsy. To make matters worse, friends testified that the epilepsy made Curtis deeply embarrassed, even ashamed, which added to his artistic alienation. And, of course, as Joy Division's fame grew, so, too, did the stress, until they were like parallel snowballs running downhill. The situation may have been exacerbated by the medication Curtis was advised to take for the epilepsy, which, at the time, was experimental, a case of hit and miss, often with depressing side effects. Indeed, there are those who believe that it was the pills that drove him to his death.

If Curtis had been a normal "rock star" with a bloated sense of his own self-importance, he could, perhaps, have surfed this bay of sharks like some tragic superhero from a Wagner opera, seeing his epilepsy as an equivalent of Christ's stigmata, marking him out as a "chosen" one. But he wasn't; the exact opposite, in fact. Indeed, everyone seems to agree that he was extremely sensitive to the needs of others, to a painful degree, in fact, which, of course, explains why he was considered an excellent disablement resettlement officer and a reliable band leader. It's also quite striking how relatively few direct expressions of despair there are in his lyrics, despair being an extreme form of self-pity, although almost the entire period of his mature song-writing coincided with the tug of war between self and soul, desire and truth, that threatened to tear him apart. But, and it's a big but, Joy Division's most famous song and their only, relatively minor, hit before Ian Curtis's suicide – like Bob Dylan, Joy Division were more cult influencers than commercial hit-makers – referred very directly to that tug of war. This was "Love Will Tear Us Apart".

One striking similarly that characterised Bob Dylan and Ian Curtis was the fact that both found the life of an artist incompatible with marriage. Dylan's marriage to Sara began to fail when he gave up his attempt to live a happy family life. "Love Will Tear Us Apart" details a similar situation, although Curtis attempts to universalise the situation in order to express the fact that an unconditional commitment to truth, the "love" in the song title, is forever incompatible with any human attachment, the "us", that likewise sets out to be exclusive, hence it's the "love" that will always tear the relationship apart rather than make it stronger, as might be expected. In this respect, the first verse makes clear reference to "Something Must Break", with its "two ways to choose". "Something Must Break" also prefigures "Love Will Tear Us Apart" with its comment that, committed to truth though he is, Curtis "still" sees "your face in my window". The "window" here is clearly the soul's window of opportunity for freedom through free will, while "your face", one might guess, is that of his wife, who, Curtis says, "won't set me free", from the desire for power, that is. Now, in "Love Will Tear Us Apart", Curtis writes of them "taking different roads".

To clarify that it's earthly love, the love between two people, that's incompatible with the love of truth, spiritual commitment, he then turns to the intimate side of his marriage, which is now a cold bedroom and a wife turned away on her side. But, in a clear echo of that "still" in "Something Must Break", he writes: "Yet there's still this appeal." The third verse has his partner crying out in her sleep, underlining his "failings", leading to feelings of "desperation" as "something so good" can no longer function. As with Dylan's "Don't Think Twice, It's Alright", his song of intended separation from his own first love, in which he writes: "Still I wish there was somethin' you could do or say/To try and make me change my mind and stay," there's clearly regret here, but also an artist's understanding that there can be no rival to the spirit of truth, hence spiritual "love" will always tear apart any couple that claims absolute love for their relationship when one of the two is an artist. It's this that makes the song a work of art, whatever insights it might offer into Curtis's marriage.

As such, "Love Will Tear Us Apart" provides a handy introduction to Joy Division's second, and final, album, *Closer*, which they began recording in London on the 18th of March, 1980, two months to the day before Curtis's suicide. Like The Beatles with their record producer, George Martin, Joy Division were fortunate to have a profoundly sophisticated and sympathetic producer in Martin Hannett, a Mancunian raised in a working-class Catholic family and who attended Catholic schools before gaining a university degree in chemistry and subsequently finding his vocation in music. Hannett was something of a techno-whizz-kid who pioneered many musical innovations but probably found his greatest fulfilment in the voice and lyrics of Ian Curtis. Understanding, soon after he began work with Joy Division on *Unknown Pleasures*, what he had in Ian Curtis, Hannett worked closely with the singer on realising his potential as a recording artist. Indeed, he certainly had no little influence on the great singer that Curtis became on his records. In this respect, the album's title, *Closer,* can be seen as meaning closer to the voice, closer to the soul, closer to the meaning of the music, closer to the spirit of truth. Hannett claimed that *Closer* was his most "mystical" album, while Bono, singer and lyricist of Irish band U2, who was present at some of the recording sessions, later spoke of "the holy voice of Ian Curtis". As for Annik Honoré, a Belgian fan with whom Curtis had an intense, albeit technically platonic relationship in the last few months of his life, she remembered a sacred quality to the laying down of his vocals, as if "some kind of inner Holy Communion were taking place". When the album was released on the 18th of July, 1980, however, two months to the day after Curtis's suicide, some reviewers read the title of the album as a closer, with a hard 's', as in "The End", one of the singer's favourite songs from The Doors. Not surprisingly, perhaps, in the circumstances, the album was a commercial success, even as the band reformed under the name "New Order".

The album kicks off with "Atrocity Exhibition", which quotes the JG Ballard book of dystopian short stories, although Curtis said that he wrote the lyrics before he actually read the book and that it was pure coincidence that some of the ideas in the book were similar to some of the ideas in the lyrics. In fact, the song can probably best be compared to Canadian singer-songwriter Leonard Cohen's title song of his 1992 album, *The Future*, in which Cohen tells us that he's seen the future, brother, and it is murder, a song, it should be noted in which Cohen lumps together the Soviet totalitarian dictator Stalin and St. Paul, a founder of that "imperialistic house of prayer", the Roman Catholic Church.

Annik Honoré has been quoted as saying that Curtis was a very kind man, polite and soft spoken, and much of the potency of "Atrocity Exhibition", and of *Closer* as an album, is in Curtis's gentle understatement, a very British quality, which only serves to give a frightening emphasis to the horrors described in the song, with Curtis's invitation to the listener to "come this way and step inside" having a particularly ominous tone. Perhaps the song's most telling line is Curtis's equating torture and violent deaths in the Roman Coliseum with all those people "who try hard to succeed", a strange relation, at first sight, until we realise that they're all part of the *same* striving for power of people who "can't relate" to truth. The "inside" of the invitation, in other words, is that hired car of power, with its windows closed. The song concludes with Curtis asking the listener to take his hand and he'll show them "what was and will be", an invitation subsequently made by Leonard Cohen in *The Future*.

Closer's second song, "Isolation", faces the artist's alienation squarely. "Isolation" can also be seen, certainly in its first verse, as a development on Dylan Thomas's definition of the religious in his verse sequence "Altarwise by Owl-Light" as "tipsy from salvation's bottle". Curtis describes such people as in constant fear, calling for aid "from above", loving their idea of the divine, but only, in Bob Dylan's definition, because they see God as "an errand boy" to satisfy their desires. Such religious devotion, says Curtis, "touches perfection" but is just as painful as any other expression of desire. His response is the one-word chorus: isolation.

From religious aberration, Curtis switches abruptly to himself. The first word of the verse, "Mother", toys with the idea of the religious praying to "Mary, the Mother of God", only then to bring the song down to earth with his own birth-mother, telling her that he tried, "please believe me", that he's doing the best that he can. He then confesses, sincerely, in contrast to so many religious with their hopes of salvation as a reward, that he's "ashamed" of his actions, ashamed of who he is, hence the chorus: isolation.

The final verse summarises the compensations of isolation for the truly spiritual life, of the artist, the truth-seeker, the mystic, whose starting point is precisely the humility of the second verse, the exact opposite of the pride of the first. Now, Curtis describes "the beauty" of truth, the knowledge he "could never describe", "pleasures" which, in the world's eyes, are "a wayward distraction". It's in this context that he considers that his isolation just might, in his manifold torments, be his "one lucky prize".

The positive benefits for the soul of isolation, of alienation, were obviously very much on Curtis's mind at this time because he returns to the theme in "Colony", whose title is based on the Franz Kafka short story, "In the Penal Colony", which describes an elaborate torture and execution device for condemned prisoners, which doesn't necessarily relate to the song, although it does suggest that Curtis was wracked by indecision. Indeed, the song begins with "a cry for help", goes on to cover "broken homes" and a woman cradling a man in her arms as he lies asleep. He then tells her that there are things he has to do, but that he doesn't mean her any harm. A worried parent's tearful last goodbye follows as "a cruel wind", in an echo of Dylan's wind howling "like a hammer" in "Love Minus Zero/No Limit", leaves him standing in the "cold" of disillusionment and the alienation of "this colony". All this seems to point to Curtis leaving his emotional attachments behind for the sake of truth but, nevertheless, with a degree of regret.

This is confirmed in the next verse, when we find him asking why such dislocations are necessary; the absence of any family life, he adds, makes him feel uneasy. But, then, in the final verse, he makes an overwhelmingly positive riposte, stating, with absolutely no room for misunderstanding, that God took him by the hand and made him understand that the artist's alienation is inevitable, part and parcel of the process of disillusionment. It is, in short, a means to an end, which is precisely the title of *Closer*'s next song. "Means to an end" provides a moving summary of Curtis's love of truth. "Committed still, I turn to go," he concludes, as he tells his muse: "I put my trust in you."

These songs are important artistic statements. But, undoubtedly, the heart of *Closer* is a trio of songs that describe the dilemma of the artist in the "no man's land" between self and soul, desire and truth, a dilemma that Ian Curtis's genius makes very much his own. Tellingly, the first song, "Passover", recalls the Jewish holiday which commemorates the liberation from slavery of "the Children of Israel" by "God" after inflicting ten plagues on the Ancient Egyptians, as described in the *Old Testament*'s *Exodus* Chapters 11 & 12. The final, and ultimately persuasive, plague was the death of each Egyptian firstborn. The Israelites were told to mark the doorposts of their homes with the blood of a slaughtered lamb so that the plague would pass them over, hence the English name given to the holiday. Curtis refers to this in the song's third verse, where "a mark on the door" is said to provide "sanctuary" for the artist, rather than for the Jews, from the "feverish smiles", an inspired description for the pursuit of happiness. The "sanctuary" in question is free will, and the opportunity it offers the artist to detach himself from desire in order to receive inspiration, for which the requisite condition is a childlike humility, characterised as "infancy's guard" in the song.

"Passover" is a beautiful example of the combination of the universal and personal that marks the lyrics of Ian Curtis, a balance that provides much of their drama. Appropriately, the song describes a crisis he "knew had to come", one that threatens to destroy a balance he'd managed to keep, a balance that can only be between the human attachments of his self and the commitment of his soul to truth and, crucially, the resulting process of self-extinction. Curtis's self-soul dilemma is conveyed through a series of questions and answers in the song's first three verses before arriving at a final resolution in the fourth verse.

The first verse describes his doubts and vacillations, his fearful questions on the consequences of disillusionment, before asking himself whether he would prefer to live a "role" rather than a real life. To do so, he says, would be to live an illusion that would fall apart "at the first touch" of reality. The next verse, however, provides a counterweight to this conclusion. It starts off quite brilliantly by characterising the disillusioning remembrance of things past as a brutal process of "watching the reel" of the film of his life pass as his human attachments are slowly strangled to death. Can he, he asks, go on disturbing and purging his mind in this way when it amounts to renouncing his family duties. His answer is ambiguous in the extreme as Curtis tells us that, if he does, then he knows that he'll lose every time. Does this mean that Curtis can't bear to pay the personal price of abandoning his duties to his loved ones or that, by cutting off his attachments, he'll lose the chains of the desire for power? The answer is implied in the dependent clause "when all's said and done", which conjures an idea of the end of life, when such duties would have to be abandoned anyway. Self-extinction, in other words, is simply bringing forward the inevitable. Another way of expressing this is the adage that the cemeteries are full of people who were indispensable.

The third verse provides Curtis with a reminder of his artistic vocation, his need to answer the question *why*, "the gift that he wanted to give" mankind. In pursuit of this he tells himself that if he does give up on disillusionment now, "forgive and forget" is how he terms this, he'll only have to pass through the "deserts and wastelands" of the process a second time when the question *why* returns to haunt him. This is because disillusionment, self-extinction, is the condition of finding the meaning of life. Bob Dylan expressed this same idea in "Stuck Inside of Mobile with the Memphis Blues Again" on *Blonde on Blonde* as he wrote of "sitting here so patiently" – Curtis echoes this with his "sat by the fire" – waiting to find out what price to pay to avoid going through the same things twice. The principle is here established that there's no alternative to pursuing the road of truth, whatever the consequences. Curtis then repeats the song's first line about the crisis he knew had to come, destroying the balance he'd kept, before moving on to the next set of selves for disillusionment, wondering what their extinction will reveal.

The second in our trio of "no man's land" songs, "Heart and Soul", is an instant classic, a template for the artist that compares to the very best of Bob Dylan's work, indeed, surpasses much of it. The song encapsulates the dilemma facing every artist between the attachments of the self, the "heart", and the commitment to truth, the "soul". Three verses deal, firstly, with vacillation, then with the absurdity of a world based on the pursuit of happiness, before finishing on the day-to-day reality of the life of the artist.

Thus, we begin with the fact that, however committed the artist, they're "still" always susceptible to be led astray by the "instinct" for self-preservation, and to believe in happiness, "a journey to the sun". But, however it's constituted, this journey is always, by definition, "soulless" and doomed, whatever moral "justification" might be made for it. Like the Jesus Christ who shed a tear at the thought of Jerusalem's future sufferings, Curtis observes all this "with a pitiful eye", but, as an artist ultimately concerned only with reality, he's obliged to say that there can be no compromise between heart and soul: "one will burn".

The second verse belongs firmly to the literature of the absurd, which was very much Curtis's favourite reading. Curtis describes the illusionary world of the desire for power as "an abyss that laughs at creation", an echo of Hermann Hesse's novel *Steppenwolf* with its reference to "the awful ambiguity grinning over all" the "hopeless tragedy and waste" of the lives we lead in "the dreary machine" of that world for fear of the alternative, which is to stare "into the void…into bottomless darkness", which is what the world amounts to once we see it in the light of reality. He goes on to echo the Dylan of "Mr. Tambourine Man", with its "circus sands", and "Desolation Row", where "the circus is in town", by characterising the dream world as "a circus" with "foundations" going back through "the ages", that the artist must nevertheless tear up by the roots.

Echoing Kurtz's "The horror, the horror" of *The Heart of Darkness,* Curtis then memorably encapsulates "the terror" of the desire for power as "the grip of a mercenary hand", whose merciless control sometimes drives its puppets to savage distraction, but there can be "no turning back" or "no last stand" for a pawn whose every action is controlled, only the unconditional choice between heart and soul, where "one will burn".

The first two verses of the song are consistent in having eight lines followed by the one-line chorus. The final verse reduces the body of the verse to just four lines, with a repeated chorus of three, as it succinctly and quite brilliantly summarises the essential view of the artist. This is that "existence", which is to say the "normal" world of pride and dreams, doesn't *really* matter; the artist attempts simply to "exist" in it on "the best terms" he can manage, as he gets on with the real business of life, which is to rip up the roots mentioned in the second verse: his "future", as Curtis, puts it, depending on his "past", while his "present" is "well out of hand", because he's in the hands of the spirit of truth, which echoes Stanley's "No hands" in Harold Pinter's *The Birthday Party*. This "well out of hand" also underlines the constant necessity for the artist perennially to renew their marriage vows with the spirit of truth because of the absolute incompatibility of truth and desire, hence the repeated final chorus that "one must burn".

"Twenty-Four Hours" has something of Bob Dylan's "All Along the Watchtower", made famous in the Jimi Hendrix cover version, as that song's "hour is getting late" is echoed in its final words, "before it gets too late", words of enormous poignancy considering how little time Curtis actually had left. Ironically, the song begins with mankind's perennial search for "permanence", in this case the happy-ever-after of marriage, but it could just as easily represent the eternal joy of salvation or any other kind of happiness, which, by its very nature, is a striving for permanence. In the case of "Twenty-Four Hours", Curtis seems to be referring to his own failing marriage, which he places squarely in the realm of pride, now "shattered", an innocent belief in happiness, now overturned, leaving him "under a cloud" that marks his every move, colouring the entire experience of that marriage, as each experience is defined by its outcome.

Curtis then details his attempts to save his marriage and how "just for one moment" he thought he'd found a way, only for destiny to unfold, leaving him to watch as it slipped away. Ian Curtis took his lyrics extremely seriously, writing and re-writing all the time to find the exact word, phrase or expression to correspond to the experience he was describing, and, always, as an artist, in tune with the spirit of truth, in a manner that would define that experience in a true, which is to say, universal and timeless way. Joy Division guitarist Bernard Sumner recalled in 2007, for instance, that, while the band was working on *Closer*, Ian had told him that doing the album felt strange because he felt that all his words were writing themselves. There is a description, for instance, of Curtis scribbling new lyrics for the songs on *Closer* even moments before they were finally recorded in the studio, just as Bob Dylan had done for so many songs before him.

The memorable phrase "destiny unfolded" in "Twenty-Four Hours" is a case in point, encapsulating as it does the iron laws of reality that govern all human experience, Bob Dylan's "The Law" in "She Belongs to Me", even as Curtis uses it to describe the situation of one individual, himself, at a particular time and place. The phrase brings to mind British Prime Minister Harold

Macmillan's one-word reply to a journalist who asked him what was most likely to blow Governments off-course. "Events," he replied. "Destiny unfolded" expresses the same thing, but with an artist's deeper understanding of the world, since it incorporates the inevitability of cause and effect. Reality is what is, it says, and what happens is simply a particular expression of that reality. In this way, Curtis lifted his experience from the ground of a particular situation onto the higher plane of the universal.

Curtis then expands on this idea of the inevitable failure of all human efforts to find "permanence" in an illusionary world in the next verse, where he moves on from his marriage to tell us that his attempts to hold on to all his most cherished attachments proved "beyond all reach", as in the "touching from a distance, further all the time" of "Transmission". He then invites the listener to step outside their closed world with him to see why this should be, showing us that it's because the events of a life are merely the inevitable consequence of "hopes and desires" that are "valueless", valueless because they're illusions.

The next verse drives home this understanding as Curtis follows in the footsteps of a legion of previous artists when he says that he "never realised" how far he would have to go to find true permanence, "the darkest corners" that would need to be illuminated before he could see clearly. Echoing the "just for one moment" of the second verse, he tells us that he thought he heard a "call" that offered hope for human happiness, but, looking beyond "the day in hand", i.e. stepping outside his own closed world, he saw that there was nothing there at all. For permanence, an unchanging reality, cannot be found in an illusionary world.

The final verse encapsulates all that Cutis has learned as an artist, a knowledge that can best be summed up in the fact that all human desires are doomed to failure, and that the only way to find one's "destiny", where permanence lies, is by going "deep into the heart" of each of one's desires, every attachment where "sympathy held sway", to free oneself from them once and for all before it's too late. For the artist or truth-seeker, in other words, life is an allotted time span to find freedom from desire, a time span that ends with death; ideally, perhaps, death of the self, but, if not, then inevitably with physical death.

The final two songs on the album, "The Eternal" and "Decades", were clearly inspired by the idea of wasted lives, young deaths, and, most pertinently, by the song "Where Have All the Flowers Gone?", composed, with lyrics for the first three verses, by Pete Seeger in 1955, with two additional verses added in 1960 by folk singer Joe Hickerson, who turned it into a circular song, which is probably what appealed to Ian Curtis. The song begins by asking where all the flowers have gone, with the answer that they were all picked by young girls. The question then becomes where all the young girls have gone: taken husbands. The next question is where all the young men have gone: gone for soldiers. Where have all the soldiers gone, gone to graveyards. Where have all the graveyards gone, gone to flowers. The repeated chorus with each verse asks when they'll ever learn. The song is a perfect characterisation of the circular effects of the centuries-old grip of the desire for power on the human mind as tit-for-tat wars wipe out whole generations, a round dance of death, the English nursery rhyme "Ring a Ring a' Roses" with the thorns to the fore.

"The Eternal" takes this a step further in an echo of Philip Larkin's poem "This Be the Verse", with its "Man hands on misery to man", as a man is possessed by impotent fury at the waste as a Remembrance Day parade, praising the glory, passes by, while the old men scatter flowers in an echo of "Where Have

All the Flowers Gone?". The second verse then shows how a child is conditioned to be the cannon fodder of the next generation by being encouraged, in contrast to Dylan's "younger than that now" of "My Back Pages", to respond to setbacks by becoming "older" or more determined to prevail. The child of the second verse, as with most children, longs to be older, innocently conspiring with his influencers, seeing his time with children as "wastefully spent", when, tragically, the adoption of a childlike humility would enable him to access inspiration and understand that he's setting himself up for a fall. The song ends with the child, blinkered in his power-enclosed world, seeing only the trees, with their roots, a clear reference to the "foundations" of "Heart and Soul", not realising that the trees' falling leaves are a metaphor for his own demise.

The album's final song, "Decades", significantly entitled "Cross of Iron" before a late change, is even more obviously inspired by "Where Have All the Flowers Gone?" It deals with young men, weighed down by the idea of doing their duty, pushed into "Hell's darker chamber" before – those who survived, that is – looking back "from the wings" to see themselves as actors in a play redolent of the 1963 absurdist piece *Marat/Sade* by Peter Weiss, in which the inmates of an insane asylum, directed by the original sadist, perform the assassination of a radical French revolutionary.

In contrast to the question in "Where Have All the Flowers Gone?" about when will they ever learn, Curtis's question in "Decades" is where have the young men been? For all their dreams of glory as they set out to war, the answer is nowhere. This is driven home by the abridged final verse, which shows the surviving soldiers, in spite of the horrors, missing the fear and "the thrill of the chase", a "ritual" that, like a matador with his red cloak taunting the impotent bull, shows them the door to that elusive glory, only for them to find it slammed in their face.

"That last track, the young men with the weight on their shoulders," commented Annik Honoré, "was the way he was talking in his last days, with that same soft voice, because he was so tired and confused and sad." Bernard Sumner added that, during the recording of *Closer*, Curtis told him that "he had this terrible claustrophobic feeling that he was in a whirlpool and being pulled down, drowning."

In the circumstances, the cover of the album, when it appeared in July 1980, had something of a fated quality about it. Graphic designer Peter Saville, a partner at Factory, Joy Division's record company, had created one of the most iconic album covers ever for *Unknown Pleasures*. It was Sumner who spotted an image in *The Cambridge Encyclopaedia of Astronomy* that showed 100 consecutive pulses from the first radio pulsar. Saville reversed the image so that it became white with a black background. For *Closer*, Saville had been impressed by a series of images in a magazine of ornate family tombs in a graveyard in Italy and suggested that he use one of these for the cover, even though he hadn't heard the album or knew the meaning of the lyrics. The band, and particularly Curtis, agreed.

The ominous undertones of all these signs were compounded when, in a frenetic series of London concerts following the completion of the album on the 30th of March, Curtis had two epileptic seizures in a row when Joy Division performed two concerts back-to-back at different venues on Good Friday, the 4th of April. Returned to Macclesfield for Easter Sunday, he took an overdose of barbiturates. Worried that they might not be enough to kill him but sufficient to damage his brain, he told his wife what he'd done and she called an ambulance. Just two days later, still recovering from his suicide attempt, Curtis agreed to perform at a scheduled concert in Bury, just north of Manchester, but only managed to sing "Decades" and "The Eternal", before breaking down, which led to a riot by some members of the audience.

Feeling that he'd let down everyone who depended on him, Curtis wrote to Annik, "I feel a deep self-hate." As for his suicide attempt, he confided to a friend, "It wasn't a cry for help. I actually want out."

Curtis's last lyric, "In a Lonely Place", whose title echoes the alienation theme of "Isolation" and "Colony", must be one of the most incredible ever written for its combination of mysticism and graphic suicide rehearsal, soul and tormented self. British writer and broadcaster Jon Savage has pointed out that the lyric, certainly in its first two verses, appears to relate to the 17th century Baroque Italian sculptor Bernini's *Ecstasy of Saint Teresa*. This life-size marble statue depicts a vision of the 16th century Spanish mystic and close associate of John of the Cross, Teresa of Avila, as described in her autobiography, in which a beatifically smiling angel is about to pierce her heart with a spear as she swoons in the ecstasy of the title. Beginning with a reference to a marble statue, the Ian Curtis lyric contrasts a "special, unique love" that "caresses" the sculpture against a hot, feverish waste. It's likely that Curtis means to contrast the spirit of truth here with the desire for power. The chorus then expresses a fervent longing for "you", as in the spirit of truth, to be "here with me now".

The second verse provides a vivid description of what could be Bernini's sculpture, with "that awful daylight", probably a synonym for the cold light of reality, which might refer to the illumination of the statue by a natural light filtering through a hidden window in the dome of the Cornaro Chapel of the Church of Santa Maria della Vittoria in Rome. That hidden window would certainly have appealed to Curtis, who describes a body curled around the feet of another, just like a warm dog, that "curls in and dies". The description would certainly fit the *Ecstasy of Saint Teresa*, with Teresa at the feet of the angel. The fervent longing for the return of the spirit of truth is then repeated.

The final verse provides a change of tone so dramatic that it must be unique in the history of popular music. Consider: we're now presented with a hangman who looks round as he waits, presumably for the condemned prisoner to approach. We then leap forward to the execution as the "cord stretches" before it breaks. "Someday", Curtis confides to his spiritual mentor, we'll "die in your dreams", but not the death of the self in a reality that he never reached before it got too late. The chorus is now an inclusive longing to be "here with you now", as if Curtis, sensitive to the last, wished for all mankind to be introduced to the spirit of truth before he died.

Ian Curtis hanged himself in the kitchen of his home in Macclesfield in the early hours of the 18th of May, 1980, just two months before his 24th birthday and the day before Joy Division were due to fly to the United States for their first American tour. He left a note for his wife that concluded with the remark that it was now dawn and he could hear the birds singing. His suicide involved tying the rope from an old-fashioned clothes rack on a pulley around his neck. By the time he was found, the rope had stretched and he was kneeling on the floor as if in prayer.

David Gray

WHITE LADDER

Singer-songwriter David Gray has come to represent something of a cardinal case where triumph over adversity is concerned. Gray produced three albums in four years (1993-6) under major record labels only for all three to flop. A period of drink-and-drugs-excess followed after which he, with a little help from his friends, recorded an album of new songs in the spare room of his north London terrace house. This was self-released in November 1998 in Ireland, where Gray had an incipient following, and was subsequently re-released via the record label route in the US and UK in 2000. That record, *White Ladder*, went on to become the best-selling album of all time in Ireland and currently the 11th best of the 21st century in the UK, selling a total of seven million copies worldwide and encouraging a legion of new singer-songwriters in the process.

But there's another way of seeing David Gray's experience, one that places him alongside Bob Dylan and Ian Curtis as a genius, as a simple channel for divine inspiration. As Gray himself recalls in the commemorative book that accompanies *White Ladder*'s 20th anniversary edition: "Standing inside the songs and looking out on the audience, we were starting to sense the amazing power that the music seemed to have. As our success and the audiences grew, this strengthening conviction became more like an unshakeable belief in the strange magical power of these humble but powerful songs."

Gray's words, whether intentionally or not, recall the line in the album's iconic song, "Silver Lining": "only things worth living for innocence and magic – amen", "innocence" being a synonym for "humble" where the "magic" of inspiration from the spirit of truth is concerned. Indeed, "Silver Lining" might qualify as one of the most spiritual lyrics ever written with its eternally reassuring line: "know that the light don't sleep", "the light", of course, being a synonym for truth. "Silver Lining" appears to have been the first lyric Gray wrote for the album and, although many of the songs seem different in tone, more prosaic or mundane, as well as more in tune with the contrasting "darkness deep" reference in the song, yet "Silver Lining" undoubtedly defines the underlying theme of *White Ladder*, which is that of a bird's-eye detachment from human suffering: perspective, in a word, one from which its millions of admirers could find some relief from their own travails.

This theme of a bird's-eye view chimes beautifully with Gray's recollection of writing *White Ladder*'s opening song, "Please Forgive Me", in January 1998, while trying out some newly-purchased technology. As the song's chords presented themselves to him, so, too, did the lyrics, "seemingly arriving out of nowhere…The whole song just dropped out of the sky…I remember this weird but very distinct feeling while it was happening. It was as if I had split into two parts – the subjective part that had tears in his eyes as he wrote down the words and felt the whole mysterious lift of the music, and the objective part that stood above looking down at the whole writing process… The experience was completely unforgettable and beyond any that I'd ever had whilst writing any of my previous songs."

Where the song's meaning is concerned, Gray is quoted in Michael Heatley's *David Gray: A Biography* as saying: "It seems like a very simple song – not so much about falling in love for the first time, but re-falling in love. It's a love song tempered by experience, but almost more passionate for the re-discovery."

The "experience" Gray refers to here is undoubtedly linked to that of the adversity of his career "fall" and its consequence in consolatory drink and drugs. It's also linked to falling in love for the first time *without* the benefit of that subsequent experience, but, crucially, not in love with another human being, rather with the spirit of truth. In this, Gray was following his mentors, Bob Dylan and Van Morrison, who first alerted him to the meaningful possibilities of song-writing.

So, who is David Gray? He was born on the 13th of June, 1968, in Manchester to a well-to-do family of shopkeepers. He first came across Dylan through his *Greatest Hits* album, followed by the early acoustic songs and on to Dylan's later albums, particularly *Blonde on Blonde*. The other great influence was Van Morrison's iconic early album *Astral Weeks*, a song cycle released in the year of Gray's birth and whose mystical overtones he came to appreciate after hearing the Irish songwriter's overtly spiritual "Into the Mystic" on the 1970 *Moondance* album.

No surprise, then, that after completing a degree-course at Liverpool College of Art, where John Lennon also studied, Gray went on to a career in acoustic folk, slowly merging into alternative rock music, both heavily influenced by Dylan and Van Morrison.

Thus, in "Coming Down", from his second album, *Flesh*, a favourite with his Irish fans, we have the essential lines, where David Gray's vocation as singer-songwriter is concerned: "I'm trying to spell/What only the wind can explain."

There would seem to be little doubt that the reference to Bob Dylan's "Blowin' in the Wind" was intentional and that Gray, like Dylan and Morrison before him, was aware of the "wind" of truth from an early age. Again, in "Lullaby", also from *Flesh*, we have: "Stand up and let the wild wind blow/Right into your soul till the night is dead."

Essentially, then, David Gray's explanation of "Please Forgive Me" as a love song tempered by experience, as a re-falling in love, with the repeat benefiting from being more knowing, is tantamount to Bob Dylan writing in his *Chronicles: Volume One*, "Invoking the poetic muse is something I didn't know about yet. Didn't know enough to start trouble with it, anyway."

Gray, in other words, may have known about the spirit of truth from an early age, but only in a theoretical way, from hearsay, as it were, which is very different from experiencing it, embracing it unconditionally and letting it work through you. As Gray writes in "Sail Away", *White Ladder*'s penultimate song, "of all the times I've tasted love, never knew quite what I had, little darling if you hear me now, never needed you so bad."

Suffering is a great teacher. In David Gray's case, following an orgy of self-pity, the pain of his triple whammy of album flops finally persuaded him to be rather more detached about his situation, which, in turn, triggered the inspiration that lifted his songs onto another level, just as it had for Bob Dylan and Van Morrison before him. "Silver Lining" and "Please Forgive Me" are as infinitely superior to Gray's earlier songs as "Blowin' in the Wind" and "A Hard Rain's A-Gonna Fall" are to Bob Dylan's and *Astral Weeks* and "Into the Mystic" to Van Morrison's, notwithstanding those songwriters' natural talent. Masterpieces need more than talent.

David Gray's early albums present us with a body of work by an earnest young man, one who is rather judgemental towards perceived human failings. Heatley quotes him as saying: "I used to be like a bull in a china shop. I had all the best intentions, but sometimes you have to take a step back and relax…I thought I was a happy, chipper chap and then I listen to the early stuff. The anger! …There was obviously real anger at the fact that no-one was listening…"

Here, then, was a classic case of "Physician, heal thyself", hubris inviting nemesis, which, when it came to pass with Gray's career falling flat on its face, prompted the spiritual re-set that produced *White Ladder*. Accessing the spirit of truth through detachment from the self – whether the self-righteousness of some of his early songs or the self-pity that followed the failure of his early albums – is clearly expressed in *White Ladder*'s hit single, "Babylon", with its appeal to "let go your heart, let go your head and feel it now."

Like "Please Forgive Me", "Babylon" appears on the surface to be a conventional love song. But both include lines that reveal the underlying spiritual agenda. The former has the plea to truth to "help me out here, all my words are falling short and there's so much I want to say" as well as the need for the self "to die" in order to experience the "deep mystery" of reality. As for "Babylon", the song's catharsis in a reunion with a lost love occurs while "climbing on the stair" after "turning back for home", which echoes Bob Dylan's "I was born very far from where I'm supposed to be so I'm on my way home."

As for "climbing on the stair", this relates to the album's title song, "White Ladder", an impressionist lyric quoting biblical passages, most pointedly that of Jacob's ladder of *Genesis* (28:12-17), when Jacob dreams of a ladder joining earth to heaven offering mankind a gateway courtesy of divine intervention, which is the meaning behind "water and wine" in the song, a reference to

Christ's first miracle at the marriage at Cana, as told in *St. John's Gospel* (2: 1-11). This might be a "tall order", as Gray puns in the song about both events, but one he accepts as the only escape from the feeling that "there's no rhyme or reason to life."

Now, it's necessary to point out here that none of this has anything to do with religion. Just because many people turn to religious organisations at times of difficulty or despair doesn't mean that David Gray did, just as Ian Curtis dismissed religion early on in his own spiritual development. Gray, like Curtis, is unapologetically spiritual and dismissive of religion: "Most of my songs could be interpreted as virtually spiritual statements, which is what they are – and we're in an age of reigning spirituality, to the detriment of everything," Heatley quotes Gray. "And I'll say unabashedly that we need spiritual guidance – but I don't like organised religion one bit. I think it's corrupt crap, and boring as well..." No grey area there.

As for the remaining songs on *White Ladder*, it's perhaps safe to say that they're far more in tune with the day-to-day concerns and difficulties of the album's listeners, although Gray phrases those preoccupations rather more poetically and philosophically than they might. "My Oh My", for instance, asks "What kind of world is this we're living in where you never win?" "We're Not Right", meanwhile, deals with an alcohol problem with which some in the UK and Ireland will be familiar: "now my hands are shaking but I just can't stop," yet one which he knows is an impediment to any kind of achievement: "can't tell the bottle from the mountain top". "Nightblindness", meanwhile, asks two questions familiar to many: "What we gonna do when the money runs out...how we gonna find the eyes to see a brighter day."

Yet the bird's eye view of human experience prevails throughout, as if some spiritual therapist is guiding the singer's hand as he faces up to his desperate situation. "This Year's Love", for instance, written for the 1999 British film of the same name, while bemoaning the difficulty of finding lasting love, nevertheless points out that, even in the midst of heartbreak, life goes on.

Similarly, Gray's cover of the Soft Cell hit "Say Hello, Wave Goodbye", written by Marc Almond and David Ball, the story of a failed relationship, changes the meaning of the song by ending his own interpretation with quotes from the Van Morrison songs "Madam George" from *Astral Weeks* and "Into the Mystic", the former a meditation on eroticism, the latter on spirituality that cites the wind of truth in its opening line.

Whatever its concerns, however, whether "darkness deep" or "light don't sleep", *White Ladder* is something of a miraculous work-of-art, allowing us a front row seat as an apprentice moves from being a Bob Dylan/Van Morrison wannabe to become a fully-fledged artist in his own right. Reassuringly, where equal opportunities are concerned, he does so by tapping into the same source of inspiration as his mentors.

What's more, we, the listeners, are invited to better understand our own difficulties by imbibing Gray's hard-won sense of perspective, initially through the words, of course, but also through the music, whose beat aspires to be both cheerful and comforting whatever the subject matter. Where Gray had often shouted his lyrics in the past – "I used to be so sure you know I used to be so def-in-ite," he sings with studied irony in "My Oh My" – his newly measured, sometimes contemplative tone is now infinitely more persuasive. Even as desperate a lyric as "We're Not Right" ends with a "yeah yeah yeah yeah" like some latter-day "She Loves You" on tranquilizers.

In such circumstances, it's hardly surprising that, while it may have taken a while, the turn of the century saw David Gray belatedly recognised as a true artist by increasingly large and enthusiastic audiences throughout the world as he spent three years touring in support of the album.

a new day at midnight

Although *White Ladder* was David Gray's fourth album, the commercial failure of his first three created a general impression that it was his first. His next studio record, then, effectively qualified as the "difficult" second album of music industry folklore. In the event, *a new day at midnight*, released in late 2002, sold well over two million copies. The reviews, however, were mixed.

Certainly, it would have been difficult to follow-up an album as unique as *White Ladder*. But it was possible. Bob Dylan had done it with his trio of surreal albums in the mid-'60s, each one arguably better than the last, with the third, *Blonde on Blonde*, Gray's favourite. Dylan's inspiration, however, had been running at white heat throughout that period. Gray's, in contrast, had gone cold.

He tells us as much in the album's second song, "Caroline". Although on the surface a conventional love song, or song of unrequited love, there's absolutely no doubt that "Caroline" echoes Dylan's "I Don't Believe You (She Acts Like We Never Have Met)" in bemoaning the fact that the spirit of truth has gone missing: so much for "the light don't sleep". As we know, though, truth requires commitment, and Gray admits in the first verse that he "tried hard as I could" to forget her.

The worldwide success of *White Ladder* meant that David Gray found fame and fortune. But, unfortunately, he also found that fame wasn't what he expected, indeed, that it had something of a nightmarish quality. As with most artists, Bob Dylan prominent among them, Gray found it profoundly dislocating. Dylan recalls in *Chronicles*: "The actor Tony Curtis once told me that fame is an occupation in itself, that it is a separate thing. And Tony couldn't be more right." And, again: "After a while you learn that privacy is something you can sell, but you can't buy it back." And, again: "People have one great blessing – obscurity – and not really too many people are thankful for it."

Where Gray is concerned, he recalled in an interview in *The Observer* in August 2010 that when he returned home after three years on the road with *White Ladder* he tried to settle back into his previous life, "but nothing is the same". "Fame," he said, "is not something you can do a course on…and, yes, for a moment, it was all a bit too much for me. I realised instantly that I like my privacy."

Again, in a November 2016 interview in Glide Magazine, an independent online site covering music, movies and the arts, Gray recalled: "Fame intimidated me for a while, and success. You know, I lost my bearings trying to think about it and questioning what it was I was doing."

The upshot is that, while *White Ladder* is an inspired album, inspired, that is, by the spirit of truth, *a new day at midnight* is not, or only to a limited extent. In "Caroline", for instance, an overwrought Gray actually sees himself facing the force of the desire for power itself: "a steel eyed dinosaur" in a "final war", a situation in which he desperately needs the aid of truth while feeling that it gets "further and further away".

One of the songs Bob Dylan had written during the initial period of his own allergic reaction to fame had been "Long-Distance Operator", included on 1975's *The Basement Tapes* album. In the song, he tries to contact the distant spirit of truth from a phone booth that's "on fire". The song that follows "Caroline" on *a new day at midnight*, meanwhile, is "Long distance call", where Gray similarly tries to contact truth, imagines his soul flying in her wind only to look back and see "the fire now taking hold". He might well be rich and famous: "I'm up so high…", but where truth is concerned, he's fallen "so far from it" and is "nowhere at all", or, where knowledge of reality is concerned, "Knowhere", which is the title of a similar song on the album.

Ironically, Michael Heatley's biography of Gray quotes him as saying that he'd lost his early respect for The Smiths' fellow-Mancunian Morrissey when he heard his song "Please, Please, Please, Let Me Get What I Want" and thought "Wait a minute, you were a pop star, with loads of money, playing big shows. What are you talking about?" Now, hoist with his own petard, Gray knew all too well. As he finds himself in the "hurricane" of fame in "Knowhere", he recalls that he, too, had said that he wanted to be rich and famous, but "I lied." And as he complains that he no longer knows where he is or who he is, so a voice says that it seems "you're doing all right". And so he is: as the ambitious singer-songwriter he once considered himself, but not as the artist who wrote *White Ladder*.

The point is made by quoting from "A Hard Rain's A-Gonna Fall", Bob Dylan's vow at the outset of his vocation as an artist to speak truth to "all souls". That song starts with Dylan asking "my blue-eyed son" where he's been. Gray's ironical echo has him recalling the interminable touring with a cheeky cheerleader's "Go on my blue eyed son," go on, that is, to "Knowhere". (Incidentally, the Dylan song also contains the image of a "white ladder", which may have influenced Gray where that song's concerned).

David Gray's parlous mental state, his exhaustion and feeling of vulnerability, are encapsulated in "Easy way to cry", where he tells us that the "one night stands" of touring are "making me crazy I know". The song has an "if only" lyric, "if only things were different, I'd be happy; if only reality were conditional and not absolute, we could all be happy." But it isn't. In the case of "Easy way to cry", the condition Gray craves is that his father survives a terminal illness. The song, in fact, is one of five on the album related to the death from cancer of Gray's father, Peter, to whose memory *a new day at midnight* is dedicated.

As if things weren't bad enough already, just as David Gray found himself facing a crisis of identity, of disabling alienation, so, too, was he faced with a family bereavement, with the resulting grief exacerbated by his mental confusion. "December", for instance, is almost unbearable as it bemoans the "killers underneath our skins".

Peter Gray had always been supportive of his only son, whatever he decided to do with his life, and was his greatest fan once David settled on a career in music. He even left his hospital bed during chemotherapy in the summer of 2000 just in time to see David perform on the main Pyramid Stage at Glastonbury, where he was filling in for Burt Bacharach on the last night.

Gray senior died in February 2001. His son was still grieving more than a year later when he wrote most of the songs for the album. Thus, the first, "Dead in the water", quotes "the old man" for the title, while also expanding the inevitability of his father's death to that of all our deaths and seeing it as happening under "an armageddon sky", recalling the Armageddon of the book of *Revelation* (16:16) in the *Bible*, the "final war" referenced in "Caroline" between the "steel eyed dinosaur" of desire and the spirit of truth. The death in the song is not only our physical death, from which none of us can escape, but also our spiritual death: if, that is, we simply "stand in line" and conform or worship "some forgotten god", whether physical or metaphysical.

Arguably the two "big" songs on the album dealing with grief are "The other side" and "Freedom". "The other side", which, like "Babylon" in 2001, won the Ivor Novello Award for Best Song Musically and Lyrically in 2003, is pure wishful thinking, very different from "Babylon" philosophically or spiritually. In common with millions of others seeking comfort from grief, David Gray imagines re-uniting with his father after death. "I have no belief that I will meet (him) again," Heatley quotes him, "but in this song I'm calling out and wishing I could."

"Freedom" is more philosophically interesting but also ends with wishful thinking as Gray closes his eyes and imagines his father dancing and laughing out loud, "undiminished".

True to his alienation, however, the song begins with a blunt demand to stop staring at him: "Take your eyes off me/There's nothing here to see," later echoed by Bob Dylan in "False Prophet" on 2020's *Rough and Rowdy Ways*: "What are you lookin' at – there's nothing to see." "Freedom" then notes that nothing good lasts forever before moving on to consider the nature of freedom in a world without meaning. Where the wishful thinking of Gray's reaction to grief is concerned, this is balanced throughout the song by the need to return to the road of truth: "It's time to clean these boots" while "bending to the task" of the artist in a work that's "never finished".

Whatever the worldly distractions of fame and grief, in fact, Gray is not unmindful on *a new day at midnight*, as its title suggests, of his vocation as an artist to seek the light even in the midst of darkness. And this, he knows with absolute certainty, involves the spirit of truth. As he tells us in "Caroline", facing the facts without the benefit of truth is merely "paper on the cracks".

Similarly in "Last boat to America", whose title offers a spiritual interpretation of sailing to the land of opportunity, he acknowledges that while he lives in a world of "makebelieve", there's nothing that "any fool can do" about it, "any fool" incorporating the entire human race. Only the "unseen hand" of the spirit of truth can lift "the veils of mystery".

The song offers Gray's take on "lead us not into temptation" from "The Lord's Prayer", which he expresses as "Don't pin that line on me oh no," the line in question being that of attachment to desire. Now, acknowledging the initial commitment to truth that he showed in *White Ladder*, he pleads with the spirit to take him "all the way" to reality, while accepting that this involves leaving the warmth of human attachments behind: "Frost on my windowpane is forming." The image recalls Bob Dylan's "On a Night Like This" from 1974's *Planet Waves* album, where frost gathers on the "window glass" with each "kiss" from the spirit of truth. Gray, too, sees the touch of truth in "Last boat to America" in terms of a kiss.

Where angst is predominant in many of the songs on the album, "Last boat to America" is more serene, more detached in the manner of *White Ladder*. And this also applies to "Kangaroo", which also benefits from humour, something for which David Gray is not generally noted in his song-writing.

The humour is apparent throughout but most particularly in the "kookaburra kangaroo" he employs in the song as a jokey variation on the "abracadabra" incantation used in stage magic tricks, in this case to signal the magic of truth, to which he refers in "Silver Lining".

Where detachment is concerned, the song begins with the advice to himself (and to us) to pay no mind to it, whatever his, and our, "it" might be. As any psychologist would say, letting it go is essential to preventing psychological damage. Gray had already told us as much in "Babylon" with its "let go your heart, let go your head and feel it now". The "Jeez" that follows in "Kangaroo", as Gray laments his own – and our – inability to learn offers an ironical aside.

This is followed by a stand-up routine in which Gray employs trite commercial phrases that are used ad nauseam as "good practice" to signal that he's not offering advice here that can be found in any manual.

The body of the song involves a conversation between Gray and the spirit of truth in which he offers himself as a "volunteer" in collaborating to make "the whole thing disappear", i.e. escape from the world of desire, including "the avalanche" of human problems.

Gray then offers his own take on the impossibility of happiness: "Nothing ever comes out good," while asking the spirit to free him from his fame and fortune only then to leave them "just outta reach" when he screeches at their removal, this amounting to a cold turkey cure for his addiction to them. A clear signal follows that we're talking spirituality here with the mention of "that burning bush", a reference to Chapter 3 of the book of *Exodus*, where God appears to Moses as a burning bush and promises deliverance.

Gray finishes by asking the spirit to give him something that lasts and is out of the cacophony of temptations. The refrain then acknowledges that, after touring the world, he is "so far behind" in his journey along the road of truth.

Keeping the best until last, David Gray's two most heartfelt songs to truth on *a new day at midnight* are undoubtedly "Be mine" and "Real love", both show-stoppers providing aural evidence that if the artist was down he wasn't out.

"Be mine" is the kind of song that could be sung by any person proposing to their partner, acknowledging as it does that nothing matters next to probably our deepest wish, which is to be loved, as Harold Pinter showed in *Betrayal*. The song reveals Gray at the peak of his creative powers, while its spiritual significance is shown in the fact that, where this love is concerned, his "eyes are so wide" in contrast to the closed eyes of wishful thinking in "Freedom". That we're talking spirituality here, rather than religion, is suggested in the lines: "Jumpin' Jesus holy cow!/ What's the difference anyhow."

Just as "Be mine" is contrasted to "Freedom", so is "Real love" contrasted to another grief song on the album, in this case "The other side", which ends with Gray complaining that he still doesn't know what love is. Well, he does in "Real love". Aside from the manifest excellence of the song, "Real love" also amounts to a major philosophical statement from Gray which proves that his disturbed state hadn't blinded him to the whole point of truth, which is to free us from our attachment, our imprisonment in illusion by the force of the desire for power. Gray uses the image of "bars of iron rain" to symbolise this imprisonment, again quoting the "rain" of Dylan's "A Hard Rain's A-Gonna Fall" where the rain symbolises human illusions and their catastrophic consequences. The image then becomes "iron wheels" in the second verse, wheels that "chain my heart" through attachment. Gray's reaction to this slavery then becomes an "iron rage" – or rage-at-the-iron-bars – which "paints my soul upon the page", i.e. brings his soul, the mind-turned-towards-truth, into play in his song-writing.

Where the spirit of truth is concerned, this comes in the form of "I hear the voice of Eden cry", which suggests Bob Dylan's "something calls for you" in "It's All Over Now, Baby Blue" as well as his "Gates of Eden", both on 1965's *Bringing It All Back Home* album. Truth lifts Gray up to walk "on high" until she makes him want to "lay down and die", self-extinction, in short.

This is real love, or the love of reality, which is whatever it is that the spirit of truth represents, God, in a word, not the God of the churches, the God of "With God on Our Side", but the real God, the God of the spirit of truth.

While *a new day at midnight* might be a disappointing album relative to *White Ladder*, then, it does have its compensations, with two of David Gray's greatest songs.

But that wasn't the end of his proving that he could still write inspired lyrics because there was another, making up a trilogy of spiritual love songs. That third song, however, wasn't included on *a new day at midnight* but on his next album, *Life in Slow Motion*, released three years later, in September 2005.

Life in Slow Motion

Like "Be Mine" and "Real Love", "The One I Love" can be taken as a conventional love song, particularly with its dénouement as the singer and his partner twist and shout on the dancefloor of the bay hotel. But, again, as with its predecessors, it's full of details that make this unlikely, suggesting instead a spiritual, rather than carnal, relationship.

It begins with Gray stating his intention to close his eyes and watch his partner leave, a partner who runs through his life "like a field of snow". This relates to "frost on the windowpane" of "Last boat to America", signifying a move away from the warmth of familiar attachments into the relative cold of reality through the inspiration of truth. Closed eyes, in contrast, signify his having chosen desire and, hence, illusion, rather than truth.

Gray clearly sees this partner in terms of an episodic relationship, like a tracer rising and falling in his sky to leave him praying for her return as darkness descends. Her absence in the next verse, moreover, coincides with an absence of wind – symbol of truth – and bullets flying, a consequence of illusion. Gray also sees their separation in terms of things he might have said, but didn't, suggesting a lack of commitment on his part, which leaves him feeling dead inside.

The final verse then tells us that his relationship has nothing to do with heaven and hell, i.e. reward and punishment, but with "lights up bright" and a life-affirming dance. This might be ambiguous but points in one direction, as does the chorus. This has Gray re-affirming his commitment to his one true love in terms of "the stars above", which can only mean to his destiny as an artist, and of "the repo man".

This is ambiguous in the extreme. A "repo man" is a person whose job is to repossess something from someone, usually after defaulting over a long-term purchase. It's surely not too much of a stretch to see this as covering two different interpretations, firstly, the impossibility of happiness, no matter how hard we might try to "buy" it, and, secondly, the repossession of the soul by its "owner", which is to say ultimate reality or God, with which the soul reunites to become one with that reality, recalling Emily Dickinson's poem "My Life had stood – a Loaded Gun", in which "The Owner passed – identified – And carried me away."

That this is Gray's intended meaning is confirmed by the fact that the absence of his love is synonymous with the absence of any interior life, life for his soul, that is. So here we have a love song to the spirit of truth, which, through a lack of commitment on Gray's part, is absent, but one whose return he fervently wishes. Just as with "Caroline", then, "The One I Love" defines the theme of *Life in Slow Motion* as one of a despairing separation from truth.

This doesn't necessarily mean an absence of inspiration since that depends on commitment, and facing up to one's situation in a dispassionate manner is a commitment in itself, which accounts for the excellence of "The One I Love".

This applies equally to "Ain't No Love", which is outstanding in the force of its depiction of the human condition, life without meaning in the absence of truth. This song is Edvard Munch's painting *The Scream* in musical terms.

The song begins with a categorical rejection of religion, which Gray states is "just a lie"; but if the God of religion is false, not so the inspiration or "ecstasy" of truth, which he says he can "feel" as if "it's heaven sent", *when* it's given. All illusory attempts to find a substitute only leave the recipient feeling "right as rain", yet another ironic reference to Dylan's "A Hard Rain's A-Gonna Fall". This is confirmed in the next verse where "the fruit of rain", Gray's equivalent to Dylan's "pellets of poison" of illusion in "Hard Rain", brings back the "familiar fear" that life has no meaning: "nothing ain't no good".

The song's verses are rushed as if Gray is dismissively stating the obvious, what's certainly obvious to him. What he takes his time over is the chorus, which consists of the repetition of: "This ain't no love that's guiding me" expressed with tremendous feeling as Gray vents his frustration and desolation at having to eat up "the boredom on an island of cement" due to his separation from truth. To be absolutely clear here, "No love guiding" means not being guided by truth and, hence, being guided by the only alternative, which is desire, hence Gray's "the horror, the horror" reaction. The song finally achieves an apotheosis in its final lines, where Gray suddenly remembers the magic of *White Ladder*'s bird's eye perspective and pulls off the same trick, "pulling back" to see the human condition from a distance, "so laughable and small", and to understand that attachment to this situation is pure madness.

It has to be said that much of the rest of the album is along similar lines but without the same persuasive force. Perhaps the most revealing lines with regard to David Gray's artistic frustration are those that involve "running" or "running wild", presumably what he felt like doing but couldn't – wishful thinking, in short – which occur in three separate songs on the album.

Thus, in the album's first song, "Alibi", he clearly seems to be reflecting on how far he's come down since the artistic high of *White Ladder,* which he imaginatively calls his "Friday night enfant". This is because he produced it in his own time: after the working week, as it were, on a "Friday night"; and as a "foreign" offspring of the music industry, hence "enfant", "enfant", of course, being French for "child", in this case meaning the childhood innocence necessary to receive the inspiration of truth, which accounted for the excellence of the album. Yes, but that was then. As for now: "Where d'it all go wrong?" he asks. His alibi for his continuing failure to rediscover his inspiration is the fact that he's in the grip of desire, under its "spell", its "all night busz on a line" of attachment in the dark night that leads him on, wrecking his head, leaving him "stone blind" and eating "the lie". It's from this mental imprisonment that, in a moment of wish-fulfilment, he imagines "running wild".

Again, in "Lately", he asks: "Someone tell me where did it go/ Darling I'm damned if I know," as he says "Goodbye" to "a time that ain't no more."

With "Nos Da Cariad" (Welsh for "Goodnight, love"), we're back to the make-believe of "running" as Gray admits that he's had "a bucketful of Babylon", his biggest hit, and asks himself: "What is it you're waiting for?" He provides the answer himself in the song's conclusion, which has him "all wired up" to attachments as the "dawning ray" of a new day mocks him.

In "Slow Motion", he's "hypnotized" by desire, while the resulting life "don't feel real" and truth is his "long lost friend".

"From Here You Can Almost See the Sea" has him as "just another fool in the line" of conformity he so despised in "Dead in the Water", while the "running wild" occurs in the form of the electric shock treatment of a dive into freezing water. As for the sea view, that's Gray's distant sight of the sea of reality, a favourite Dylan image.

With "Hospital Food", we're remembering the good days of *White Ladder* again when David Gray "basked in the road" and "stood in the roar" and all because of the inspiration of truth, hence: "You've tasted the snow" of cold detachment. But the songwriter admits that, while he's seen the beauty of truth and "the way it oughta be", he turned away.

Still, Gray tells us in "Now and Always" that truth is always on his mind as he feasts his eyes "on sacred lies" and wishes that "these demons would let me rest." The song ends with dogs "running wild" this time.

Gray keeps the most outrageous wish-fulfilment until last with "Disappearing World". The song could serve as the theme for a save-the-world-from-global-warming green movement as the singer laments the beauty of a disappearing world. That Gray intends the song as a spiritual statement, however, is clear from the outset.

As we saw with Bob Dylan, it's a fact of the spiritual life that as the soul travels along the road of truth and the perception of reality becomes stronger so does the illusionary world of desire fade. This is the situation that Gray imagines in the song. Although he knows that his reality is one of the "trailing wire" of attachment to desire, still he sees himself "sticking" there with the spirit of truth, creating art that hits its listeners "'tween the eyes".

In fact, rather than the world, it was his listeners who were disappearing. Commercially, *Life in Slow Motion* continued to benefit from Gray's *White Ladder* reputation. But the public's patience had reached its apogee.

David Gray's patience had also run out. As he recalled in a 2010 *Observer* interview about his next album: "My previous records were inward most of the time. But suddenly with *Draw the Line*, I'd kicked the front door down and I was outside."

Draw the Line

The hankering to run free which is the dominant theme of *Life in Slow Motion* finally found its expression with *Draw the Line*, released in September 2009. Unfortunately, where his two follow-up albums to *White Ladder* had Gray damning himself for pusillanimity, he now simply widened his scope to damn everyone for the same thing. That hadn't worked too well with his first three albums and it didn't impress too many this time either. Even duetting with Annie Lennox, one of the most successful female British singer-songwriters of all time, on the album's final song, "Full Steam Ahead", failed to convince.

In truth, the song, which berates humanity for its lemming-like qualities, running full steam ahead towards destruction, in spite of countless warnings, is the kind of diatribe that might lead some listeners to quote the David Gray song "Hospital Food" from his previous album: "Tell me something I don't already know."

Similarly, the album's first song, "Fugitive", which warns that we can't take our wealth with us when we die, might prompt some listeners to reply: "Not everyone is as rich as you, David. Most of us don't have anything to take." In doing so, they'd simply be echoing David Gray over Morrissey's moaning.

"Fugitive's" twin rallying cries, however, "Gotta live" and "Gotta try", do provide catchy stimulation for anyone contemplating setting out on the road of truth.

"Draw the Line" itself provides a less effective stab at the same thing with its dire warnings of time running out and the prospect of death but it does include a memorable line that what the truth-seeker seeks isn't material, "not the flesh", but spiritual, "the howlin' ghost within".

But, of course, David Gray, being a consummate artist when he has a mind, knows all this. Indeed, he tells us so in "Stella the Artist": "You're only saying what they all say," admitting that he felt "the sting of my own rebuke" as it came "spinning back like a boomerang", while dismissing self-righteous preaching as a "sea of psychotic puke".

Arguably, *Draw the* Line's outstanding song, one which benefits from no little inspiration, both lyrically and musically, is "Nemesis". In this context, the word can be defined as an inescapable agent of someone's downfall, the inevitability of failure if we fail to respect the natural laws, or, here, the metaphysical laws.

In the song, however, David Gray sees the word in the widest-possible context from a spiritual point of view, as everything that can instigate a movement away from illusion and towards reality, from "an intangible sense of loss" to the "ecstasy" of the spirit of truth itself, from the childlike innocence we shelter within ourselves: "the babe that sleeps through the Blitz" to the sense that real life is elsewhere: "I'm life sweet life itself". In this respect, the song echoes Saint Thérèse of Lisieux's "Tout est grâce!", which might be translated or transliterated as "Everything leads us to God," popularised as the famous last words of the sickly priest in the 1936 novel, *The Diary of a Country Priest,* by French writer Georges Bernanos, subsequently made into a celebrated film in 1950. What's more, Gray's song has the same detached, matter-of-fact rendition as many of the songs on *White Ladder.* The badgering tone of much of *Draw the Line* is entirely absent.

If the album as a whole, however, was an attempt by Gray to make himself more relevant to popular taste, then it's probably fair to say that it failed miserably. As we've seen with "Stella the Artist", Gray seems to have known this even at the time. But it obviously bothered him enough to try to set things straight by returning his work to its spiritual foundations with another "inward" album in double-quick time.

Foundling

It's no surprise, then, that David Gray called *Foundling,* released less than a year after *Draw the Line,* a "private record".

"I've never taken the dynamics so low as I have done on this record," he explained in the 2010 *Observer* interview. "I had to have faith in writing and understatement – the things I hold as my strengths." As for the album's prospects of commercial success, Gray was philosophical: "This record is going to disappear off the face of the earth." He was obviously coming to terms with the new commercial reality of his situation.

Certainly, *Foundling* is unmistakeably spiritual in tone and direction, or not quite entirely so. The first song, "Only the Wine", could be – and probably was – interpreted as a drinking song by some fans and perhaps that's why it has proved such a favourite. So many people have streamed the track, in fact, that Gray later felt obliged to include it in his *Best of* album, released in October 2016.

The theme of the rest of the album, however, suggests that song's chorus, a plea for help in finding the way home, is an echo of "Babylon's" "turning back for home", while the "Gone forever, ah whatever" of the song likewise recalls the nothing-to-lose detachment of *White Ladder,* in this case either at the prospect of there being nothing left to drink or of a spiritual life without drink.

The "going home" theme continues in the next, title song of the album, whose final line chorus is simply: "Take me home." "Foundling" is clearly inspired by the second chapter of *Exodus*, where the basket child Moses is discovered in the reeds by Pharaoh's daughter. She feels sorry for him as he cries and adopts him as her own son. Gray is using the story as a handy metaphor for his own condition of feeling abandoned by the spirit of truth, which, as in many other songs, he confounds with "love" and to which he appeals for similar compassion. The love becomes manifestly spiritual by the end of the song, when it's "transcendent" and "luminescent".

"Foundling" shows David Gray's impressive way with words and meanings, co-opting the expression "strictly on a need to know", usually associated with trade secrets, to convey the fact that the spirit is only available to those absolutely committed to truth and hence strictly on a need to know *why.*

In the song, however, although Gray testifies to his readiness to be ducked in freezing water to separate him from his warm worldly attachments, he likewise accepts that the road of truth is long and that he won't find himself "finally confronting" ultimate reality "till the time is right".

In the meantime, he'll have to give up so many attachments; as the spiritual shorthand has it: "forgetting" them, which is the title of the album's next song. The song sequence looks, in fact, as if Gray is working through the day-to-day reality of a spiritual commitment. That's not to say that he won't have regrets, he says, since he is "spellbound and hellbound, and caught in the netting" of the force of desire, which he is "aiding and abetting" by his own desire for happiness. As we've seen, this "netting" or "spider's web" image for the attachments of desire is also used by other artists. Gray persists with it in the album's next song, "Gossamer Thread", in which the force of desire is a "dog in the doorway" in whose wiles he's "dyed in the wool". Still, he's planning to free himself from "what that bastard did", an echo of Bob Dylan's "long-time curse" in "Just Like a Woman", and hoping that he's wrong in sometimes thinking that it's a hopeless endeavour.

As for forgetting, he couldn't help remembering *White Ladder* when writing the songs for *Foundling* because he was attempting to rediscover the closeness to truth of that earlier time, a time of "innocence and magic". Two songs on *Foundling* attest to the fact.

In "We Could Fall in Love Again Tonight", for instance, its "echoes return". For "what kind of existence" is this, he asks, to hanker so deeply after the spirit and "only feel the distance". Again, in "When I Was in Your Heart", he compares the effectiveness of the inspiration he received with *White Ladder* in reaching others to the "now" when his every word falls "on stony ground".

The "cold water ducking" treatment for worldly attachments in "Foundling" goes overboard in "Davey Jones' Locker", in whose depths Gray hopes to free and redeem himself, a wish he also feels in "A New Day at Midnight".

For all his attempts to find a renewed commitment to truth, for which *Foundling* provides copious proof, however, Gray is never complacent. The reality, as he tells us in the mesmerising "Holding On", is that, although "we are just passing ghosts… vapours of joy and hurt", yet we desperately hold on to the world to the bitter end. Our conditioning sees to that and, most pertinently, our instinct for self-preservation. For, as we've already seen, it's only with the death of the self that the soul can find its own life.

Thus it is that while the song's hypnotic repetitions and images of "inert stone" and "empty streets" might bring to mind the "boredom on an island of cement" of "Ain't No Love", yet a central bridging verse changes the whole feel of the song with its joyous imagery of love as spring bursts from the ground, a ground where Gray's dismantled self has been interred and from which his soul unfurls.

This abiding image echoes the album's very first line in "Only the Wine", where his soul is "sprung like a wild orchid".

Mutineers

The next studio album appeared almost four years later, in June 2014, but the singer-songwriter's focus hadn't shifted a jot. The determination to be considered a serious artist was undiminished.

In an interview with the *Financial Times*, just prior to the album's release, when asked what frightened him, Gray replied: "To be dismissed as insubstantial – that's definitely a fear…don't dismiss me as some wobble-headed inconsequential fuckwit; listen to the thing – there's intricacy and depth as well as immediacy."

If by this description Gray was hoping to relate *Mutineers* to *White Ladder*, which most certainly had bags of "intricacy and depth as well as immediacy", then he was being unduly optimistic. For, while *White Ladder* is undoubtedly spiritual, yet its wider concerns were recognised by many as their own. This is less the case with *Mutineers*. Indeed, Gray says as much in the album's title song, where he asks the spirit of truth what "they" could know about their relationship, "they" presumably being the public.

There's a suspicion here that Gray might have been feeling insecure, as in those desperate pre-*White Ladder* months, since "Mutineers", like "We're Not Right", is suggestive of an alcohol problem as he sees the yearning for drink and, more generally, human addictions and attachments, as mutineers trying to take over a ship bound for reality. But while "We're Not Right" and, indeed, "Only the Wine", suggested that we're all in the same boat, "Mutineers", as we've seen, is more exclusive, although it starts with inclusion: "You know the way it is…"

If all this shows that David Gray is a man as well as an artist, then the album as a whole does acknowledge that the artist has a self as well as a soul. Indeed, "As the Crow Flies" is precisely concerned with this fact, contrasting inebriation with sobriety, stupidity with wisdom, while asserting that reality, "the good stuff" is "not far…as the crow flies", which suggests that it's available to everyone who is prepared to open up to truth. What's more, Gray goes on to insist that "a part of me", which is to say, his self, is "dying/For the truth to be told", and that he has "never wanted something more", i.e. he's divorcing himself from his self in order that he can express the reality of the human condition.

Certainly, *Mutineers* is different from Gray's previous albums, with the exception of *White Ladder*, in that he claims to be back in touch with the spirit of truth; a curse has been lifted, he's no longer "stony eyed…like the living dead", as he tells us in the album's opening song, "Back in the World". The "world" in this song is not the illusionary world in which we're all forced to live by our attachment to desire. It's the real, parallel world we inhabit when we're in touch with truth.

Here, for the first time in his creative output, Gray names "God" as a possible alternative for "Love", the name he usually gives to the spirit of truth, while declaring that definitions don't really matter. All that matters is that "joy" has returned to his heart and, while it's not hugely important, it has to be said that the image of Gray on the album's sleeve shows a remarkably joyful man.

This isn't to say that the road of truth is one long joy-fest as any artist or truth-seeker knows well. There are many dry periods, but the difference now is that David Gray appreciates that these are all part of the process of disillusionment, as he tells us in "Beautiful Agony". Again, in "Last Summer", he tells us that truth comes when "it's good and ready".

"Snow in Vegas" is a meditation on Christ's "The things which are impossible with men are possible with God" from the *Luke Gospel* (18:27). The "Baby" in the song is the spirit of truth as she and Gray are reunited at long last. Their journey along the road of truth is continued and new amazing revelations arrive "like snow in Vegas", Las Vegas in Nevada being in the Mojave Desert, not known for its snow. The "magic" of truth, as "Silver Lining" had it, is then reiterated with "Now pigs can fly" and a reference to the legend of the 11th century King Canute, who was said to have tried to command the tide, "these breakers" in the song.

The relevance to the comment by Christ quoted in *Luke* is given added resonance in a startling ending to the song in which Gray says that he, and the rest of humanity, might be "vain and greedy", "selfish and needy", but that "it's just the way God made us". The point of this is that the magic of truth is necessary to lift us out of our darkness.

This is also the meaning of "Girl Like You" in which Gray acknowledges his limitations as a man and the difficulties in achieving an absolute commitment to truth, which is the "girl" in the song. He is, however, "working on it". For when he fails in the degree of his commitment, as he acknowledges in "The Incredible", he unleashes "the wrath of angels", which is a dramatic way of saying that truth is absent, and that there's "no going home tonight", "home" being the soul's ultimate destination.

David Gray is very much a-heart-on-sleeve artist and nowhere as much as in *Mutineers.* The album might be seen as more esoteric than *White Ladder*, but it's no less revealing of an artist's soul. It's hardly surprising that Gray tells us in "As the Crow Flies" that sometimes when he's "open wide" part of him "tries to hide". As we've seen before with David Gray, fame doesn't make a spiritual life any easier. There's a very good reason why legions of truth-seekers in the past have chosen a life apart. Quiet and solitude are essential to inspiration. As Gray explains in his *Financial Times* interview, one theme that runs through *Mutineers* is that "of far-flung places losing the human taint".

"I've come to realise," he says, "that there's always a part of me wishing I was somewhere like that; wishing I was on St Kilda, living with storm petrels, sitting on a cliff. It's probably to do with the level of saturation…It's escapism: getting out of the churning mechanism of the human environment."

It's also connected in Gray's mind, as he tells us in the *FT* interview, with his fascination with birds: "The more I understand about them, the more enraptured I become. There's a world of obliteration in birds – I lose myself in nature, forget about my thoughts…It's vital balm for the soul… I bought binoculars – then you go further into the world of the bird. They are 'other', they sing, they're of the sky." David Gray's description follows in a distinguished tradition, as we saw in the Introduction, in which artists and mystics have often seen the soul – the "other" side of the human mind to the self – as a bird seeking to take wing away from earth-bound concerns, with their song a celebration of their inspiration.

There's no question that David Gray feels the same way. "A part of me earth/A part of me sky," he sings on "As the Crow Flies". This is taken further in "Birds of the High Arctic" where the birds are compared to "blue distances calling", another echo of Bob Dylan's "something calls for you" in "It's All Over Now, Baby Blue".

A third song on the album also deals with birds while clearly linked to the "wind" of truth. "Gulls" is the final song on *Mutineers* and the most obviously mystical. Just as the album's first song, "Back in the World" sets the tone for what follows, so does "Gulls" leave a lingering spiritual essence, clearly Gray's intention.

The song is based on an eight-line poem by Belgian writer Herman de Coninck:

"Just as this island belongs to the gulls
And the gulls to their cry
And their cry to the wind
And the wind to no one

So is this island the gulls
And the gulls are their cry
And their cry is the wind
And the wind no one's."

In an interview in *The Daily Telegraph*, Gray spoke of "a yearning for removal from earthly stuff" in relation to the poem and of the inspiration he received from it: "I was finding something new and it was a major shard of light coming through." The poem is clearly profoundly spiritual, indeed, suggests that the spiritual element is all that exists, that the so-called physical world is purely illusory, a mirage that must be traversed in order to reach the reality on the other side.

Gold in a Brass Age

David Gray's next studio album, *Gold in a Brass Age*, was released almost five years after *Mutineers* but continued the spiritual development of its predecessor. At first hearing, it most resembles *Foundling* in that its "dynamics" are "so low" as to suggest that it's a "private record". But that doesn't mean it's lacking in intensity. Indeed, the fact that, like *Foundling*, the songs show Gray's "faith in writing and understatement", as he said of that earlier album, merely reveal here that he continues to feel, indeed, feels increasingly, that less is more. As novelist Charlotte Brontë of *Jane Eyre* fame put it succinctly: "Don't explain," which is probably true for the creative artist, if not for the critic. What Gray felt for this album in particular, although it was already apparent with *Mutineers* and even earlier, was that what the songs needed were open vistas for the music to fill, creating a constantly changing emotional and spiritual envelope around the lyrics.

Interestingly, too, its first song, "The Sapling", returns to the formula that made *White Ladder* so successful. That formula, in a word, involves perspective.

Gray explained in an interview on writewyattuk.com in February 2019 to publicise the album: "...there's this cyclical nature of things. I watched a raindrop fall in a puddle, saw these concentric circles emanate out from that.

"I was in a park and they'd cut down a tree, I was looking at the rings and suddenly an acorn fell on the ground next to me and I thought, 'God, it's the same thing – the acorn creates the ring, just like ripples in a puddle, but over 150/200 years rather than a couple of seconds. But that's still a blink of an eye in terms of the measurement we now have for the universe."

The point is that the natural world, like the real world of truth and reality, as we saw in the Introduction, operates cyclically. And, as Gray tells us in the song, that cyclical nature, which we see in the seasons, is asking us a question that "we barely comprehend", but, whatever it is, "The answer's YES." The question, of course, is whether we're willing to give up our ego and live for the soul alone in answer to the question *why*.

Gray contrasts this real world with the illusionary linear world of happiness, which we believe we're travelling towards, by interjecting "human cries" or excuses for the fuck-ups, cries such as "I kept it bottled up too long" and "Days I can't tell no right from wrong" to express the fact that, for all our efforts, we just can't seem to get things right.

Gray then pulls a rabbit out of the hat, echoing the reason *White Ladder* was such a success, in having a chorus respond to the cries with "I know that feeling too yeah" and "Tell me about it." These responses involve us all in the situation, which is only natural since Gray is simply describing the human condition.

This prepares us for the album's title song, "Gold in a Brass Age", which is a line from American writer Raymond Carver's short story *Blackbird Pie*. *Gold in a Brass Age*, Gray explains in the writewyattuk.com interview, "felt like the right title for the album. You can interpret it very obviously as something special that rings true in a world of noise and meaninglessness. But the way (Carver) puts it in the story is more humorous. It's something of infinite value almost, in a world of utter absurdity, his life taking an absurd twist. Something happens and he says, 'That's gold in a brass age'. So that's where it comes from, and it's got an uplifting quality. And this certainly is a brass age – let's make no mistake."

"Gold in a Brass Age" is a meditation on the "infinite value" of the inspiration of truth: "How much it means", in contrast to the "buzzing flies" of the force of desire's assaults on our senses. It also refers to the process of inspiration, described earlier by Gray with regard to "Please Forgive Me" as "The whole song just dropped out of the sky", which he here memorably lyricises as "I gave my best by accident."

Also unforgettable is Gray's description of the mysterious nature of the process, its other-worldliness, which means that "It's gone the moment I reach towards."

Gray explores the process further in "Furthering", seeing the artist as "the ghost of Christmas past" as he takes on the mantle of Christ's message of truth in exploring "what we don't know", losing "the weight" of the self until the spirit of truth's "arms enfold", an image around which he built the song "Spiral Arms" on his subsequent album, *Skellig*.

The process of truth is echoed in "A Tight Ship", which, as in the songs "Mutineers" and "Sail Away", sees the soul's journey as a ship sailing towards the sea of reality, letting "the senses/Be our guide" and snipping "these strings" of human attachment. The slimming down of the self from "Furthering" is now seen as becoming "sleek to dive in mirrored pools" as the mind breaks through the illusion that the self we see in the mirror is who we are.

These songs often echo those of Bob Dylan and Van Morrison as Gray follows in the footsteps of his mentors. In "It's Late", for instance, Gray echoes Dylan's "the hour is getting late" from "All Along the Watchtower" to underline the need to get on with it as human life is short, while the song's "No turning back" echoes Morrison's "Too late to stop now" from "Into the Mystic", which he also quoted in his cover of "Say Hello Wave Goodbye" on *White Ladder*.

Similarly, in "Hall of Mirrors", Gray echoes Dylan's "The palace of mirrors" from "The Changing of the Guards" on 1978's *Street Legal* album. The song covers roughly the same ground as "Full Steam Ahead" on *Draw the Line* but reveals how Gray has learned from past mistakes, replacing the hectoring tone of that earlier song with a highly entertaining fairground barker's delivery which makes much of the same kind of absurd humour favoured by Raymond Carver and creating an impression of full steam ahead in the music rather than in the lyrics, "sounding the notes of the words", as Gray has it in "Watching the Waves".

The "hall of mirrors", like Dylan's "palace of mirrors" is the self-admiring illusionary world in which society takes place, a world in which we're all encouraged to dream, to get on: "Let's go Let's go Let's go" and to avoid too much contemplation: "Not ours to reason why." The inevitable effect of such hubris is nemesis, but Gray amusingly counsels its victims to avoid looking down as the "too solid ground" comes up to meet their precipitous fall, as if ignorance of their impending fate could cushion the crash.

This echoes the "What we don't know can't hurt us" of "Furthering" and the "So what do we do but make-believe" of "Hurricane Season", with Gray asserting that "the merest breath of wind" could knock him down. This echoes the "hurricane breeze" of Dylan's "Man in the Long Black Coat" on 1989's *Oh Mercy* album.

All this might sound as if *Gold in a Brass Age* is depressing fare but that's far from the case. The overall impression it creates is of a sedate waltz, dancing featuring prominently in both "A Tight Ship": "Tonight we dance like no-one sees" and "Watching the Waves": "To dance like wind through the wheat".

There's also a dance in "Ridiculous Heart", but this song is probably not about Gray's spiritual marriage as, for instance, in "Watching the Waves": "I took that ghost for my bride", but about a more conventional marriage, just as, on one level, so was "Babylon": David Gray married Olivia, sister of the wife of electronic music band Orbital's Phil Hartnoll, in 1993, and the couple have two daughters.

The comparison with "Babylon" is apt because there are apparent connections between the two. In "Babylon", for instance, Gray berates himself for his jealousy and bitterness and the ridicule he has brought down on himself, while in "Ridiculous Heart"- that "Ridiculous" chiming with the earlier "ridicule" – Gray is sorry for not taking "no for an answer" and wanting you "all to its own self" – that "own self" contrasting with the soul responsible for most of his songs. In "Babylon", the solution offered was "crying out loud, the love that I was giving you was never in doubt", while in "Ridiculous Heart", it's a return to their early days, "like a sun rising", and that dance: "May we dance and erase."

This relates to the overwhelming issue faced by all artists and truth-seekers at some point on their spiritual road. This is that of their fidelity to their loved ones against that of the need for an absolute commitment to the spirit of truth. As we saw in the previous section, the issue was particularly notable with Ian Curtis as a result of one of his most famous songs, "Love Will Tear Us Apart", the love in question being spiritual with the "us" referring to his marriage with wife Debbie. Similarly, with Bob Dylan's "Sara" to his first wife on 1976's *Desire* album.

The issue is faced by Gray in the album's final song, "If 8 Were 9", where he tells us in no uncertain terms that, if the reality of the world were different, his commitment to his wife would be absolute. The song is extremely tender and makes two points. The first is that if he could he would shepherd her into heaven himself. The second is his hope that their life together could go on forever but, as it can't, he settles for the fact that the strength of their love is the equal of longevity. Certainly, "If 8 Were 9" must be one of the most remarkable romantic songs ever written.

"Mallory", too, is pretty unusual, transforming the death of British mountaineer George Mallory on Mount Everest in 1924 into a spiritual metaphor. Mallory, along with his climbing partner, Andrew Irvine, was last seen when about 800 feet below the summit of Everest. His body wasn't found until 1999. It's not known if he reached the summit.

David Gray celebrates Mallory's final climb as an escape from "the earthly stuff", which are "the shackles of the known roads" in the song, "to be free/Of all that is". What Gray means by this is the illusionary world of desire, "the whale of a lie", with its overwhelming demands, "the wave/That…engulfed me".

Faced with this human condition, Mallory and Gray choose "to be lost" as they cleave "to the wind", Mallory that of Everest, Gray of the spirit of truth, both "deaf to reason".

In this interpretation, Gray confounds the adventurer and the artist, both setting out fearlessly into the unknown, "far-flung places losing the human taint", as Gray once put it: "I've come to realise that there's always a part of me wishing I was somewhere like that…on St Kilda, living with storm petrels, sitting on a cliff."

Skellig

...or on Skellig, the twin-pinnacle crag less than 10 miles off the south west coast of Ireland, which would be more appropriate since David Gray named his 2021 album after the island. A UNESCO World Heritage Site, the 50 acres of rock rising 700 feet above sea level hosted a monastic settlement between the 6th and 12th centuries and first inspired Gray around 2009/10 when he wrote the title song. "Pondering that idea of setting up a monastery in such a remote place...It blows my mind to get so close to God in a contemplative way," he recalled on his website. Considering how he eventually developed the idea, it's unfortunate he didn't pursue it further at the time rather than releasing *Draw the Line.*

Skellig features a Celtic version of a Gospel choir and spiritual love songs that set a template for the genre. The laid-back let-it-be of the album is perhaps best encapsulated in Gray's idea of answering the absurdity of mankind's entrapment in desire's web by firing "laughing gas" into the crowd in the song of that name.

The album came out while Gray was planning a 20th anniversary tour of *White Ladder* and there's definitely a sense that *Skellig* is the true follow-up to that earlier tour-de-force. Certainly, Gray is conscious that he's "tarried too long" since then, that it's time he "come home right away", as he puts it in "House with No Walls". The song is built around the image of the fish out of water featured on the cover of the album, an album whose poles, he explains in an interview on the forbes.com website, are "the renouncing of the world and the giving yourself to contemplation and a different level of existence". Wouldn't that be something: a rock star becoming a monk, except, of course, that David Gray has never had any truck with religion so will have to settle for a monastery-of-the-soul as a mystic-about-town.

That's the beauty of both Ian Curtis and David Gray, the fact that both are no-nonsense Mancunians who bring spirituality to the widest possible audience through their songs. Where they're concerned, the desire versus truth dichotomy is no esoteric fairytale but an everyday reality of pressing interest to us all.

And, with *Skellig*, it's certainly true to say that David Gray rediscovers the profound responsibility of his vocation as an artist to inspire others just as he was first inspired by the spirit of truth on *White Ladder*. As he explains in the title song, the escape he seeks in such a far-flung place is only so that the inspiration he receives will be clear and consistent in order that he can inspire others in turn.

This wish for inclusivity begins the song, and the album, since "Skellig" is the album's first song. The "we" of "Skellig" then becomes the "us" of "Dún Laoghaire", Dublin's port town, the Irish connection further cementing the connection with *White Ladder,* which found its first home there. The song sees the struggle against the desire for power as one involving us all, Gray then explaining something of its nature in "Accumulates", as desire insinuates itself into every aspect of our lives. The idea is further developed in "Can't Hurt More Than This", whose gorgeous tune compensates for the bloody chaos the desire for power unleashes on the world, but, for David Gray, the resulting pain can't hurt more than living a life without meaning.

The rest of the album focuses more on the compensations of truth, initially with the inspired spirituality of "Heart and Soul", whose title recalls the similarly inspired Ian Curtis lyric, and in which the "I'm younger than that now" of Dylan's "My Back Pages" becomes Gray's: "Wonder shining in my eyes/Like I'm three years old".

Another comparison with Dylan can be made with "No False Gods", since his "False Prophet" on *Rough and Rowdy Ways* contains roughly the same general message, which Dylan encapsulates as: "I'm the enemy of the unlived meaningless life," Gray as: "We are love's body or we are undone," which means that our purpose is to merge our souls with God or ultimate reality. In both cases, the message has something of an essential quality.

This is particularly apt because Gray tells us at the bottom of the printed lyrics that they were inspired by the poem "Real Presence" by the Scottish nature writer, poet and novelist Nan Shepherd. The poem deals with transubstantiation, not in any dogmatic religious sense, but in that of the merging of substance and essence, which is to say soul and God, informed by love, which is to say promoted or facilitated by the spirit of truth. The difference is in the fact that dogma deals with belief, which is an idea, while what Nan Shepherd, David Gray and, indeed, Bob Dylan and Ian Curtis are writing about is experience, an actual process that leads to a practical conclusion. Nan Shepherd contrasts the two by rejecting the former as "No false gods now" and accepting the latter as: "We are love's body or we are undone," two lines which make up the body of David Gray's song, which he only interrupts twice to comment on the contrast between the belief of religion and the experience of spirituality.

In the first instance, in a rare outbreak of humour, he comments that following Nan Shepherd's counsel means being "damned if you do", which is to say condemned to hell according to religious orthodoxy if you follow the heresy of an individual path to salvation, and "damned if you don't", which is to say unfulfilled. In the second, he recreates the experience of inspiration by the spirit of truth as a repetitive process that seems unique each time we experience it. It is, in other words, outside time, a fact also expressed by Bob Dylan in his songs. This recalls the process described by David Gray in writing "Please Forgive Me", quoted at the outset of this critique and bringing it full circle.

For if *White Ladder* could be said to have promised so much, then there's little doubt that, while David Gray has written more than a few really great songs over intervening years, particularly spiritual love songs, he, now, finally, seems to have found a more consistent level of inspiration, one in which an album such as *Skellig* presents a satisfying whole. Certainly, that's the way it looks to David Gray. It can't be a coincidence that the final song on the album is entitled "All That We Asked For" and that, with the return of the consistent detachment that made *White Ladder* so wonderful, his life and output appears once more to be full of innocence and magic.

James Cowie

The blessing of obscurity

Most of the artists whose work is analysed in this book enjoyed – or, perhaps, endured would be more accurate – a degree of fame. Bob Dylan is one of the most celebrated artists of the last century and his name and 1960s image are widely recognised; Harold Pinter is generally considered one of the greatest post-war playwrights by theatregoers worldwide; millions of people own David Gray's *White Ladder* album, and, while Ian Curtis died before he and Joy Division could become more than an underground sensation, interest in his work has continued to grow since his death. Scottish painter James Cowie is an exception to this rule. He spent most of his life as a secondary school art teacher and is now largely forgotten.

Yet his best paintings are truly startling in their revelation of the nature of reality. His life, meanwhile, shows that widespread recognition is not a prerequisite for an artist to fulfil their vocation. Towards the end of his life, writing to his daughter, who was unhappily working as a teacher, he expressed this with admirable self-awareness:

"There is a sense in which it is true to say that every one of us lives a life 'alone'. Nor do I think that it is much to be regretted...The thing to do is to make your job serve its purpose of providing the necessary means of life and go on expanding your inner life as hard as you can. I can truly say of myself that I do not in the least regret my long years of teaching and I liked it no better than you do. The truth is it gave me the means of developing my artistic mind in peace. I made it subserve my real life always...you will be surprised to find that your everyday experience even of teaching will supply you the material you need and can make use of in your real work."

The fact is that being an artist involves a commitment to truth. This excludes all wishful thinking, all dreams of a different life, which only create dissatisfaction and interfere with that commitment. What's more, as we've seen with Harold Pinter, Bob Dylan, David Gray, and Ian Curtis, commercial success can also prove a serious distraction, to the point where it even threatens an artist's status, a danger of which all four were painfully aware. Fame is a curse that has often proved infinitely more damaging to creativity than obscurity, which, in light of that fact, can be a real blessing. In this respect, James Cowie was indeed fortunate to be largely anonymous.

So who was he? James Cowie was born on the 16th of May, 1886, on a small farm not far from the city of Aberdeen in north east Scotland. He came from a long line of farmers but his destiny was always going to involve the arts. At first, this wasn't painting but literature, which eventually led to his enrolling on the Honours English course at Aberdeen University. At the same time, Cowie, who was always highly pragmatic, also became a King's Scholar at the teacher training college in the city. And it was there that he found his lifetime's vocation, abandoning his university studies and finishing the course in drawing with distinction.

In turn, this prompted the move into teaching, initially in Fraserburgh on the North Sea coast. But in 1912 a determination to develop his art led to his being accepted, at the relatively advanced age of 26, at Glasgow School of Art, where his limited savings forced him to qualify for the school's Diploma in just two years rather than the usual three. He then resumed his career as an art teacher, this time in Bellshill, a coal mining town near Glasgow, shortly before the outbreak of the First World War. Where this was concerned, Cowie was a conscientious objector, which resulted in him spending two years in the Pioneer Corps, an army support unit, based at a camp near Edinburgh. He resumed his teaching at Bellshill in 1918, when he also married a fellow-student he'd met at Glasgow School of Art. Six years later, however, Cowie suffered a personal tragedy when his wife died of tuberculosis just ten months after the birth of their daughter, Ruth, to whom he'd later offer his own hard-earned experience of learning detachment in the letter quoted above.

Indeed, it was while he was teaching at Bellshill that Cowie developed his unique style as a painter, with the classroom effectively serving as his studio. A "lone wolf", he didn't belong to any contemporary school and took his influences from early Italian Renaissance painters, particularly Botticelli, as well as more surrealistic modern artists. The major paintings that resulted were a unique combination of Classicism and Modernism, preceded by many preparatory drawings and built up over years, their lack of spontaneity balanced by a precision in the expression of an idea, which Cowie took to be the function of painting.

It's this philosophical attitude that makes his most representative work universal and timeless. The paintings are full of a profound mystery suggesting an alternative world of serene contentment contrasted with human despair when separated from it.

Two Schoolgirls, for instance, painted in 1934-35, in Cowie's last years at Bellshill, and now in Aberdeen Art Gallery, is at once disturbingly modern in its consciousness of existential angst, yet with a sense of paradise found.

The two girls in the picture sit on art-room stools staring fixedly out of the picture in different directions. Behind them is a backcloth of heavy drapery pinned up across two easels. Each of the girls, moreover, has masses of drapery in her lap, so that both seem almost engulfed by it, particularly as the picture plane is so shallow as to suggest confinement. However, while one girl is clutching hers, the other has seemingly abandoned the drapery, having let it fall. But it is the girls' expressions that are most arresting. The one on the left appears frozen in anxiety and fear, as if about to break into Munch's painting of *The Scream*. The other has the calm, contemplative look of a Renaissance saint, while the mysterious circular gesture she makes with her visible hand suggests completeness and fulfilment.

The gesture is repeated in Cowie's *A Portrait Group*, started before *Two Schoolgirls* but completed five years later and now in the Scottish National Gallery of Modern Art in Edinburgh. Here, we have a group of four people, two boys, a girl, and, in the immediate foreground, a woman, who is the one making the mystical circle with her hand. They sit around a table in the open air, again in a shallow space, confined by a hedge. And, as with the two schoolgirls, the figures all stare out of the picture, but, here, straight at the onlooker. It's as if we've disturbed them and they're challenging us as to the reason why.

What's striking about this group is its immense serenity, closeness and solidarity and the sense that the four share some profound truth. In this respect, they're like the saintly girl in *Two Schoolgirls*, particularly the woman.

It's been suggested that the boy on the left of the picture is based on the young James Cowie; and, considering that Cowie had an elder brother and a sister, the group may, whether consciously or not, represent a family gathering, with the woman being the mother. This idea is supported by the fact that this image, in contrast with *Two Schoolgirls*, has a background, a distant landscape, which, as in many of Cowie's pictures, is based on the countryside around his childhood home near Cuminestown, suggesting the influence of "home" or upbringing. If so, however, this is a family of a different kind, a family joined together by a secret knowledge. Moreover, the painting has a number of clues as to what this might be.

The background, for instance, is partly obscured by mist and drapery, which, surrealistically, seems to be suspended in mid-air. The drapery provides a link to the masses of drapery in the *Two Schoolgirls* painting. Combined here as it is with mist, it points to the distracting power of human illusions. Drapery has often fulfilled this function in literature and painting, whether as veils or as curtains shutting out the light, as in Harold Pinter's *No Man's Land*. Moreover, the Cuminestown background suggests further that Cowie sees these illusions as having their source in childhood conditioning, from which the artist must break free in order to release their soul. It's certainly striking how the group faces outwards from the picture plane, firmly turning their backs on the background.

This interpretation is supported by a picture painted by Cowie in 1935 called *Intermission*, now in Liverpool's Walker Art

Gallery. This shows five schoolgirls in a classroom, one reading aloud from a book whilst the others listen. The standing girl in the centre of the picture provides yet another version of Cowie's serenity. Most significantly, a large window in the background with thick drapery on one side theatrically pushed aside shows a similar Cuminestown prospect to that in *A Portrait Group*, only this time with broken fencing starkly outlined in the open space. Freedom has been achieved from the influence of the past, lost time redeemed in terms of Marcel Proust's *À la recherche du temps perdu* (In Search of Lost Time) and Bob Dylan's asking how he can "redeem the time" in "Crossing the Rubicon" on 2020's *Rough and Rowdy Ways* album.

Another recurring motif in Cowie's paintings is that associated with images of macho aggressiveness as an expression of the desire for power. In *A Portrait Group*, for instance, this is represented by a red-coated huntsman riding through the landscape in the background. In *Two Schoolgirls*, we have the central image of a plaster cast of the muscular Discobolus that divides the girls. In contrast, Cowie's "enlightened ones" all adopt a detached humility.

It seems unlikely that Cowie intended any of this to have religious or theological connotations. There's no evidence that he was at all religious in a conventional sense. His father was a member of the Free Church of Scotland, an evangelical Calvinist denomination, but, from the evidence of the paintings, it would seem that Cowie regarded this as an element of the childhood influences or early conditioning from which he needed to disillusion himself rather than an attachment to which he related. The two apples on the table in *A Portrait Group* do suggest the fruits of the tree of knowledge from *Genesis*, but that's now hardly a religious image, rather the opposite. No, there's little doubt that the truth to which Cowie's work attests is of a spiritual or mystical kind.

The final proof is simply in the arresting beauty that paintings such as *Two Schoolgirls* or *A Portrait Group* possess, their spirituality, which applies equally to the most profound songs of Bob Dylan, Ian Curtis or David Gray. With Harold Pinter's great plays, the feeling of wholeness or fulfilment is rather in their philosophical perfection, although they do have their transporting spiritual moments.

In 1935, Cowie was appointed head of drawing and painting at Gray's School of Art in Aberdeen He moved again two years later to the post of Warden of Hospitalfield, the Scottish Art Colleges school for postgraduate students near Arbroath, on the North Sea coast, 45 miles south of Aberdeen. Here he remained until his retirement from teaching, influencing among others those enfants terribles of London's Soho in the 1950s, Robert Colquhoun and Robert MacBryde, and Joan Eardley, one of Scotland's most popular artists.

The long periods of leisure he enjoyed at Hospitalfield allowed Cowie to pursue his art in a new, increasingly surreal way. His themes remained the same as those in his Bellshill pictures, although now with more sinister and erotic overtones. Whereas the earlier work had concentrated on the apprehension of some beautiful inner truth, his major new works were far more concerned with facing up to the ugly illusions that needed to be eclipsed in order to reach that truth. This may have had something to do with the horrors of the Second World War, although, with Cowie's work, there's far more a sense of inner demons being exorcised than outer demons being acknowledged.

Perhaps the most striking of his paintings of this period are *Noon* (1946) and *The Evening Star* (1937-44).

Noon, a work owned by the Scottish Arts Council, is quite terrifying in its sense of oppression. A young girl lies fast asleep outdoors in sunshine within a Cuminestown prospect shimmering in a heat haze of desire. The girl is dreaming and in the foreground we see the subject of her dream, the aggressively male figure of a satyr, its face in profound shadow, its tail shown in a mirror suspended threateningly in mid-air directly above the girl. The macho symbolism of the Discobolus and the huntsman is now "up front" and all-conquering, while the theme of illusions or dreams arising from childhood influences are now linked to erotic sex.

This theme reached what Cowie himself considered its high point in his work with *The Evening Star*, now in Aberdeen Art Gallery. Here, we're presented with a nightmarish combination of Dante's *Inferno* and Plato's parable of the cave of human illusions, where mankind mistakes the shadows thrown on the wall by a fire for reality. A number of nude male figures and a Cupid with a bow, its arrow lying abandoned, are seen lamenting their fate within a desolate rock formation, while one stares through an empty picture frame.

Cowie achieved a measure of recognition on his retirement to Edinburgh in 1948 when he was appointed Secretary of the Royal Scottish Academy. Typically for such a self-deprecating figure, however, *Self-portrait: The Blue Shirt*, painted around this time and now owned by Edinburgh University, shows him with an expression of wry humour, perhaps his version of Rembrandt's late, laughing, self-portrait.

It was his last major work. Soon after, Cowie suffered a severe stroke that brought his career to an end. He died three years later, less than a month away from his 70th birthday, and was buried in the graveyard near where he was born, appropriately rounding off his life.

To: Esmé

Artists

" with respect "

Michael Karwolss E.

Artists

Michael Karwowski

Matador
Unit E2 Airfield Business Park,
Harrison Road, Market Harborough,
Leicestershire. LE16 7UL
Tel: 0116 279 2299
Email: books@troubador.co.uk
Web: www.troubador.co.uk/matador
Twitter: @matadorbooks

ISBN 978 1803133 317

British Library Cataloguing in Publication Data.
A catalogue record for this book is available from the British Library.

Printed and bound in the UK by TJ Books Limited, Padstow, Cornwall
Typeset in 11pt Minion Pro by Troubador Publishing Ltd, Leicester, UK

Matador is an imprint of Troubador Publishing Ltd

Contents

Preface 1

A Necessary Introduction 3

Harold Pinter: Illustratio Interruptus 23

Bob Dylan: Sooner or Later 155

Ian Curtis: Wounded Genius 193

David Gray: White Ladder 229

James Cowie: The Blessing of Obscurity 269